Revision Guide

Cambridge IGCSE ®

Business Studies

Medi Houghton

CAMBRIDGE
UNIVERSITY PRESS

CAMBRIDGE
UNIVERSITY PRESS

4843/24, 2nd Floor, Ansari Road, Daryaganj, Delhi - 110002, India

Cambridge University Press is part of the University of Cambridge.

It furthers the University's mission by disseminating knowledge in the pursuit of education, learning and research at the highest international levels of excellence.

www.cambridge.org
Information on this title: www.cambridge.org/9781107661622

First published 2013
Reprinted 2015

Printed in India by Shree Maitrey Printech Pvt. Ltd., Noida

A catalogue record for this publication is available from the British Library

ISBN 9781-107-66162-2 Paperback

Additional resources for this publication at www.cambridgeindia.org/cibsrg.asp

Cambridge University Press has no responsibility for the persistence or accuracy of URLs for external or third-party internet websites referred to in this publication, and does not guarantee that any content on such websites is, or will remain, accurate or appropriate. Information regarding prices, travel timetables, and other factual information given in this work is correct at the time of first printing but Cambridge University Press does not guarantee the accuracy of such information thereafter.

Table of contents

Introduction

This revision guide has been written to help students studying for Cambridge International Examinations IGCSE Business Studies. The structure of the guide broadly follows the syllabus headings, and is designed to accompany the IGCSE Business Studies course book (by Nuttal and Houghton).

Each unit includes:

- Definitions and explanations of key concepts for each of the syllabus areas
- Summary charts or diagrams to highlight important ideas
- Tips and notes to provide helpful guidance on key points
- Links to show where concepts in different units overlap
- Progress checks to allow you to test your understanding
- Model questions and answers to highlight common mistakes or misunderstandings
- Sample examination style questions for your practice.

There are sections on examination technique and guidance notes to help you prepare for your exam.

Key skills

Business Studies is a skills based subject. The four main skills that will be assessed are as following.

- **Knowledge** – demonstrate knowledge and understanding of facts, terms, concepts, conventions, theories and techniques.
- **Application** – using knowledge and understanding of facts, terms, concepts, conventions, theories and techniques to business problems or issues.
- **Analysis** – selecting, explaining or interpreting information to show good understanding of terms and effects of decision.
- **Evaluation** – present developed arguments or reasoned explanations, and be able to make judgements and decisions.

To gain higher grades, you must be able to demonstrate analysis and evaluation skills.

Examination style questions

There are three main styles of questions that you are likely to be asked. These can take various forms, including interpretation of tables or graphs or performing simple calculations.

1. **Knowledge questions.** These types of questions are trying to assess how well you understand the basic terms and concepts. You could be asked to write down simple definitions of terms, provide examples or work out simple calculations.

   For example:

   'What is meant by the term 'fixed cost'?'
   'Identify two examples of fixed costs.' or
   'Calculate the fixed costs for business Y.'

   There is a difference between what each of these questions require. So it is important to always read the question carefully to make sure you have understood the question properly. They are testing your knowledge and understanding of business studies.

2. **Application questions.** Application is usually assessed along side other skills such as knowledge, analysis and evaluation. The examiner is looking for you to use your knowledge of business studies, and **apply** it to the particular business that the question is based on. It is therefore, important that you avoid making general statements and **focus** your answer on the specific business mentioned.

   For example:

   > *'Identify and explain **two** possible consequences of a high labour turnover for Homer's business.'*

   If you fail to apply your knowledge to Homer's business in your answer, you will lose marks as you have not fully answered the question set.

   Key command words to look for include 'Explain how company A', 'Why might Company B', 'Using the information in Appendix 1' or 'Identify two fixed costs of C's business'.

3. **Analysis questions.** These questions require you to develop or explain concepts or information to show a more detailed understanding of key terms or ideas. You could be asked to interpret information from a table, or the implications of decisions for a business. This type of question could ask you to apply your knowledge and understanding to a particular issue or business. Always check to see if the question refers specifically to the business in the question or any business.

   For example:

   *'Identify and explain **three** reasons how company A might be affected by a rise in interest rates.'*

All questions will include key 'command words'. These are important as they will tell you what the examiner is looking for.

Learn the key facts. You do not have to write a lot to score full marks on knowledge questions.

Check the wording of the question carefully. Does it refer to a specific business or any business?

Do not just list points. Try to expand on points. Think in terms of 'this means' ... AND write it down.

Or

*'Identify and explain **three** reasons how a company might be affected by a rise in interest rates.'*

Key command words to look for include 'identify and explain three ways, 'explain why' or 'explain how.'

4. **Evaluation questions.** This type of question asks you to make a decision or give your own opinion or suggestions on a topic. These are the hardest questions to answer.

For example:

'Using the information in Appendix 2, and other case material, do you think Snappers was right to close factory B. Explain your answer.' [12]

This type of question is assessing your ability to make judgements *(evaluate)*. It is therefore, important that **you do make a decision**. But, remember, a decision on its own is not likely to score many marks. You must also provide suitable reasons to support your point of view.

Usually, the question will allow a range of possible answers. So do not worry if you have different opinions (or suggestions). Focus on identifying and explaining relevant points that support what YOU are saying. If possible always try to include at least one point which offers an alternative view. This will give your answer a better balance, and should give you a better chance of scoring a higher mark.

Key command words to look for include 'Do you think', 'Recommend', 'Which do think are the most important factors', 'Do you agree' or 'Justify'.

> Note that the first question refers to a specific company. If you do not apply your reasons to company A you will lose marks.

> ALWAYS make a decision.
> Make sure what you write supports your decision.
> Remember: there is usually more than one possible answer.

Focus on the **command** words used in the question. This is the best guide to help you answer the question. It will tell you which skills are being tested in each question.
Looking at the number of marks available for each question can also help you work out which skills are being assessed. The more marks available for a question means a wider range of skills is likely to be assessed.

Important tips to remember for **all** questions:

- Always read the question carefully to ensure you provide the correct response to the question being asked.
- Use the marks available as a guide to how much you should write.

Preparing for examination

There are lots of ways to revise. Everyone is different, and methods of revision that work for one person might not suit someone else.

Here are just some simple points to bear in mind.

1. **Know what you need to learn.** Do not spend time learning about things that are not included in the syllabus. Business Studies is a vast topic which covers many more concepts than the ones you will need to understand for IGCSE Business Studies. Your teacher will tell you what you need to revise.

2. **Make a revision timetable.** Set aside a dedicated time every week for study. You will be sitting exams in more than one subject so allow yourself plenty of time to revise for everything. Remember to give yourself time to relax as well.

3. **Revise effectively.** Do not spend hours just looking at the textbooks. Split up your time into smaller revision periods, say 30 to 40 minutes, then give yourself a break so you have time to reflect on what you have learnt.

4. **Make your revision active.** Rather than just reading, make notes, construct summary charts, create mnemonics, think of picture associations for key themes so that you can remember ideas later.

5. **Test yourself regularly to check that you have understood.** If you have not understood or cannot remember something, go and refer back to your course book. If there are topics or concepts you still do not understand, ask your teacher for help.

6. **Practice past or sample questions.** This will help you familiarise yourself with the style of questions that you will come across in the exam and will also help you to time your answers accordingly.

Five important things to remember in an exam

1. Read each question carefully. Look for the command words such as identify, calculate, explain, and justify. These words will guide you as to which skills the examiner is looking to assess.

2. For calculation questions, always show your workings out. Everyone can make a mistake when copying down a number, but if you show your method, the examiner is often able to give candidates some credit.

3. Always write in sentences and explain any point you make. Lists and bullet points can only be credited as a level one answer.

4. For case study questions, you must base your answers on the information in the case study. Do not just quote the company name, but refer to what the business produces or sells, and highlight the issues they face. Use the information provided to help you when you write you answer. Do not make general statements – make sure all points are relevant to this business.

5. If a question asks for a decision, make sure a decision is made. Include reasons for that decision. In many cases, there are a number of possible outcomes. It is important that students explain how and why they have come to a particular decision. Any decision made must be consistent with the points they have made.

Section 1:

Business and the environment in which it operates

Unit

1 Introduction to business activity

Learning Summary

By the end of this unit you should understand:

- *The difference between needs and wants*
- *The purpose of business activity*
- *The link between scarcity and opportunity cost*
- *The four factors of production*
- *The meaning of 'added value'*

The difference between needs and wants

A business produces goods and services because everyone has needs and wants that they would like to satisfy.

Needs are things that we must have in order to survive such as shelter, clothing and food.

Wants are things that we would like to have to make our lives more enjoyable.

The difference is – we **cannot** live without meeting our needs, whereas we **can** live without our wants.

The purpose of business activity

> Profit is a key concept for you to understand. It affects many areas of business behaviour.

A business is any organisation (or group of people) that makes goods or provides services. They exist to provide the goods and services that people need or want.

The main reason why people start a business is to make a **profit** by providing the goods and services people are willing to pay for. But this is not the only reason to start a business.

Other points to remember

A 'business' can be one person (**sole trader**), a large global company (**multinational**) employing 1000s of people or even a charity.

Businesses can be owned and controlled either by Government (**public sector**) or by private individuals (**private sector**).

All organisations in the public and private sector are involved in some form of business activity – it is only the objectives (what, for whom and why they produce goods and services) that differ.

The link between scarcity and opportunity cost

- The basic problem facing businesses is **scarcity**. People have unlimited wants but there are limited resources available to meet them all.
- Business activity is trying to make the best use of these resources to meet as many needs and wants of the people as possible.
- Choices must be made between what is made or bought. Resources (including money) used to make one item cannot be used for another purpose. The option which is not chosen is called the **opportunity cost**.

The four factors of production

All business activity involves the use of resources – these are called factors of production. They are as following:

- **Land** – includes all resources that occur naturally; example, oil, fish, minerals as well as the space used for production. Note this also covers the sea.
- **Labour** – this is the physical effort of the workers and the manpower used.
- **Capital** – refers to all items used in the production of goods and services; example, buildings, machinery as well as money to buy them.
- **Enterprise** – refers to the people who organise the other factors of production. They are the risk takers who invest their time, skill and money to ensure that the goods and services are available for people.

> **Useful links:**
> **Buying land and capital**
> **Unit 20: Finance and Unit 35: Accounts**
> **Role of capital**
> **Section 3: Production and productivity**
> **Labour**
> **Units 37–39: Motivation, management, laws and training**

The meaning of added value

Most businesses need to buy in materials to make products. Changes are usually made to these materials to make them worth more, so that they can sell them at a higher price.

Example: Tickers make watches. They buy materials costing $50 and sell on the finished watches to local shops for $150. Tickers pay their workers $60 and rent and heating is $15. What is the added value?

The answer is $100. Is this profit for Tickers? **No**. The amount of value added also includes other costs such as wages and other expenses. Only the amount left after all the costs have been covered is profit.

Added value is NOT profit. This is a common error. Make sure you know the difference.

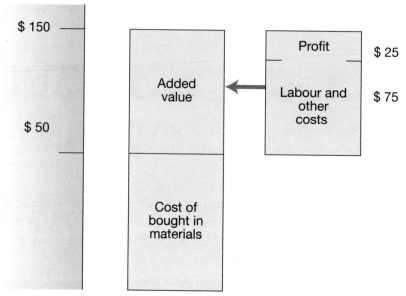

Summary chart: Added Value at Tickers Watches

$ 150

$ 50

Added value

Cost of bought in materials

Profit — $ 25

Labour and other costs — $ 75

Useful links:
Unit 31: Costs

Units 24–29: Marketing

Ways for a business to add value:

- Turning raw materials into finished goods,
- Branding,
- Packaging,
- Adding extra features to products.

Progress check

1. Define the following terms, as accurately as you can:
   - Scarcity
   - Public sector
   - Opportunity cost
2. What is the difference between a need and a want? Give an example of each.
3. Explain what is the main purpose of business activity.
4. State **two** factors of production for a market trader.
5. Write an explanation of added value, using a fisherman as an example.
6. State **two** ways in which a business can add value.

Sample question – worked example

1. What is meant by 'added value'? [2]

   Student's answer:
   Added value is the amount of money a business adds to a product to make it worth more.

Comment: This answer is too general. There is some understanding of 'increasing value' but it is not clearly explained. Overall mark: 1/2

Key terms to learn

Added value: the difference between the selling price of a product and the cost of raw materials used to make it.

Opportunity cost: the cost of something in terms of the next best option.

Public sector: any business owned, run or controlled by the Government.

Private sector: any business owned, run or controlled by private individuals.

Scarcity: the limited availability of resources to meet the unlimited wants of people.

> This unit covers some basic ideas – including why businesses exist. You need to understand the problems that businesses are trying to solve. This should help you to understand why some actions and decisions are taken or why they are important.

Examination style question for you to try

> Gee is a fruit farmer. He sells his fresh fruit to local shops and markets. He is always looking for ways to add value to his products.

1. What is meant by 'opportunity cost'? [2]

2. What is meant by 'added value'? [2]

3. Identify and explain two ways that a business could add value to their products.
   Way 1:
   Way 2: [4]

Unit

2 Classification of business

Learning Summary

By the end of this unit you should understand:

- *The difference between primary, secondary and tertiary sectors*
- *The chain of production*
- *Why different countries are involved in different business activities*

To make the best use of limited resources, businesses try to focus or specialise on activities they can do well.

The difference between primary, secondary and tertiary sectors

Businesses are grouped into 3 main types of activity (sectors):

Do not confuse these terms with types of market research.

(i) Primary
(ii) Secondary
(iii) Tertiary.

Primary sector

- First stage of production process;
- All production involves some form of **extraction** of raw materials;
- Provides the raw materials from which goods and services are made in secondary sector;
- Typical examples of the sector includes farming, fishing, mining etc.

Secondary sector

- Second stage of production process;
- Any business that uses the raw materials to make finished goods;
- All production involves some form of manufacturing, assembly, processing, refining or construction;
- Businesses will either make a finished product or make parts for another business to use;
- Typical examples of the sector includes manufacturing, building, refining etc.

Note: Some businesses might be involved in more than one stage of production.

Tertiary sector

- Any business that provides services to other businesses or individuals;
- Goods that have been made have to get to the final consumer. So other businesses need to use services such as transport, retailing, warehousing and finance;
- Individuals also have needs. Services for individuals can include health care, education etc.;
- This is a growing sector in many countries.

Useful links:

Units 24–9: Marketing including distribution

Unit 6: Role of government

Unit 9: Types of economy

Summary chart

Name of sector	Primary	Secondary	Tertiary
Main activity	Extract	Make	Service or sell
Possible example	Gold mine	Clothing factory	Transport company

The chain of production

All **three** sectors are linked together. They each rely on the other to produce goods and services. If any part of the chain breaks down, the customer will not get the goods and services they want or need. For example:

- A farmer grows fruits which he needs to sell to make a profit;
- A canning factory needs the fruits to make its tinned products;
- A shop needs the tinned products to sell to customers.

Primary	Secondary	Tertiary

Farmer	Canning factory	Shop

Why different countries are involved in different business activities

- Resources are **limited** not just in terms of how much there is but where they are found.
- Different raw materials will be located in different countries. South Africa is rich in minerals such as gold, whilst the Middle East has oil and gas reserves. Other countries have the right climate to grow certain foods such as Africa where cocoa beans grow.

Useful links:

Unit 32: Location

Unit 10: International trade

Unit 6: Government influence

- Countries might have skilled workers who are good at making certain things. Certain countries with large workforces, such as China and India, might be able to make or produce products for less money which means lower cost.
- Some countries, such as Singapore, specialise in providing services to other businesses or people. This could be due to the talents they have or because of the lack of natural resources.

Every country tries to make the best use of the resources and skills that are available to them.

Progress check

1. Write down the definitions of the following terms, as accurately as you can:
   - Primary sector
   - Secondary sector
   - Tertiary sector
2. Give **two** examples of a secondary sector business.
3. Give **two** examples of a tertiary sector business.
4. Think of a product and write down a possible chain of production for it.

Sample question – worked example

1. What is meant by 'secondary sector'? [2]
   Student's answer:
   It is the sector <u>which makes goods</u>; for example clothing business will take fabrics and make clothes out of them.

Comment: This answer has some understanding that the secondary sector manufactures goods. But this statement is not enough for full marks on its own. However, the example supports the explanation so would gain the second mark. Overall mark: 2/2

Key Point You do not need to use exact text book answers as long as you can clearly explain what the term means. You can often include an example to help show good understanding.

Activity Find out what percentage of people in your country work in each of the 3 sectors. Try to think of any reasons for this.
- Which sector employs the most people?
- Which sector employs the fewest people?

Key terms to learn

Primary sector: the sector of the economy which extracts or produces raw materials out of which finished products are made.

Secondary sector: the sector which takes raw materials and turns them into finished goods.

Tertiary sector: the sector of industry that provides services to businesses and individuals.

> This unit provides some key concepts that will become important later in the book. **Remember the links**. Always try to think about the links between different areas of the syllabus. You will often be able to bring these ideas into your exam answers. This helps in showing a good understanding of the subject.

Examination style question for you to try

The employment minister in country A is worried about recent changes in employment in the country. He has been given the following information (see Table 1) outlining the percentage of labour employed in each sector of the economy.

Table 1

% of labour force employed in	Country A	Country B
Primary	43	8
Secondary	20	22
Tertiary	37	70

1. Identify **one** type of business that could be found in the:

   (I) Primary sector

   (II) Secondary sector   [2]

2. Identify and explain **two** possible reasons for the difference in the percentage of labour employed in each country.

   Reason 1:
   Reason 2:   [8]

> You could be asked to interpret charts and tables.
> 1. Check to make sure you look at the right year or country.
> 2. State what you see and use the numbers to support what you are saying.

> Kape Confection is a large company that manufactures chocolate. They produce and sell a wide variety of products in several countries around the world. Their policy has always been to sell as many items as they can, cheaply. All products are made by machines. A recent piece of market research has shown that the customer tastes are changing towards better quality chocolates. They have recently agreed to take over Bradbury's, a small independent chocolate maker. They announced this information on their website.

3. Kape Confection is in the secondary sector but they also use the services of many businesses from the tertiary sector, such as insurance to help them run a successful company. Identify **four** other examples of tertiary sector businesses that Kape Confection might use and explain how each will help their business. [8]

4. Suggest **three** important businesses Kape might use from the tertiary sector. Justify your choices.

Tertiary business 1:

Tertiary business 2:

Tertiary business 3: [12]

3 Business growth and the measurement of size

Learning Summary

By the end of this unit you should understand:

- *The different ways of measuring size of a business*
- *The problems of using different methods to measure size of a business*
- *The various ways a business can grow*
- *Why businesses want to grow*
- *The problems of growth*

The different ways of measuring size of a business

A business can vary a lot in terms of size. Think about a sole trader, who might have only one person who owns, controls and does all the work. Whereas, a large multinational company might have thousands of employees working for them in different places around the world.

Knowing the size of a business matters because:

- Growth is an objective for some businesses. It therefore needs to know whether it is increasing in size or not.
- Workers might not like working for large businesses as they feel too remote from the management.
- Workers, in turn, might think there is more job security with a large firm.
- Banks might be more willing to lend to a large firm as there is more chance of the money being repaid.
- The government needs to know the effect of policy decisions on different sized businesses.
- Businesses want to know about size and strength of the competition.

Main ways to measure the size of a firm are:

- Number of employees;
- Capital employed (amount of money invested by owners);
- Size or level of output;
- Sales value or revenue.

> Remember the higher the value or number, the larger the business is judged to be.

The measures do not include profit. Other factors besides size of a business influences the amount of profit made. It's inaccurate and is, therefore, avoided as a measure of the size of a business.

Problem of measuring size

Do not forget that there are other issues with each method. Can you think of any?

You could be asked calculation questions on size. So make sure you know which measure the question refers to.

Measure	How it's measured	Issue with method
Number of employees	Number of workers in the business	What happens if one business uses a lot of machinery? Are they large or small?
Capital employed	Amount of money invested by owners/borrowed from lenders	Any size business can have a lot of expensive machinery so high amount of capital is employed.
Level of output	Amount of output over a given period	How to compare if different types of products are made?
Sales	Value of sales over a given period	A small firm might sell a few high value items whilst a larger firm may sell many cheap items.

Why businesses want to grow

Useful links:

Unit 10: International trade

Units 11–15: Objectives and types of organisation

Unit 19–20: Finance

Section 3: Production

Units 24–29: Marketing

The main reasons why businesses want to grow are as following:

- **Economies of scale** – to benefit from lower average costs per unit.
- **Diversification/spread risk** – to be less reliant on one market or product.
- **Financial reasons** – larger firms are more likely to survive or be able to borrow money.
- **Personal objectives** – power and status wanted by owners.
- **Market domination** – increased power or share of market in existing markets.
- **Access new markets**.

Economies of scale

Learn the main types of economies of scale. Make sure you can explain why they are important.

Type	Example
Technical	– Can afford to buy expensive specialist equipment – Able to use mass production methods – Easier to afford investing large amounts in research and development as costs spread over more units
Financial	– Easier for large firms to access more sources of finance – Larger is seen as less risk, so lower rates of interest likely
Management	Can afford to employ specialist managers

Type	Example
Marketing	Cost of advertising spread over more products, so can prove relatively cheaper
Purchasing	Large scale production means can buy materials in bulk, so able to access discounts
Risk bearing	Large companies often operate in more than one market. So if one market is struggling they have other markets to rely on

> **Note that there are many examples of economies of scale. These are just some of main ones.**

Economies of scale matter because:

- Larger firms tend to have lower average costs than smaller businesses.
- As a firm grows, they can take advantage of economies of scale.

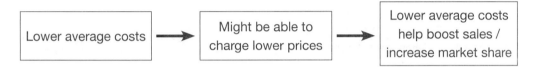

| Lower average costs | → | Might be able to charge lower prices | → | Lower average costs help boost sales / increase market share |

The problems of growth

Not all businesses want to be large because:

- Bigger firms are harder to manage and control. This can lead to diseconomies of scale. When a business reaches a certain size, it can become too large to manage effectively. Typical diseconomies include communication problems, bureaucracy, motivation issues etc.
- Competition rules. Governments often put legal restrictions in place to protect the interests of consumers and other stakeholders.
- Cash flow and financial problems are also a reason. A business may not have access to enough money to fund external growth.
- The size of business can affect ownership. Owners might have to give up some or all control of the business as they grow.

> **Useful link:**
> **Unit 6: Government influence**

> **Useful link:**
> **Unit 33: Cash flow**

There are also other factors to consider as discussed below.

Market issues

- The market may not be large enough. There might not be enough demand for larger companies to bother with a particular market.
- Most large firms are not interested in specialist goods (niche markets) as it is not cost effective to operate in such markets.

Personal reasons of owners

- Some owners want to be their own boss.
- Small firms tend to be more flexible, and are able to react to market changes more quickly.
- Small firms are more creative which can be lost in large organisations.

Progress check

1. Write down definitions of the following terms, as accurately as you can:
   - Economy of scale
   - Diseconomy of scale
2. Explain **two** reasons why the size of a firm might be important.
3. Explain **one** difference between a merger and a takeover.
4. State **two** ways a business can grow internally.
5. Identify **two** reasons why some firms stay small.
6. Would you want to work for a large or small business? Give reasons for your choice.

Sample question – worked example

Ronaldo and his brother are partners in a small but successful glass making business. They make a range of products from windows to bottles in an old factory, near the city centre. They have been looking to expand their business. A local window fitting business wants to join the two businesses together. Ronaldo likes the idea but his brother wants to keep control of the business.

1. Identify two reasons why Ronaldo might want to expand the business. [2]

   Student's answer:

   The business wants to grow to be a bigger business.

   Comment: This answer is too general. There is some understanding of the word 'expand' but it does not explain any reasons why Ronaldo might want to grow the business. Overall mark: 0/2

2. Identify and explain **one** advantage and **one** disadvantage for Ronaldo's business of joining the two businesses together. [8]

   Student's answer:

   This is where the business grows by itself – internally
   Advantage: Access to more finance – Ronaldo and his brother want to expand their business as they only run a small glass making business. The two brothers, although successful, might not have enough finance to expand the business on their own as they are only a partnership. Partners will have limited access to

Lots of application points.

fund compared to a larger business, particularly if they form a limited company. By joining together with the window business they will have access to more funds.

Disadvantage: Ronaldo's brother might have personal reasons for being against the merger. He might like being his own boss. He wants to <u>remain in control</u> of the business. This would mean the brothers would be able to take all the decisions without having to listen to the views of other owners. As the business was <u>successful,</u> he might feel there is no great need to change their approach.

Comment: This is a good answer. The advantage, access to finance, has been clearly explained to show why a merger would help Ronaldo's business. The reference to being a small business and a partnership shows good application.

Likewise, the disadvantage caused by a loss of control is explained to show how this could be a problem for the original owners if they joined together with the other business. Overall mark: 8/8

Key terms to learn

Merger: where two businesses agree to join together to become a single company.

Diseconomies of scale: factors that lead to an increase in average costs when a business grows beyond a certain size.

Takeover: where one firm buys out the other business.

> There are plenty of concepts that you need to learn here. Remember to look at the links. 'Growth and size of firms' overlaps with many other syllabus areas. Remember, you can include any relevant issue in your answers.

Examination style question for you to try

1. What is meant by an economy of scale?   [2]

2. Identify **two** diseconomies of scale.   [2]

3. Identify and explain **two** problems for a business if it grows too large. [4]

4. Identify and explain **two** ways a business could grow.   [8]

5. Do you think it is a good idea for Ronaldo to join together with the
    local window fitting business? Justify your answer.   [12]

4 National wealth and business activity

Learning Summary

By the end of this unit you should understand:
- *Impact of business activity on the environment*
- *Impact of business activity on the national wealth, the depletion of natural resources and sustainable development*
- *The reason why sustainability is important*

Impact of business activity on the environment

Business activity is all about producing goods and services to meet people's needs and wants. But this uses up scarce resources, and can damage the environment.

Should businesses try to protect the environment?

You can be asked for your opinion on this topic. Always remember to give reasons to back up your decision.

Advantage	Disadvantage
• Good for public relations as a better image and reputation leads to more sales.	• It can take a long time to adapt the processes and make them environment friendly.
• New business opportunities to meet growing customer demand for 'environmentally friendly' goods.	• Might not be able to source materials any other way.
• Might lead to new production techniques which also cuts wastage.	• Adds to the costs of business which could reduce the level of profits.
• Avoids government regulation/ fines if reduces the business pollution.	

Externalities

When business activity has an impact on others outside the business, the effects are called externalities. The effect can be good (**social benefit**) or bad (**social cost**).

The table presents some typical examples.

Social costs	Social benefits
Environmental factors such as pollution from factory	Increased jobs for the community
Spoiling natural beauty sites	Improved facilities such as schools and hospitals
Destruction of natural habitats for wildlife	Improved or new roads built
Increased risk of global warming from cutting down trees/burning coal	Regeneration of areas if new businesses are attracted to the area
Social factors such as loss of local jobs if another company has to close	

When a business makes a decision, a business will focus on the costs and benefits to itself (internal costs). The monetary value of these costs is called **financial costs.** Any money gained from the decision for the business is called a **financial benefit.**

Other influences to consider

1. **Government action:** Governments can influence/restrict business activity through a range of measures. These can include taxes, direct controls, and laws to limit/restrict externalities.
2. **Role of pressure groups:** Groups can try to influence government and business decisions through a range of actions.
3. **Business objectives:** Some businesses want to be environmentally friendly so will try to limit/avoid harmful external costs.

Useful links:
Unit 41: Pressure groups
Unit 5: Objectives
Unit 6: Role of government

Impact of business activity on national wealth

The wealth of a country lies in its natural resources and other productive assets. How well the country uses these resources will affect the general standard of living in the country.

⇒ An increase in the number of goods and services produced will lead to economic growth. This is measured by changes in Gross Domestic Product (GDP).
⇒ A rise in GDP should lead to a rise in living standards for people in that country.

Remember that the basic problem is that most resources are scarce and people have unlimited wants and needs. But it's not just about people now, what about people's needs in the future? This is where sustainable development comes in.

Remember this is a business studies paper, not economics. You do not need to understand these terms in depth, only the basic ideas.

Useful link:
Unit 1: Purpose of business activity

The reason why sustainability is important

Useful link:

Unit 42: Influences on business activity

Sustainable development is 'development that meets the needs of people now, without compromising the ability of future generations to meet their own needs'.

Sustainability is important because people have unlimited wants and there are limited resources – if all the resources are used up for production now, there will not be enough resources left to meet the needs of future generations.

What can people do to support this idea?

- Businesses can change how or what they produce to become more environment friendly.
- Governments can introduce measures and laws.
- Pressure groups and other stakeholders can influence the decisions of businesses and government.

There are usually no right or wrong answers to questions on this topic. If you are asked to make a judgement, make sure you make a decision, which your answer supports.

But this is not easy to achieve:

- All business activity has an effect on the environment.
- Resources are not shared equally between countries.
- Developing nations are still developing – their needs are different to those countries that enjoy a higher standard of living.
- Actions of one country has an impact on others – a certain country may not agree with the idea of sustainable development.

Progress check

1. Write down definitions of the following terms, as accurately as you can:
   - Financial cost
   - Externalities
2. What is the difference between a social cost and social benefit?
3. Give an example of a social cost.
4. State **one** example of how the national wealth in your country could be increased.
5. Explain **one** reason why the idea of sustainable development is becoming more important for businesses.

Sample question – worked example

T&U Partners is owned by two brothers. T&U Partners produce building blocks made by recycling waste plastic. The blocks are very cheap to make. They believe the blocks are ideal for low cost housing.

Despite having no business experience, the brothers set up their business making 'green blocks'. Funded by a government grant, they rent an old factory near the city centre. Rubbish is delivered to the site, twice a week. Demand has grown quickly from 1000 to 15,000 blocks per week. The business has just received new orders for an additional 10,000 blocks per week. Usman, one of the owners is concerned that they might have to relocate. "We will need to triple the number of deliveries, and take on extra staff. The government are planning new pollution laws. We have to cope with rules for everything – workers, the quality of the bricks. When is it going to end? It all costs us more money. We are trying to be as sustainable as we can. We could either try to build a larger factory here or move to another country." Usman is thinking of using a cost benefit analysis to work out what the best thing to do is.

1. Usman is concerned about having to cope with more environmental protection laws. Do you think T&U should do more to try to protect the environment? Justify your answer. **[6]**

    Students answer:

    No. Usman and his brother are using old waste plastic that would otherwise be rubbish. There might not be another suitable material for them to use for the housing blocks so they have to do this. At least they are making an effort to reuse some waste material unlike some large multinationals that just dig up green fields and take all the profit they can. How can the government stop them if they gave them the money in the first place? They could try to do more because if they do not they could face legal action or fines for the pollution caused by the block making. It could also damage their reputation if they are not seen as 'green'. If they change how they make things, it could increase their costs even more which they might not be able to afford and people would have to pay more for their housing or they could end up on the streets.

> **Application and knowledge shown.**

> **Opinion on multinational is not needed here.**

> **Attempt at evaluation supports the NO but the point is about the role of blocks than whether they should do more to protect the environment.**

Comment: This answer has identified a number of valid points both in support and against the statement, and there is clear and relevant development of some of these points. The answer is in context and there is some attempt at evaluation which is rewarded.

Overall mark: 5/6

Key terms to learn

Environmentally friendly: activities that conserve the environment or do not use up scarce resources unnecessarily.

External costs: costs incurred by the wider society from a business decision.

Externalities: the costs and benefits of business activity borne by the wider community.

Financial benefit: refer to the internal advantages to the business of a decision, expressed in monetary terms.

Financial cost: refer to the internal disadvantages to the business of a decision, expressed in monetary terms.

Social benefit: is made up of the financial benefits to the business itself plus the wider benefits to the community.

Social cost: the total cost to society as a result of a business decision. This is made up of the costs to the business itself plus the wider cost to the community.

Sustainable development: development that meets the needs of people now, without compromising the ability of future generations to meet their own needs.

There is plenty of overlap with the role of government in this unit. Make sure you can identify measures that governments might use. Remember to look at individual units on location, marketing, international trade for relevant actions governments might take. Do not worry if your country does not use these measures, they are only options.
The idea of sustainable development is an issue for many people.
Do you know what your government plans to do about it? (It could be nothing) Do you agree with them? These are all themes you could include in your answers.

Examination style question for you to try

1. What is meant by 'financial benefit'? [2]

2. Identify and explain **two** possible social benefits of the T&U partners planned expansion.

    Benefit 1:

    Benefit 2: [8]

3. Identify and explain **three** externalities that T&U Partner's current factory might cause.

    Externality1:

    Externality 2:

    Externality 3: [6]

4. Explain, using examples of social costs and social benefits, whether you think T&U should built a new factory in country K. Justify you answer [12]

Unit 5 The organisation

Learning Summary

By the end of this unit you should understand:

- **The main business objectives and their importance**
- **The different stakeholders and their objectives**
- **The objectives of private and public sector enterprises**

The main business objectives and their importance

An objective is simply a target which a business wants to achieve in order to fulfil its aims. They provide direction for a business, and a guideline against which to judge success.

Most businesses have the same main objectives.

- **Making a profit:** This is the most important objective. Without profit, a business is unlikely to survive in the long term and might have to close down.
- **Survival/break even:** New businesses want to survive its first year of trading; alternately a business might be facing difficult trading conditions. Just 'keeping going' can be as important as profit.
- **Increasing sales revenue:** If sales revenue rises more than costs it should lead to more profit.
- **Increasing market share:** A larger share should mean more sales.
- **Growth:** It means either entering new markets or expanding their product range. This can help spread the risk for a business, and could (if successful) help achieve other objectives such as increased sales and higher profits.

There are also other objectives such as:

- Providing jobs for themselves or employees;
- Providing quality products;
- Customer satisfaction;
- Business independence;
- Social responsibility;
- Providing an income for their family;
- Being a good employer;
- Protection of the environment.

> **Useful links:**
> Unit 20: Finance
> Unit 31: Break even
> Units 24–28: Marketing
> Unit 3: Size of firms

> **Remember objectives will vary for different businesses.**
> - Objectives can be influenced by size and type of business.
> - Objectives can change depending on factors like economic situation, differing aims of stakeholders etc.

The different stakeholders and their objectives

Business activity can have an impact on a lot of people both inside and outside the business.

A **stakeholder** is any group of individuals who have an interest in the activities of a business.

Different stakeholders will try to influence what a business does, based on their own interests and objectives.

> Stakeholders are not the same as shareholders. Shareholders are only one stakeholder group. Carefully read the question to make sure you talk about the right group.

Stakeholder group	Typical objectives	Possible influence
Shareholders	– Increased dividends from profits – Rise in value of shares	– Power to vote out directors – Sell off or refuse to buy additional shares
Employees	– Good working conditions – Better pay – Job security	– Could take industrial action – Not work hard so affect quality of products – Leave job
Managers	– Success leading to promotion – Status and power	– In charge of day to day activities so have some control over actions
Customers	– High quality products – Good customer service – Competitive prices	– Could stop buying goods
Banks and other lenders	– Want financially secure business who can afford to pay back loans – Good return on investment	– Can demand money back – Refuse to lend to business
Local community	– Social/environmental issues such as jobs, less pollution, available local services etc.	– Could organise pressure groups to influence business or government
Government	– Economic growth – Increased employment – Protection of workers and customers	– Through legislation – Financial support – Government policies

Conflicts are inevitable.

More pay for workers might result in less profit available for shareholder dividends.

Higher levels of output could lead to more jobs and pollution for the community.

> **All businesses will have more than** *one* **stakeholder. If a questions says 'stakeholders' try to refer at least** *two* **individual groups in an answer. Do not talk about stakeholders generally. They all have different objectives.**

The objectives of private and public sector enterprises

	Public sector	Private sector
Definition	Any business owned, run or controlled by the Government	Any business owned, run or controlled by private individuals
Examples	Health care, education, police force	Most sole trader, limited companies and partnership businesses
Typical objectives	– Provide a service – Control natural monopolies – Protect key industries	– Profit – Growth – Market share – Sales revenue
Aim to benefit	Everyone	Individual owners

> **Examples will depend on the country.**

It can be confusing trying to work out the difference between the public and private sector. It might help to think about who they are trying to help.

- Public sector is run to benefit **everyone**.
- Private sector is run for the benefit of their individual **owners**.

Progress check

1. Write down definitions of the following terms, as accurately as you can:
   - Objective
   - Public sector
   - Stakeholder
2. Identify **two** objectives of a public sector business.
3. Explain **one** possible objective for a business if the economy is experiencing growth; and **one** objective if the economy is in recession.
4. Write down **two** examples of public and private sector businesses found in your country.
5. Give an example of how the objectives of shareholders and employees might clash.

The idea of stakeholders is important. There is a lot of cross over with units 40–42: Roles of government, trade unions and pressure groups. Remember a business cannot exist in isolation from other stakeholders.

Sample question – worked example

Note the type of business here.

T&U Partners is owned by two brothers. It is a private sector business that produces building blocks made by recycling waste plastic. The blocks are very cheap to make. They believe the blocks are ideal for low cost housing.

Despite having no business experience, the brothers set up their business making 'green blocks'. Funded by a government grant, they rent an old factory near the city centre. Rubbish is delivered to the site, twice a week. Demand grew quickly from 1000 to 15,000 blocks per week.

The business has just received new orders for an additional 10,000 blocks per week. Usman, one of the owners is concerned that they might have to relocate. "We will need to triple the number of deliveries, and take on extra staff. The government are planning new pollution laws? We have to cope with rules for everything – workers, the quality of the bricks. When is it going to end? It all costs us more money. We are trying to be as sustainable as we can!"

1. Increasing production at the current factory will affect many stakeholders of T&U partners. Explain how **three** stakeholders would be affected by the increased production. [12]

Student's answer:

This is incorrect. Only Limited companies have shareholders.

Stakeholder 1: The shareholders want to know how much profit is expected from the increased orders so that they will receive dividends. If the business is very profitable it might also mean that the value of the shares they own could increase which means they would receive more money if they sold their shares.

Stakeholder 2: Banks would want to know how much money the business is likely to make so that they can work out whether T&U can afford to pay back any money lent to them. If the business is not likely to meet repayments, it will increase the risks for the bank as they might not get the money back.

Stakeholder 3: Community – they will want to know when and how many extra deliveries there will be. People living nearby could suffer from all the extra traffic caused. The fumes could add to air pollution which could affect their health, so they will be worried about it.

Comment: Two relevant stakeholders have been identified in points two and three. The answers have been explained to show how they might be affected by the increased orders. There is good application to the scenario so all the available marks for these two points can be given.

The first Stakeholder is incorrect. T&U is a partnership so they do not have shareholders so the point is not valid.

Overall mark: 8/12

Key terms to learn

Objective: a target which a business wants to achieve in order to fulfil its aims.

Private sector: any business owned, run or controlled by private individuals.

Public sector: any business owned, run or controlled by the Government.

Shareholder: any individual or organisation that own shares in a business.

Stakeholder: any group of individuals who have an interest in the activities of a business.

> You need to understand what objectives are, and why they are important to a business. Remember that different types of business organisation will have different objectives, and these objectives will change depending on the stakeholders, and current situation (example, financial or size) of the business.

Examination style questions for you to try

1. What is meant by 'private sector'? [2]

2. Identify and explain **two** possible objectives that T&U Partners might have

    Objective 1:

    Objective 2: [4]

3. T&U Partners is in the private sector. Explain how the objectives might be different if the business was owned by the government. [8]

4. Increasing production at the current factory will affect many stakeholders of T&U partners. Which **two** stakeholder groups do you think will be most affected by their decision to increase production? Justify your choices. [6]

> Remember to say why you have chosen these two groups. Make sure you support this view by what you write. Stakeholders selected could either benefit or be disadvantaged by this decision.

6 Government influence

Learning Summary

By the end of this unit you should understand:

- **The need for government intervention in business activity**
- **The role of government in influencing business decisions**
- **The impact of tax and interest rates**

Government intervention in business activity

Governments own, run and control organisations, which are found in the **public sector**. But their impact on business activity does not stop there.

Reasons why governments want to influence business activity are:

- Ensure essential goods and services are produced and available to those who need them;
- Stop or control the production of harmful goods;
- Control the activities of suppliers and protect customers interests;
- Provide assistance to businesses to help trading conditions, both home and overseas.

Government influencing business decisions

Useful links:

Unit 9: Economic system

Unit 10: International trade

Unit 32: Location

Unit 39: Employment

Unit 40: Competition

Governments have a range of ways to influence business decisions locally, nationally and internationally. Measures include:

- Laws and regulations,
- Financial support such as grants and subsidies,
- Training and education schemes,
- Tariffs and quotas.

The amount of influence often depends on the economic system used by each individual country.

The impact of tax

Reducing taxes and/or increasing Government spending have the same effect i.e., **MORE** spending in the economy.

Key Point You only need to know the basics of tax and interest rates. It is more important you understand the effect of such policies on businesses.

If government wants to expand the economy they could either:

⇒ try to cut taxes for individuals and businesses to encourage them to spend more.
⇒ increase the amount of government spending.

This works in the following manner.

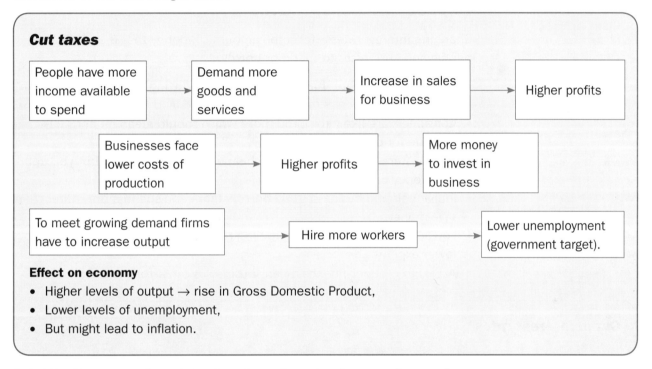

Cut taxes

People have more income available to spend → Demand more goods and services → Increase in sales for business → Higher profits

Businesses face lower costs of production → Higher profits → More money to invest in business

To meet growing demand firms have to increase output → Hire more workers → Lower unemployment (government target).

Effect on economy
- Higher levels of output → rise in Gross Domestic Product,
- Lower levels of unemployment,
- But might lead to inflation.

But if the Government wants to slow down the rate of economic growth or reduce inflation they could **increase** taxes. This has an opposite effect.

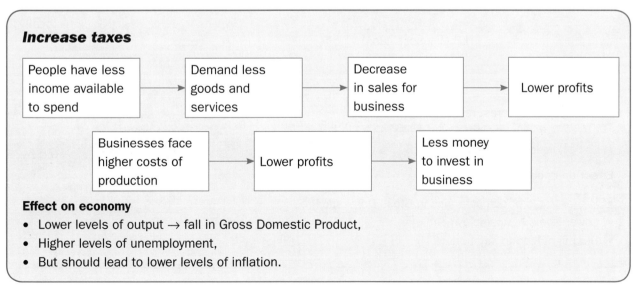

Increase taxes

People have less income available to spend → Demand less goods and services → Decrease in sales for business → Lower profits

Businesses face higher costs of production → Lower profits → Less money to invest in business

Effect on economy
- Lower levels of output → fall in Gross Domestic Product,
- Higher levels of unemployment,
- But should lead to lower levels of inflation.

Inflation refers to a general rise in the level of prices. This can be a problem for businesses as it could mean the following:

- Cost of materials could increase leading to higher business costs (so less profits).
- Higher prices could affect consumer demand leading to fewer sales.
- Prices could be higher than competitors based in other countries so businesses become less competitive.
- To afford higher prices, workers might demand higher wages, again, increasing costs.

Impact of interest rates

Changing interest rates affects the amount of money that is available for people and businesses to spend or borrow.

- Cutting interest rates has a similar effect as cutting taxes on the amount people and businesses might spend. It should lead to **more** spending.
- Consumers are likely to spend more which should mean higher sales revenue for business.
- When interest rates are cut, it is cheaper to borrow money but you get less money back on any savings.
- Individuals and businesses will borrow more and **spend more** rather than save money.
- Lower rates mean cost of borrowing reduced, so business benefits from lower expenses.
- Access to cheaper finance means businesses can afford to expand.

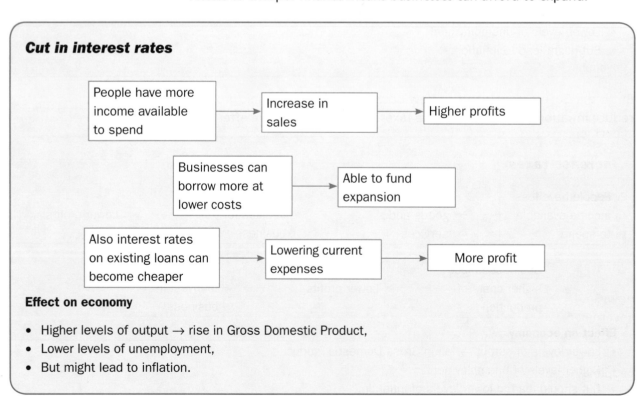

Cut in interest rates

People have more income available to spend → Increase in sales → Higher profits

Businesses can borrow more at lower costs → Able to fund expansion

Also interest rates on existing loans can become cheaper → Lowering current expenses → More profit

Effect on economy

- Higher levels of output → rise in Gross Domestic Product,
- Lower levels of unemployment,
- But might lead to inflation.

But if Government raises interest rates, this has the opposite effect.

- Individuals tend to **save** rather than spend money.
- As it is more expensive to borrow money, individuals will delay or stop buying some products.
- Businesses will face higher costs as they have to pay back more in interest.
- They are also less likely to invest in new capital/expansion ideas.

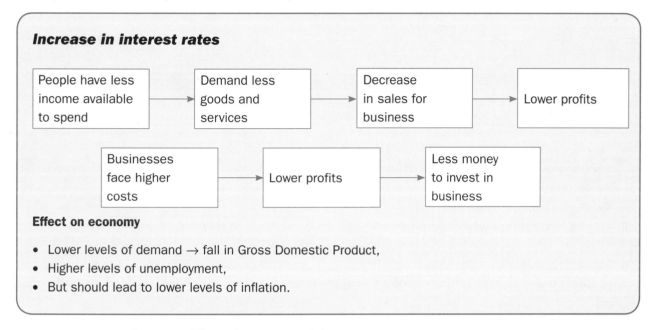

Increase in interest rates

| People have less income available to spend | → | Demand less goods and services | → | Decrease in sales for business | → | Lower profits |

| Businesses face higher costs | → | Lower profits | → | Less money to invest in business |

Effect on economy

- Lower levels of demand → fall in Gross Domestic Product,
- Higher levels of unemployment,
- But should lead to lower levels of inflation.

Summary: Effect of government influence

Government aim:	Grow economy	Slow down economy
Government action:	CUT taxes UP spending CUT interest rates	UP taxes CUT spending UP interest rates
Effect on economy:	UP growth CUT unemployment UP inflation	CUT growth UP unemployment CUT inflation
Effect on businesses:	Increased sales Increased profits Invest more/hire more workers	Lower sales Lower profits Reduce size/close down

Make sure you know the effect of both tax and interest rate policies on businesses. You need to know their impact in terms of costs, sales and profits.

How Governments spend their money can be just as important. A government could decide to build a new hospital. This will lead to more work for construction businesses and suppliers, increasing their sales and possible profits. It could also lead to new jobs being created, so increasing peoples' incomes and spending. This should benefit other businesses as well.

Note: Remember these are general effects. The impact of any change will vary depending on the business. Read the question carefully to see if there are other factors that you need to consider. Look for clues in the information provided:

- Is it a basic or luxury goods (if luxury – demand more likely to be effected by rise in interest rates).
- Is the business looking to expand – if so, the cost of finance will matter.

Progress check

1. Write down definitions of the following terms, as accurately as you can:
   - Inflation
   - Public expenditure
2. Name **two** reasons why governments try to influence the economy.
3. Explain why economic growth is important to a country.
4. What is the money supply?
5. Explain **one** effect on consumers of a rise in tax rates.

Sample question – worked example

Ronaldo runs a successful small glass making business with his brother. They make a range of products from windows to bottles in an old factory, near the city centre. They have been looking to expand their business. A local window fitting business wants to join the two businesses. Ronaldo likes the idea, but his brother wants to keep control of the business.

1. Identify and explain **two** effects of a rise in interest rates for Ronaldo's business [8]

   Student's answer:

   Effect 1: It will increase the amount they would have to repay if they take out a loan to help finance their planned expansion. This will push up their costs. If it is too expensive they are likely to delay buying expensive items of capital that they might need.

   Effect 2: Customers might delay or stop spending money. It could be better to save the money that they might have spent as they will earn money in interest payments. This will reduce sales for a business.

Reference to 'planned expansion' is application.

The effect on business well explained for analysis marks.

Comment: This is a good answer. Both points show a good understanding of the impact of a rise in interest rates on a business.

However, effect two is a general point about the impact of interest rates which is not applied to Ronaldo's business so the second application mark cannot be awarded. Answer needs to refer to idea that windows are likely to be expensive to buy so customers might delay buying them.

Overall mark: 7/8

Key terms to learn

Economic growth: measures the rate at which a country is expanding.

Gross Domestic Product: Gross Domestic Product (GDP) is the total value of goods and services produced in a country.

Inflation: a general rise in the level of prices.

Examination style questions for you to try

1. What is meant by 'inflation'?   [2]

2. Identify and explain **two** ways that a fall in interest rates could affect Ronaldo's business.

    Method 1:

    Method 2:   [4]

3. Identify and explain **four** measures a government could use to influence business behaviour.   [8]

4. Do you think that a rise in the rate of taxation is always bad for a country? Justify your answer.   [6]

Learning Summary

By the end of this unit you should understand:
- *The impact of technological change on business*
- *The impact of internet and e-commerce on business*

The impact of technological change on business

ICT is a general term that refers to all information and communications technology.

Technology can have an impact on all areas of a business. You need to be able to explain possible effects of new technology in terms of cost, workers, the method of production used as well as marketing.

Below are just some of the issues to think about.

Production

- It allows opportunity to automate production or use mass production techniques. This leads to greater **efficiency**. Machines are generally faster, more accurate and productive than people. This can lead to lower **unit costs**, better quality, continuous production and larger levels of output.
- Break down in technology has an adverse impact on business. There is a need to continually update and maintain it.

Distribution

- **Just-in-time** techniques are possible reducing the levels of stock necessary. But the suppliers will have to adjust to the system.
- It leads to better stock control as computers (often linked to tills) are able to monitor levels of sales more accurately.

Finance

- Possible cost savings from better **productivity** and lower unit costs can lead to lower costs and possible rise in profits in the long term.
- Capital can be expensive to buy meaning a business may not be able to afford it or even finance the purchase.

> **Efficiency is an important reason for using technology. You need to know what the term means.**

> **Useful links:**
> **Unit 30: Production**
> **Unit 33: Improving efficiency**

> **Useful links:**
> **Units 19 and 20: Finance**

Human Resources

- Electronic clocking on systems allow for easier monitoring of workers' hours so more accurate payment is possible.
- Some workers could lose their jobs – trade unions could campaign against the company which could damage reputation.
- **Motivation** of workers – new jobs might be boring; workers might be frightened by change so productivity and quality is affected.
- Training costs – new systems will mean additional training costs for the business, in addition to capital costs.

Marketing

- Use of e-commerce as a means to sell to wider market.
- Use of websites and email for on-line marketing.
- Possibility of designing new products.
- Increased competition as more businesses can sell to the customers.

Administration

- Use of new methods of communication helps to improve accuracy and speed of communications both inside and outside the company.
- Technical problems can result in paper work or messages not sent.

This can have an impact on effectiveness of communication across the organisation.

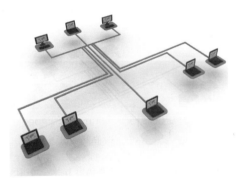

> **Useful links:**
> Units 37–39: Motivation and training

> Technology has a big impact on workers. You also need to know what a business can do to help overcome some of these problems.

> **Useful links:**
> Units 24–29: Marketing

> The impact of technology on marketing is not just about e-commerce.

> **Useful link:**
> Units 17–18: Communication

> There are many links for this topic. Read the question carefully to make sure you know which issues you have to focus on.

The impact of internet and e-commerce on business

E-commerce is the buying and selling of goods and services on-line.

E-commerce is growing which creates opportunities and threats for both businesses and consumers.

For businesses

Opportunities	Threats
Reduces some business costs as less workers are required; shop and printing costs are also reduced leading to lower prices and more profit.	Extra cost of maintenance and security of expensive equipment adds to expenses of business.
New sales opportunities as global market means more potential customers.	More competition as competing against firms around the world; it becomes hard to get customer attention.
Better information possible as greater ablity to store and access information from one place.	Viruses and technical problems could slow or even stop orders.
Flexibility as product and price lists can be updated in seconds avoiding extra printing costs.	Concerns about computer security could result in loss of customers.
Speed can reduce time from customer order to delivery as one does not wait for the post to receive order.	Not everyone has access to computers so reducing potential size of the market.
Better customer service as one can introduce tracking services on line.	Additional transport costs as the business could be anywhere in world.

For customers

Opportunities	Threats
Convenience as one can place orders at any time of the day.	Cannot see goods before purchase so one is not sure about the product.
Choice as one can select from wider range of products from around the world.	Cannot have goods immediately and have to wait for delivery.
More competition can lead to lower prices.	Not everyone has access to computer so cannot take advantage of choice and lower prices.
Can check instantly whether goods are available so less time wasted.	One must have a bank account online and there is always the fear of details being stolen.

Progress check

1. Write down definitions of the following terms, as accurately as you can:
   - E – commerce
   - ICT
2. State **two** ways that computers can help improve office productivity.
3. Give **two** reasons why some workers might not like it if a business introduced new technology.
4. Explain **two** benefits of e-commerce for consumers.
5. Identify **two** steps a business could take to help workers if new technology is introduced.

Sample question – worked example

Any Baked makes a range of products from cakes to breads. Sales have grown steadily over the last five years. It needs to increase production again. A number of their old machines keep breaking down. Homer, the Production Manager, wants to introduce new technology. The older workers are worried about what the change will mean for their jobs.

1. Identify and explain **two** ways that new technology could benefit Any Baked's business. **[8]**

   Student's answer:

   Benefit 1: Old machines are usually less reliable so are more likely to break down as has happened at Any Baked. This will cost the business both time and money to repair the machines, which will increase the maintenance expenses of the business. Newer machines should be more reliable.

   Benefit 2: New technology will be more efficient for the business. They will be able to do things more effectively.

Comment: Benefit 1 shows good knowledge of a relevant factor. There is clear development of the point to show how this is a benefit to the business. The reference to break downs is sufficient for the application mark. 4/4

Benefit 2 identifies a second valid point but has not been developed to show how this will benefit the business. This is a general statement which is not applied to Any Baked. 1/4

Overall Mark: 5/8

Key terms to learn

E-commerce: buying and selling of goods and services on-line.

> You probably know that technology is an increasingly significant feature in everyone's lives. You need to use this information to explain and make decisions about how technology has affected us, both in terms of work and our everyday lives. It is important that you understand the reasons why technology is not always good news.

Examination style questions for you to try

> You only need to refer to general factors for these questions.

1. Identify **two** reasons for a business to introduce technology.

   Reason 1:

   Reason 2: [2]

2. Identify and explain **two** problems that the introduction of new technology might cause a business.

   Problem 1:

   Problem 2: [4]

3. Identify and explain **three** disadvantages that the introduction of new technology might cause Any Baked.

   Disadvantage 1:

   Disadvantage 2: [6]

> There are both advantages and disadvantages to technology. Always try to include points for both in your answer.

4. Do you think the advantages of introducing new technology are greater than the disadvantages for Any Baked's business? Justify your answer. [12]

Business reaction to market change

Learning Summary

By the end of this unit you should understand:

- *The reasons why consumer spending pattern may change*
- *Why markets have become more competitive*
- *The impact of increased competition on consumers and businesses*

The reasons why consumer spending pattern may change

What people are willing and able to buy is called demand. People will spend their money on different things, at different times. The way people spend their money are known as **spending patterns**.

These spending patterns can change because of the following reasons.

- Price – normally higher the price, the lower the demand.
- Income – people only buy what they can afford as less income means people cannot afford to buy as much.
- Taste – people like different things and tastes/fashions can change over time.
- Price of alternative goods – many goods have substitutes (similar products) and if the substitute becomes cheaper to buy, demand for the original item might fall.
- Price of complementary goods – the sales of some products depend on the price of other items.
- Population – the age and size of population can affect what and how much is demanded.
- Seasonal factors – demand can vary with the time of year.
- Government policy and laws – laws can restrict/stop the production and purchase of certain goods; fiscal and monetary policies can influence the amount of money and confidence of people to spend.
- Technological changes – makes new products possible.

Businesses also try to influence spending patterns through product, pricing and promotion decisions.

> These factors are important. They affect many business decisions – from production to marketing.

> Useful links:
> Unit 6: Government
> Unit 7: Technology
> Units 24–26: Marketing

Why markets have become more competitive

A competitive market exists where there are many businesses in the same market wanting to sell to the same customers.

Reasons why markets are more competitive are as following:

- Rising living standards mean people have more income available to spend on goods and services.
- International trade has increased the range of products and suppliers for people to choose from.
- Improved production methods have widened the range, and reduced the cost of many products.
- Introduction of some Government policies has encouraged competition.

The impact of increased competition

Businesses must remain competitive to survive. This means:

- Produce the right product – what customers want;
- At the right price – what customers are willing to pay;
- In the right place – where customers can buy it;
- At the right time – when customers want it;
- Make sure customers know that the products exist.

Producing the right product means more money spend on research and development to meet customer needs.

Useful links:

Unit 20: Finance

Unit 30: Production

Units 24–29: Marketing

Unit 39: Recruitment and training

- New products might mean new production techniques. New equipment will mean capital expenditure. Can the business afford to pay for new equipment.
- Workers may not have the right skills or they may not be needed at all. For example, existing workers might need additional training. The business might have to recruit specialist staff.
- They may need to find new or better suppliers. The materials required might have to be imported, which means the business will have to think about the additional time for delivery and transport costs.

All this takes time and money and there is no guarantee of success.

⇒ If successful, they will keep existing customers and attract new ones. This should lead to higher sales and possibly higher profits.
⇒ If successful, they might expand their market share or be able to access new markets.
⇒ If not, they risk losing customers. Sales and profits will probably fall as customers opt for competitors products.
⇒ If not, the costs are likely to exceed revenue and they suffer losses. They could go out of business.

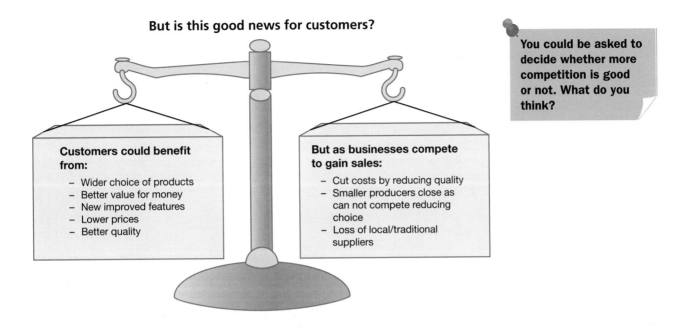

But is this good news for customers?

Customers could benefit from:
- Wider choice of products
- Better value for money
- New improved features
- Lower prices
- Better quality

But as businesses compete to gain sales:
- Cut costs by reducing quality
- Smaller producers close as can not compete reducing choice
- Loss of local/traditional suppliers

You could be asked to decide whether more competition is good or not. What do you think?

Progress check

1. Write down definitions of the following terms, as accurately as you can:
   - Market
   - Demand
2. State **three** factors that can influence demand for a product.
3. Give **two** advantages of competition for consumers.
4. Explain **two** advantages of increased competition for businesses.
5. Explain **one** possible disadvantage for customers of increased competition.

Sample question – worked example

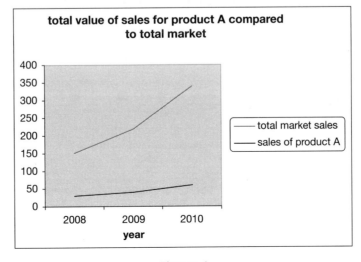

total value of sales for product A compared to total market

— total market sales
— sales of product A

year

Figure 1

1. Identify and explain **two** possible reasons for the changes shown in Figure 1. [4]

   Student's answer:
   Reason 1: Total sales for the market have increased by about $200,000 which is good.
   Reason 2: The level of sales for product A has increased, but at a slower rate than the rest of the market. This might be due to increased competition in the market so not as many of A's products can be sold.

Comment: The answer to reason one has correctly identified the change in total market sales, but unfortunately, this does not answer the question set so cannot be rewarded. The rapid growth in sales might be due to positive change in fashion for this product, it could be a new technology, change in price of other goods, or change in government laws.

The second reason does show some understanding of a valid point. Here the use of information in the diagram is sufficient for the development mark to be rewarded as well.

Overall Mark: 2/4

Key terms to learn

Competitive market: where there are many businesses in the same market wanting to sell to the same customers.

Market: place where buyers and sellers are brought together.

Spending patterns: the way people spend their money.

You need to understand the reasons behind changing demand, and be able to make decisions about how this can affect a business. Competition is important for both consumers and businesses. Make sure you understand the impact of increased competition on both consumers and businesses.

Examination style questions for you to try

Kape Confection is a large company, who manufactures chocolate. It produces and sells its products around the world. Kape Confection aims to sell as many items as it can at low prices. All products are made by machines, using batch production. A recent piece of market research has shown that customer tastes are changing towards better quality chocolate. The company has agreed to take over Bradbury's, a small independent chocolate maker. Bradbury's luxury hand-made chocolates are very popular with its rich customers. Bradbury's owner was keen to increase sales, as it only had a small local market for its product.

1. What is meant by a 'competitive market'? [2]

2. Identify and explain **two** factors likely to affect the demand for Bradbury's' chocolates.

    Factor 1:

    Factor 2: [4]

3. Which do you think are the **three** most important factors affecting demand for Kape's chocolates? Justify your choices. [12]

> Notice the different emphasis in the two questions. Question 2 simply asks you to identify and explain two likely factors. This means you can explain any relevant factors.
>
> Question 3 is more specific as it asks you to explain the most important factor. This requires you to make a decision as to which of all the various factors you think are most important in this given situation.

By the end of this unit you should understand:

- *The main differences between a mixed and market economy*
- *The impact of uncompetitive markets on consumers*

The main differences between a mixed and market economy

There is a crossover with unit 8 on this topic.

- An **economy** is a collection of people and organisations that work together to produce goods and services to meet people's needs.
- All economic systems try to solve three basic questions – what to produce, how to produce and for whom to produce.
- Each main difference between the different types of system is the **amount** of Government (State) control.
- Other economic systems also exist based on sustainability. The most common one is a subsistence economy – where the people try to meet all or most of their daily needs directly from the land around them rather than buy necessities. They aim to produce no more output than they need to consume in order to survive.

Command (Planned)	type of economy	Market
Total ⟵	amount of government control ⟶	None

Command (Planned)
Only Public sector organisations
All resources owned by State
All decisions taken by State
No profit incentive
Little or no customer choice
Limited range of goods made

Market
Only Private sector
No government control
Wide choice of products
Only profitable items made
Only needs of people who can afford to pay are met
Businesses might run monopoly

A mixed economy just tries to take the best parts of the other two systems.

Mixed economy
Both Public and Private sectors
Some customer choice available
Government influence to ensure fair prices/minimum standards
Government ensure needs of the poor are met

The impact of uncompetitive markets on consumers

Competition exists where there are two or more businesses trying to sell their goods to the same customer.

- Customers want to be able to buy as many goods as possible at the cheapest prices.
- Most consumers want competitive markets as they lead to more choice, lower prices, and better quality goods for consumers. But remember not every market is competitive.
- Businesses want to sell as many goods as possible to make the most profit. Competition will affect a businesses' ability to achieve their objectives.
- Producers want to be a monopoly so they can control prices, the amount sold and what is made. Competition is risky. The wrong pricing or marketing decision could result in fewer sales (and less profit).
- More competition in a market means less power for producers to influence the market.
- Governments do not want to stop businesses being successful, because they play an important role by helping satisfy people's needs. More businesses help create competition and choice which benefits consumers.
- If markets are uncompetitive, prices could rise, quality could fall and there could be less choice for customers.
- Governments will step in to protect consumers. Measures include: Competition Laws, Consumer laws, regulations and fines.

Useful link:

See unit 4 and 8 for more on the role of government and competition. These units cover related concepts that you might be able to bring into an answer.

Progress check

1. Write down definitions of the following term, as accurately as you can:
   - Market economy
2. How much control is the government likely to have in a command economy?
3. Explain **one** advantage of a market economy.
4. Explain **one** problem of a mixed economy for businesses.
5. State **two** ways that a government would try to control uncompetitive markets.

Sample question – worked example

1. Identify and explain **two** reasons why it is important that governments play a role in an economy. [8]

This is a general question so no application is required.

There is a clear development of the reasons provided for the additional marks.

Student's answer:

Reason 1: Government will make sure less profitable but necessary goods and services are provided for all groups in society. If left to businesses on their own to decide, some basic necessities which might be unprofitable for them to provide are unlikely to be made. Consumers would not be able to get some products which could lead to lower standards of living for some citizens. Governments could provide such low cost services themselves to make sure everyone has access to them.

Reason 2: To stop exploitation of consumers by monopolies. Otherwise consumers must pay the prices set by the monopoly supplier. This could lead to consumers having to pay higher prices than necessary to get the goods they want. I do not think this is fair because some people do not have much money to spend.

Opinion is not required here.

Comment: This is a fairly good answer. Two valid reasons are identified and are clearly explained to show why it is important that governments are involved in the economy. The last line about 'unfair' is an opinion which the question does not ask for so cannot be rewarded.

Overall mark: 7/8

Key terms to learn

Market economy: an economy based on a free market for goods and services. Government has no control over the factors of production.

Mixed economy: an economy with both a public and private sector. There is both free enterprise and state control in this economy.

You need to know and understand the differences between the different types of economic system, and how this affects **what** and **how** goods and services are produced.

Examination style questions for you to try

Sylvia and her brother run a fruit stall in the market, just selling regional produce. They have noticed that the number of customers has started to fall since a new supermarket opened two kilometres away. It advertises low prices and a better range of products for its customers. The supermarket is said to benefit from economies of scale. Sylvia does not know what this word means, but is worried for her business. The government is keen to make sure the market remains competitive.

1. What is meant by a 'mixed economy'? [2]

2. Identify and explain **two** benefits for customers of increased competition.

    Benefit 1

    Benefit 2: [4]

3. Identify and explain **two** possible disadvantages of the new supermarket for Sylvia and her customers.

    Disadvantage 1:

    Disadvantage 2: [8]

4. Sylvia is worried about the competition from the new supermarket. Do you think consumers always benefit from increased competition? Justify your answer. [12]

> Note the word 'always' here. Remember there are usually advantages and disadvantages to anything. Try to include points for both side of the argument in your answer.

Learning Summary

By the end of this unit you should understand:

- *The main reasons for international trade*
- *The problems of entering new markets abroad*
- *The barriers to international trade*
- *The effect of exchange rates on businesses*

The main reasons for international trade

- Some products are only found in certain places. If people in other countries want these products, they have to import them.
- Some countries can make products more cheaply than others. It can cost less money to import these items than try to make them.
- Some countries can make better quality products so countries choose to import these goods and services rather than make them.

> These are similar benefits to more competition in home markets. It's only where they are trading that is different.

Benefits for businesses	Benefits for customers
Able to access larger market which can lead to: – Increased sales – Greater profits – Growth – Spread risk in case demand in home market falls.	More businesses operating in a market means more competition so: – Wider choice of products – Access to better quality products – Lower prices.

The problems of entering new markets abroad

Trading overseas is not the same as trading in domestic (home) markets.

There are other issues that a business needs to consider such as the following.

- **Lack of knowledge of local markets** – customs, traditions, different laws and trading practices;

- **Lack of contacts** – where are best locations; which products to sell, how to market the product;
- **National cultures and tastes differ** – other countries may not like your products;
- **Additional costs of trading overseas** – transport, labelling, promotional costs;
- **Language problems** – is their a common language or does the business have people who can translate for them;
- **Government rules and regulations**;
- **Reaction of competitors in overseas markets** – other businesses are likely to react to threat of competition to try to protect their sales.

The barriers to international trade

Governments will often try to influence the amount of imports entering their country in order to:

- Protect domestic producers as a way to maintain jobs
- Raise money through tariffs
- Protect domestic businesses from unfair competition
- Protect important industries in the country
- Protect jobs in domestic industries.

This is done through the following:

- **Tariffs** – import taxes put on the price of goods entering the country. This makes imported goods more expensive to buy, so they become less competitive.
- **Quotas** – a limit on the amount of imports allowed in a country.
- **Subsidies** – money given by government to home producers to make home products more competitive. Domestic producers can reduce prices so as to be able to compete against imported goods.
- **Government standards** – rules set on technical specifications that imported goods must meet. Importers have to spend time and money to ensure that standards are met, which could increase costs.
- **Exchange controls** – government restrictions on amount of currency that businesses and consumers can buy or sell. This restricts the amount of foreign goods that can be bought.

> **Useful link:**
> Unit 6: Government influence

> Barriers affect consumers as well as businesses. Consumers might have less choices and higher prices.

> You must understand the effect of these changes on businesses.

The effect of exchange rates on businesses

Exchange rates are the price of one currency in terms of another currency.

Exchange rates are important as they influence the price of imports and exports.

Businesses buy raw materials from or sell finished goods to other businesses in other countries. A fall or rise in the value of a currency can have a significant impact on a business in terms of sales, costs and profit.

Falling exchange rates are GOOD for exporters but BAD for Importers	Rising exchange rates are BAD for exporters but GOOD for Importers
A fall in value of a currency is called depreciation. → Exports become cheaper as other countries are able to buy more for the same amount of money. An exporter could see a rise in sales and profits, as lower price could lead to more sales. → Imports become more expensive as businesses have to pay more to buy same amount of goods. → For producers, the costs of imported materials rise, which increases the cost of production. → Consumers in home country face higher prices, if business includes higher costs in price of goods.	A rise in value of a currency is called appreciation. → Exports become more expensive as other countries have to pay more to buy same amount of goods. Level of exports is likely to fall. → Imports become cheaper as home country is able to buy more for the same amount of money. Sales and profits could rise for importer. → For producers, the costs of imported materials fall reducing the cost of production. Business could cut prices to attract more sales, or keep prices the same for more profit. → Consumers in home country might benefit from lower prices, if business reduces price due to lower costs. This could mean higher sales for the business.

Example: Imagine an exchange rate of 1HK$= 10R.

1. A toy costing 10HK$ will sell for 100R.
2. A business buying parts costing 100R would pay 10HK$.

If value of 1HR$ fell to 5R, how would this affect the two businesses?

1. The toy would cost 50R so exports are now cheaper.
2. The parts would now cost 20R. Imports will cost more.

Progress check

1. Write down definitions of the following terms, as accurately as you can:
   - Exchange rate
   - Tariff
2. Explain the difference between a tariff and a quota.
3. Explain why a rise in exchange rates is bad for exporters.
4. State **two** reasons why governments try to influence the level of imports.
5. State **two** barriers to trade that a company could face.

Sample question – worked example

Denzel runs a sweet factory in a major European city. He imports sugar from the West Indies for use in his factory.

1. Identify and explain **two** advantages for Denzel's business of a rise in the exchange rate of the West Indian dollar. **[8]**

    Student's answer:

    Advantage 1: Imports will become cheaper as Denzel would have to pay less for the sugar, so he will benefit from lower costs of production. Lower costs could mean higher profits for his business if he keeps the prices for his sweets the same.

    Advantage 2: As Denzel is now spending less on the sugar he needs, he might be able to charge lower prices for his sweets without having to cut his profit margin. Lower prices could increase the amount bought by customers who are likely to be attracted to lower prices which will increase sales for Denzel.

> Good application here with reference to sugar and sweets.

Comment: This is a good answer. Both advantages identified are valid points which are well developed, showing how it is likely to benefit Denzel's business.

Overall mark: 8/8

Key terms to learn

Currency appreciation: a rise in the value of a country's currency in terms of another country's currency.

Currency depreciation: a fall in the value of a country's currency in terms of another country's currency.

Exchange controls: government restrictions on amount of currency that businesses and consumers can buy or sell.

Exchange rates: the price of a country's currency in terms of another country's currency.

International trade: the trade in goods and services between countries.

Quotas: a limit on the amount of imports allowed in a country.

Subsidies: money given by government to home producers to make home products more competitive.

Tariffs: import taxes put on the price of goods entering the country.

Examination style questions for you to try

> Kallis Engineering is a small engineering firm in South Africa. They make a range of farm tools. They are planning to expand the business by selling their tools in parts of Asia. Some of the managers are concerned about the idea, but can see the benefits of trading overseas.

1. Identify **two** possible reasons why Kallis Engineering wants to sell their tools in parts of Asia.

    Reason 1:

    Reason 2:   [2]

2. Identify and explain **two** possible problems Kallis Engineering might face if they decide to sell their tools in Asia.

    Problem 1:

    Problem 2:   [8]

3. The Managing Director of Kallis Engineering is keen to expand the business. Do you think Kallis Engineering should sell their tools in Asia? Justify your answer.   [6]

4. The Managing Director of Kallis Engineering is keen to expand the business. Do you think the advantages of selling overseas are greater than the disadvantages for Kallis Engineering? Justify your answer.   [12]

Section 2:

Business structure, organisation and control

Unit 11 Sole traders and partnerships

Learning Summary

By the end of this unit you should understand:
- *The role of an entrepreneur*
- *The main features of a sole trader*
- *The main features of partnerships*
- *The meaning of limited liability*

The role of an entrepreneur

An **entrepreneur** is someone who has the skill and risk taking ability to bring together the four factors of production to make goods or services.

Entrepreneurs:

- combine resources,
- identify business opportunities,
- take risks,
- make decisions.

Entrepreneurs invest their time and money into business ideas.

→ If successful, they hope to receive a return on their investment – profit. Profit is their reward for taking risks.

→ If the business fails, they will lose everything invested in the business and risk losing all their personal belongings as well.

The main features of a sole trader

A sole trader is the most common form of business. Most small businesses are sole traders.

One person owns and controls the business. They can employ others, but the owner has sole responsibility for the business.

For example, carpenter, hairdresser, local stall owner etc.

Advantages	Disadvantages
• Can make decisions quickly	• Unlimited liability
• Easy to set up	• Limited sources of finance
• Keep all the profit	• No one to share workload with
• Business details private	• Only have own skills to rely on
• Total control.	• Only have own ideas.

Key Point	**Meaning of unlimited liability** The business debts also belong to the owner; so the owner is responsible for **all** the debts of the business. If the business fails, the owner could be forced to sell their own personal possessions to repay any business debts.

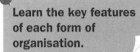

Useful links: Unit 20: Sources of funds
Unit 3: Growth of business and reasons for small firms

The main features of partnerships

A partnership occurs when two or more people decide to run a business together.

Partners will have an equal say in how the business is run in return for an equal (or agreed) share of the profits.

For example, doctors, accountants etc.

Learn the key features of each form of organisation.

Advantages	Disadvantages
• Can share workload and ideas	• Usually unlimited liability
• Covers if owner are ill or away	• Limited sources of finance
• More sources of finance than sole trader	• Must share profits
• Business details private	• Slower decision making
• Partners can specialise in tasks	• Disagreements can cause problems
• Share responsibilities.	• All owners are responsible for actions of other partners.

The meaning of limited liability

Limited liability means that the owners are only liable for the amount invested in a business. Their personal assets are safe if the business fails.

1. The biggest disadvantage of sole trader and partnerships is unlimited liability. They might be easier to set up but the risks of failure are higher.
2. Limited companies benefit from limited liability. This means that the business is seen as separate from the owners. Owners can only lose the money they invest in the business, nothing more.
3. This encourages more people to invest in the business because they know that the maximum amount of money they could lose is limited to the amount they have invested.

Progress check

1. Write down definitions of the following terms, as accurately as you can:
   • Limited liability
   • Sole trader

2. What is an entrepreneur?
3. State **two** features of sole trader.
4. Identify **one** problem for both sole traders and partnerships.
5. Why can unlimited liability be a problem for some businesses?

Sample question – worked example

Link Unit 12: Limited companies.

Alejandro is an accountant. He wants to set up his own accountancy business. He has a few customers arranged. His sister, Miranda, is a new business advisor in a local bank. She has offered to become his partner. She knows plenty of people who would use their business, and knows the problems of running a small business. She has already found rent free premises for the office. Alejandro is not sure whether it would be better for him to set up as a sole trader, in partnership with his sister or as a limited company.

1. Consider the advantages and disadvantages of each option. Which option would you recommend Alejandro chose? Justify your choice. [12]

Limited attempt at analysis in option 1.

It would be helpful if these options are explained. Example, which can restrict growth of business and problem caused by unlimited liability (personal assets are at risk if business cannot repay debts).

Only points are listed and simple evaluation is shown in recommendation.

Students answer:

Option 1 (sole trader): He is his own boss so he does not have to answer to anyone else. He keeps all profits made. It's easy to set up and he gets to make all decisions on his own. This means he can decide the direction of business. The only problems are he will have limited funds and unlimited liability.

Option 2 (forming a partnership): a partnership will have access to more funds than a sole trader. With a partner, Alejandro will have someone to share the workload with, and they might have more skills to offer the business. The only problem is that he still has unlimited liability and the partners might argue.

Option 3 (limited company): This is not a good idea. It is harder to set up as there are more forms to fill in. He might get more money from investors and have limited liability but it's not really suitable for a new business.

Recommendation: I think the best option for Alejandro is a partnership. He will have more money to use and will have someone to help him run his business. It has to be better than doing everything yourself.

Comment: This is a brief answer. For each option, advantages and disadvantages have been listed, but there is little discussion of the points to show why they are good options for Alejandro to choose.

There is no application as the points identified could apply to any business. The answer could have referred to his sister Miranda, her role in the bank, rent free premises, or the idea of a few customers as examples.

There has been some attempt at simple evaluation which can be rewarded.

Overall mark: 6/12

Do not just list points. Make sure you always try to develop any point identified to help answer the question.

Key terms to learn

Entrepreneur: someone who has the skill and risk taking ability to bring together the four factors of production to make goods or services.

Limited liability: owners are only liable for the amount invested in a business. Their personal assets are safe if the business fails.

Partnership: a business which is owned by two or more people.

Sole trader: a business which is owned by one person.

Unlimited liability: the owner is responsible for all the debts of the business. If the business fails, the owner could be forced to sell their personal possessions to repay any business debts.

The key feature of both sole traders and partnerships is **unlimited liability.** Make sure you understand what the term means, and why it is important.
There are other differences and similarities that you need to know but this is the biggest problem facing these types of organisation.

Examination style questions for you to try

1. What is meant by 'partnership'? [2]

2. Alejandro likes the idea of being a sole trader. Identify and explain **one** advantage and **one** disadvantage for Alejandro of being a sole trader.

    Advantage:

    Disadvantage: [8]

3. Miranda thinks there are more advantages for Alejandro of a partnership compared to a sole trader. Do you agree with this view? Justify your answer. [6]

Try to use information from the question to link your answer to the particular business in the question. This will help you gain any application marks as well as ensure that your answer is focused.

Limited companies

What is a limited company

You do not need to know the details about how they are set up. It's the features which are important.

- Limited companies are incorporated businesses. They are separate from their owners.
- The owners of limited companies are called shareholders. More shares owned mean the more control you have.
- The business is run by directors who do not need to be shareholders.
- The business is responsible for its own debts.
- The owners benefit from limited liability.

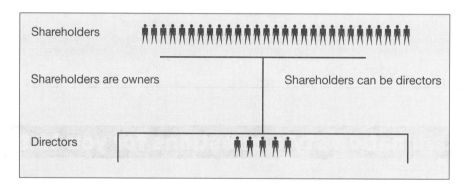

The main features of shareholders

- The owners of limited companies are called **shareholders**.
- They are only liable for the debts of the business up to the amount they have invested.
- They have little influence over day to day decisions of the business. Unlike sole traders and partnerships, they do not run the business. This is called **'divorce of control'**.
- They elect directors to run business at the Annual General Meeting.

- They have voting rights so can express opinion on major decisions.
- Main objective is profit. This should mean more dividends. An increase in profits should lead to a rise in share prices. This will increase the value of their investment.

> Shareholders only have voting rights which they use at the Annual General Meeting. They have no responsibility for day to day decisions.

The main features of private limited companies

A private limited company is a limited business whose shares cannot be sold to the general public.

- Private refers to the fact that shares can only be sold if all shareholders agree.
- Shares tend to be owned by family and friends.

Advantages	Disadvantages
• Limited liability	• More expensive to set up than unlimited
• Access to more sources of finance	• Restricted number of shareholders
	• Need agreement of other shareholders to sell shares
• Incorporated (own legal identity)	• Must disclose some financial information
• As separate entity has continuity of existence.	• Decision making slower
	• Cannot sell shares on Stock Exchange.

The main features of public limited companies

A public limited company is a limited business whose shares can be freely bought and sold to the general public.

- Anyone can own shares in a public limited company.
- Usually larger businesses than private limited companies.
- Businesses often choose to become public limited companies when they want to expand and have to raise vast amounts of money.
- Shareholders have the right to vote for directors at the Annual General Meeting.

Advantages	Disadvantages
• Limited liability	• Very expensive to set up
• Access to greatest sources of finance	• Must disclose detailed financial information every year
• Able to sell shares on Stock Exchange	• Additional costs of advertising/selling shares on Stock Exchange
• More finance to fund expansion	• Individual shareholders have little say in how business runs
• Incorporated	• Liable to takeover.
• As separate entity has continuity of existence.	

Useful links:
Unit 3: Growth of firms – how and why businesses grow

Unit 20: Sources of funds; sources available to different types of businesses

Key Point Public limited companies are in the private sector. Public just means that anyone can buy their shares. **Do not** confuse public limited with public sector.

Public limited or private limited

Advantages

- Both benefit from limited liability.
- Both benefit from access to more sources of finance as lenders see them as more secure than sole traders or partnerships.
- Both are incorporated, so business is separate from its individual owners.
- Investors are able to sell their shares if they want or need to without affecting the existence of the business.

So what's the difference?

- The main advantage for a public limited company is the **amount** of finance they can raise.
- Having access to the **Stock Exchange** means anyone can invest in the business, and you do not have to ask other owners' permission to buy and sell shares.
- More money means more funds for growth.
- Growth means a larger business. Larger businesses can benefit from economies of scale, easier to borrow funds, and easier to spread risks.

Disadvantages

- More expensive and complicated to set up and run as there is a need to disclose accounts and hold Annual General Meetings.
- Cannot keep accounts private; full disclosure of accounts is a legal requirement.
- Greater risk of takeover as business cannot control who owns the shares.
- Disadvantages caused by diseconomies of scale.
- Shareholders will expect a dividend most years.

Progress check

1. Write down definitions of the following terms, as accurately as you can:
   • Incorporated business
   • Public limited company
2. Identify **one** advantage of limited companies over unlimited companies.
3. Explain **one** difference between a private and limited company.
4. What does 'public' mean in public limited company?
5. Explain **one** disadvantage of a private limited company.

Sample question – worked example

Kallis Engineering is a small engineering business, based in South Africa. It makes a range of farm tools. Kallis is planning to expand the business by selling their tools in Asia. Some managers are concerned about the idea, but can see the benefits of trading overseas. The owners, Hans, Lars and Jacques are thinking about changing the business into a private limited company. They plan to let all the managers buy shares to reward their loyalty to the business.

1. Do you think it is a good idea for Kallis Engineering to become a private limited company? Justify your answer. [12]

   Students answer:
   The main advantage for Kallis Engineering of becoming a private limited company is limited liability. This means the owners are not liable for the debts of the business, more than what they invested. This allows a business some freedom to expand, without the owners having to worry about losing all their personal belongings should the business fail. This can encourage more people to invest in the business. The other main advantage is access to more funds. Without the threat of losing personal assets, more people will be willing to invest in the business. This means the business should hopefully be able to raise enough money to fund the planned expansion into parts of Asia. Kallis can get money from the other people so they do not have to use all their profits to expand the business. The only problems are that private limited companies can only have a limited number of

   > **Good development of limited liability showing effect of advantage on business.**

   > **Reference to Asia is application.**

   > **These other points identified are just statements showing knowledge with some basic explanation.**

Limited attempt at evaluation.

shareholders so they can only raise a certain amount of money. They also have to disclose some of the accounts so other businesses will know if they are successful or not. However these are minor points compared to the advantages of becoming a private limited company so I think this is a good move for Kallis. After all they need money to expand.

Comment: The answer starts strongly identifying two relevant issues – limited liability and access to more funds. Both points are clearly developed to show how these are advantageous for Kallis Engineering. There is sufficient development shown to earn all the analysis marks here. The other points show good understanding of relevant issues.

The reference to Asia is sufficient for 1 application mark, but this is the only application shown.

There is some limited attempt at evaluation, which is partly supported by the points raised.

Overall mark: 9/12

Key terms to learn

Divorce of control: the separation of ownership (by shareholders) from the control (by directors) in a company.

Incorporated business: business that exists separately from its owners, this means that the business has its own legal identity.

Limited liability: owners are only liable for the amount invested in a business. Their personal assets are safe if the business fails.

Private limited company: a limited business whose shares cannot be sold to the general public.

Public limited company: a limited business whose shares can be freely bought and sold to the general public.

> The main thing to remember is that limited companies have limited liability. This is a big advantage. Make sure you understand what limited liability is and how it helps a business.
> Otherwise the main difference between public and private limited companies is who can own them, and how they can sell their shares.

Examination style questions for you to try

1. What is meant by a 'private limited company'? **[2]**

2. Identify and explain **two** advantages for Kallis Engineering of becoming a private limited company.

   Advantage 1:

   Advantage 2: **[8]**

   In the future, the owners of Kallis Engineering would like to become a public limited company.

3. Identify and explain **two** possible disadvantages for a business of becoming a public limited company.

   Disadvantage 1:

   Disadvantage 2: **[4]**

4. Do you think the advantages of becoming a public limited company are greater than the disadvantages for Kallis engineering? Explain your answer. **[6]**

13 Other types of business

The main features of franchises

Franchise is an agreement that allows one business (**franchisee**) to trade under the name of another business (**franchisor**) to sell the other company's products or services.

- Franchisee pays to buy the rights to sell a product in return for a known product, marketing material and business support.
- Franchising allows people (franchisee) to run their own business without all the risks of being a sole trader.
- But unlike a sole trader, the franchisee cannot keep all the profit.
- For a franchise to work, the franchisor and franchisee must work together. Franchises are becoming very popular, example, McDonalds, KFC etc.

Franchisee

Advantages	Disadvantages
• More chances of success as selling a well known product	• Less independence than sole trader
• Banks more likely to lend them money as the risk is lesser	• Has to pay royalties to franchisor
• Has support of franchisor – advice, training and marketing	• Can only sell products of the franchisor
• Success of another franchisee can help own franchise.	• Has little or no choice of suppliers to lower costs.

Franchisor

Advantages	Disadvantages
• Expand business without investing large amounts of money	• One bad franchisee can ruin reputation of the whole company
• Risks shared with franchisee	• Costs of supporting all franchisees
• Receive regular royalty payments	• Only gets a set percentage of profit made
• Most franchisees are more motivated than employees so more chance of profit.	• If successful, only gain part not all of the profits.

The main features of joint ventures

Joint venture is an enterprise undertaken by two or more businesses pooling resources together on specific projects.

- Businesses share the costs and profits of a project.
- Each business remains separate from each other.
- Reasons for joint venture include business expansion, development of new products or moving into new markets etc.
- Joint ventures are becoming common. Many countries will only allow foreign countries to operate in their country if they set up a joint venture with local businesses.
- For a joint venture to work there must be clear objectives, and effective communication between everyone.

**Useful link:
Unit 18: Effective communication**

Advantages	Disadvantages
• Access to new markets	• Objectives of venture might not be clearly set out and communicated to everyone
• Access to other established markets and distribution channels	• Objectives of two companies could conflict
• Less risk as share costs with other business	• Have to share profits
• Access to new technology, expertise and knowledge	• Different cultures and management styles can affect level of cooperation
• Increased capacity.	• Disagreements if one party provide more expertise, finance than other.

Progress check

1. Write down definitions of the following terms, as accurately as you can:
   - Franchisor
   - Joint venture
2. What is the difference between a joint venture and a merger?
3. Explain **one** difference between a franchisee and a sole trader business.
4. Explain **one** disadvantage of a joint venture for a company.

Sample question – worked example

National Oil, a leading oil refining company and Tyle Sugar Group (TSG), a large sugar producer have agreed to a joint venture. They plan to produce sustainable bio fuel made from sugar cane. A spokesperson for TSG said "National Oil knows how to make fuel, and are keen to develop new products. We know everything about how to use sugar, it's a great idea."

No application is needed in this question.

1. Identify and explain **two** benefits of a joint venture for a business.   [4]

   Students answer:

   Benefit 1:
   They are able to share risks and costs between partner businesses so reducing the chances of failure for one business on their own.

   Benefit 2:
   Both companies are able to take advantage of each other's specialist staff or technology without having to spend their own money investing in resources.

Development shown in benefit 2.

Comment: This is a good answer which is worth full marks. Two benefits have been identified and explained to show how the point identified is a benefit to a business.

Overall marks: 4/4

Key terms to learn

Franchise: an agreement that allows one business to trade under the name of another business to sell the other company's products or services.

Franchisee: a business taking out a franchise.

Franchisor: a business granting a franchise.

Joint venture: an enterprise undertaken by two or more businesses pooling resources together.

You need to know how a franchise works – what are the benefits, problems with them for both the franchiser and franchisee. Can you explain what cooperatives and joint ventures are? Try to learn the main features of these organisations.

Examination style questions for you to try

Abraham is a car mechanic. He has always wanted to run his own business. He has saved $15 000 to invest in his own business. After some research, Abraham believes he has two options.

Option 1: Start a new car repair business. He will need to borrow an additional $10 000 to buy equipment.

Option 2: Buy a franchise for FIXIT cars, the leading repair company in the country. He will need $50 000 to buy the franchise, in addition to $10000 for equipment. All FIXIT franchisee receive full training, and marketing support. Abraham cannot decide which option to choose?

1. What is meant by a 'franchise'?   [2]

2. Identify and explain **two** advantages of a franchise for FIXIT cars

    Advantage 1:

    Advantage 2:   [8]

3. Abraham cannot decide whether to start up as a sole trader or
    as a franchise business. Which option do you think he should choose?
    Justify your choice.   [12]

14 Objectives, growth and business organisation

By the end of this unit you should understand:

- **Relationship between objectives, growth and business organisation**
- **Factors to consider when choosing a suitable form of business organisation**
- **Reasons for differences in the size of organisation**

Relationship between objectives, growth and business organisation

Useful links:
Unit 3: Growth
Unit 5: Organisation
Units 11–13:
Types of organisation
Unit 20: Finance

Relationship between type of business, objectives and profit.

Type of business	Control	Likely objectives	Main sources of funds	Use of profit
Sole trader	One owner	Profit Survival Growth	Own savings/ loans	Free to decide
Partnership	Shared between partners	Profit Survival Growth	Partners funds/loans	Share profit between partners
Private limited company	Delegated by owners to directors	Profit Growth Sales	Share capital/loans	Percentage shared with owners as dividend; rest is kept by company
Public limited company	Delegated by owners to directors	Profit Growth Sales	Share capital/loans	Percentage shared with owners as dividend; rest is kept by company

Type of business	Control	Likely Objectives	Main source of funds	Use of profit
Franchise	Franchisee but some rules set by franchisor	Profit Sales	Own savings/ loans	Set percentage goes to franchisor; franchisee decides on rest
Public sector organisation	Government	Service	Taxation	Surplus returned to government

How firms grow is similar to climbing the stairs. Most businesses will start as either sole traders or partnerships. Over time, many businesses will grow to become limited companies. Others remain as the same type as they started.

Growth is usually a gradual process for most businesses so they use internal methods. For established businesses or businesses looking to expand overseas, external methods are realistic options.

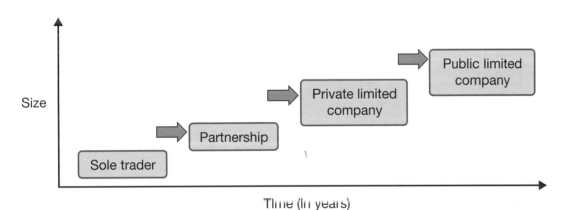

Choosing a suitable form of business organisation

- **Ownership** – Do you want to work on your own or with others? If you want total control over what you do then sole trader might be the best option.
- **Control** – How much power and influence do the owners want? Sole traders have total control whereas shareholders have little say over how a business is run.
- **Sources of funds** – Limited companies have access to more sources. If a business wants to grow, it will need finance and so might need to change to a limited company. Some businesses cannot access the finance needed to grow so have to stay small.
- **Size** – Sole traders tend to be small businesses while public limited companies are large.
- **Objectives** – Does it want a large market share, or to operate in several markets? In this case, businesses would usually look to become limited companies.

> There is no 'best' type. It is the combination of these factors which will help decide which form is best for a particular business.

Or is offering a personal service to customers more important? If so, sole traders and partnerships could be the best form of organisation.

- **Size of market** – Some markets are limited by the level of demand so a sole trader might be ideal. If the potential market is large, firms might want to choose a different form.

It is important to note that there are plenty of overlap with other units on growth, objectives, types of organisation and sources of finance. Different types of organisation have access to different sources, depending on their size and what they need the money for. Remember you could use many of these factors in answers. This can also show a broader understanding of the subject.

Reasons for differences in the size of organisation

This is only a brief summary of issues to consider. See Unit 3 for more detail.

1. Reasons to grow larger:
   ⇒ to benefit from economies of scale;   ⇒ enter new markets;
   ⇒ increase market share;   ⇒ spread risk.

But do not forget the problems of growing too large:
   – diseconomies of scale;
   – government regulation.

2. Reasons to stay small:
   ⇒ personal objectives;   ⇒ size of market;
   ⇒ access to finance;   ⇒ personal service.

Limits to size of market could restrict the amount of profit. There is a number of options that can be used to increase the size of organisation.

- Internal growth is slower so potentially easier to control the pace and impact of change; but it could also lead to missed opportunities.
- External growth is a quicker way to grow so as to be able to achieve objectives sooner.
- Franchising the business idea is also a growth option.
- Joint ventures facilitate growth as well.

Summary of main ways to classify organisations
An organisation can be grouped by the following:

- Activity: Primary, secondary or tertiary
- Sector: Public or private
- Size: Based on number of employees, value of sales, capital employed
- Legal form: Limited or unlimited company

Remember these different groupings only exist to make it easier for people to monitor business activity. All organisations are involved in trying to meet the needs and wants of people.

Progress Check

1. Write down definitions of the following terms, as accurately, as you can:
    - Private limited company
    - Public sector
2. Name **two** objectives for a new business.
3. Name **two** objectives that a public limited company might have.
4. Identify **two** factors which influence the type of business organisation.
5. What is usually the next form of organisation for a partnership which is looking to expand?

Sample question – worked example

Razzaq is a sole trader. He owns two small bread shops in the same part of the city. He does not want to open any more shops.

1. Identify and explain three reasons why Razzaq's business might want to remain small. **[6]**

    Students answer:
    Reason 1: He might loose touch with his customers if he expands.
    Reason 2: He might not have enough money so he has to remain small.
    Reason 3: There might not be enough demand for bread so he cannot expand anymore as there are not enough people nearby who want to buy his products. This means he cannot increase sales as the size of the market is limited.

> **Need to explain why or how he will loose touch for second marks.**

> **Reason 2 is a statement only; it does not explain how lack of money is a problem.**

> **Reason 3 shows good development but can only gain two marks.**

Comment: The answer identifies three valid reasons, but only reason three has been developed to show why the lack of demand is a reason for not growing. Reason three includes more detail that the question requires, but can only gain two marks. To gain additional marks, the other reasons need to be developed.

Overall mark: 4/6

Key terms to learn

Revise the following terms.

- **Limited liability**
- **Sole trader**
- **Franchisee**
- **Joint venture**
- **Public limited company**

It's important that you understand the main features of each type of business organisation, and the likely objectives of businesses. Can you give reasons to explain why businesses choose one form of organisation rather than another? Remember to think about issues such as objectives, finance and stage of business growth.

Examination style questions for you to try

1. Identify and explain **two** problems for a business if they grow too quickly.

   Problem 1:

   Problem 2: [4]

National Oil, a leading oil refining company and Tyle Sugar Group (TSG), a large sugar producer have agreed to a joint venture. They plan to produce sustainable bio fuel made with waste sugar canes. A spokesperson for TSG said "National Oil knows how to make fuel, and are keen to develop new products. We know everything about how to use sugar, it's a great idea."

---

2. Identify **two** possible objectives for National Oil of this joint venture.

   Objective 1:

   Objective 2: [2]

3. Do you think a joint venture is the best option for National Oil? Justify your answer. [6]

4. Some board members of National Oil want the company to merge with TSG. Which do you think is the best option for National Oil? Justify your answer.

   Joint Venture:

   Merger:

   Recommendation: [12]

15 Multinational business

Learning Summary

By the end of this unit you should understand:

- *The reasons for growth of multinational companies*
- *The importance of multinationals*
- *The impact of multinationals on the countries in which they are based*
- *The other issues about multinationals to consider*

The reasons for growth of multinational companies

- Not every business that trades overseas is a **multinational company**.
- A business must not only sell goods in more than one country, it has to produce goods in other countries as well.
- A multinational company is a business that has operations in more than one country.
- Improvements in technology, transport and communications mean businesses can now access global markets.
- Limited resources in some countries mean that some items have to be imported, if goods and services are to be available.
- Rising living standards around the world means people can afford to buy more goods and services. Consumers want more product choice, and the chance to buy cheaper or better quality goods.
- Governments too are encouraging international trade, as they seek to meet their objectives such as economic growth and job creation.

For businesses it means the following:

- **Increasing sales** – able to access larger international market;
- **Maximise profits** – by selling to more markets, whilst benefiting from lower costs (through economies of scale);
- **Improve customer services** – as people can buy products from anywhere, it is beneficial to have a base in all your main markets;
- **Cost cutting** – to take advantage of lower wage rates in some countries, locate nearer raw materials to cut production costs, or locate nearer customers to save distribution cost;
- **Increase efficiency** – access to cheaper labour or materials could cut unit costs, lower costs could help increase profitability;
- **Appeal to global market** – able to spread the risk if its domestic market declines or is limited in size.

> The reasons for growth are the same as any business. The only difference is the size of the business and where it operates.

> Useful links:
> Unit 3: Economies of scale
> Unit 7: E-commerce
> Unit 32: Location
> Unit 33: Efficiency

The importance of multinationals

Globalisation is a trend towards competition between small numbers of very large businesses competing in a single global market.

- Multinationals are important because of the size and scale of their operations.
- They have a head office in one (home) country.
- The operations are based in many countries (host) around the world.
- The decisions made by a multinational affect a huge number of people around the world.

The impact of multinationals

Host country

Host country is a country where multinational company (MNC) has an operating base.

Advantages

- Increased employment raises the living standards for the local population.
- Country is less reliant on imports as there is an access to a wider range of products made locally.
- Lower cost of goods as there are no duties or additional transport costs.
- Improved image for the country overseas as association with international company could lead other businesses to invest in the country.
- Access to new technology and training which was not available before.
- Profits of company could be a source of tax income for the Government who would be able to provide more services.

Disadvantages

- Jobs are often unskilled and low paid, so limited benefit to local workers.
- Increased competition for local businesses could lead to closure as they cannot afford to compete.
- They are unlikely to have any loyalty to the country if they selected it only for business reasons. Therefore, they can leave for a country with cheaper labour.
- They can have too much influence on Government and might demand grants and assistance to locate or stay in the country.

- Using up scarce resources of the country which are not available for other purposes.
- Pollution and environmental concerns can add to the problems of a country affecting the health of locals.
- There would be loss of cultural identity if local businesses close and everyone buys 'international' goods.
- Profits are usually sent to home country so there are limited tax benefits for the host country.

Home country

Home country is a country where MNC has its head office.

Advantages
<ul><li>Learn new production skills and techniques.</li><li>Business less reliant on home market so more secure.</li></ul>
Disadvantages
<ul><li>Loss of jobs if production is switched to host country leading to unemployment in home country.</li><li>Loss of exports for other producers to a new host country.</li><li>Might lead to rise in imports from host countries.</li></ul>

The other issues about multinationals to consider

Multinationals are large organisations. The reasons for growth are the same as any business. However, managing any large organisation can be difficult.

➢ How to organise the business – should it be organised by function, by region or by product?

➢ Who has control over decisions – head office (centralised) or the individual areas (decentralised)?

➢ Communication can be an issue – how does the head office keep in touch will all its markets?

➢ Motivation – will workers feel too remote from the management?

➢ Large organisations can be slow in reacting to change – could market opportunities be lost?

➢ Diseconomies of scale can lead to inefficiency and higher costs.

➢ Risk of Government regulation – as large organisations could have too much influence in the market affecting competition and consumers; regulations could add to costs.

Useful link:
Unit 16: Internal organisation

Useful links:
Unit 3: Growth
Units 17–18: Communication
Units 37–38: Motivation
Units 40–41: Government influence

Remember, multinationals face similar problems of other large businesses. It is only the scale of the business that is different as it has bases around the world.

Progress check

1. Write down definitions of the following terms, as accurately as you can:
   • Multinational company
   • Host country
2. State **two** reasons for becoming a multinational company.
3. Any business who sells goods overseas is called a multinational? True or false.
4. State **one** advantage and **one** disadvantage of multinationals for the home country.
5. Explain **one** advantage of multinationals for host country.

Sample question – worked example

Karim's Designs manufacture clothing. It only operates in country A. The company wants to set up another factory in country B, which has a large and rapidly growing population. Imports to Country B are limited.

1. Identify and explain two reasons why Karim's Designs might want to become a multinational company. **[8]**

   Student's answer:
   Reason 1: It is one way for Karim to increase sales. The growing population of country B means they would have more potential customers to sell their clothes to. If they did not open a factory there, they would only be able to sell a few goods there because imports are limited.
   Reason 2: It is a good way to cut costs. They can move production to other countries to take advantage of lower local wage rates. This will reduce the costs of production, and possibly lead to higher profits on the same level of sales.

Comment: This is a good answer. Both points show good understanding of relevant reasons, and are developed to show why a business would want to become a multinational. The first reason is worth full marks, but reason two is not applied so can only gain the knowledge and analysis marks.

Overall mark: 7/8

Key terms to learn

Multinational company: company with its headquarters in one country and operations in a number of countries.

Home country: country where multinational business has its head quarters.

Host country: country in which multinational has overseas operations.

Multinationals bring both advantages and disadvantages. You will be expected to explain what the issues are and be able to make judgements about them. Are they good or bad? There is no right or wrong answer to this type of question. You decide – it's how you argue your point of view that counts.

Examination style questions for you to try

Kape Confection is a large company, who manufactures chocolate, based in country T. It produces and sells its products in several countries around the world. Kape Confection aims to sell as many items as it can at low prices. All products are made by machines. Kape wants to set up a new distribution centre, which will create 300 new jobs. The Government of country S would like Kape to choose their country.

A spokeswoman for Kape said "We are always looking for new opportunities, we will move wherever the customers are. Government assistance does influence the exact location, but we bring jobs and the Kape brand which most customers welcome. Everyone gains. That's business."

1. Explain what type of business Kape Confection is. [2]

2. Kape are planning to set up a new distribution centre in another country, T. Identify and explain **three** effects of this decision on the host country.

   Effect 1:

   Effect 2:

   Effect 3: [8]

   > **Remember there are both good and bad points about multinationals. Always try to include and discuss both in your answers.**

3. Many countries believe the advantages of multinationals are greater than the disadvantages. Do you think a Government is right to encourage more multinationals to set up in their country? Justify your answer. [6]

   > **Question 3 does not require any application but question 4 does.**

4. Do you think the Government of country S should encourage more multinationals to set up in their country? Justify your answer. [12]

16 Internal organisation

By the end of this unit you should understand:
- *The roles, responsibilities and interrelationships of people within organisations*
- *The main features of an organisation chart*
- *The concepts of span of control, hierarchy, delegation and chain of command*
- *The reasons why organisation charts may change as a business grows*

The roles, responsibilities and interrelationships of people within organisations

→ As a business grows, it develops a structure.

→ An **organisational chart** shows how the business is arranged and various responsibilities of people involved in the organisation.

→ Sole traders usually have no or very few employees so there is no need for an organisational chart.

→ A large public limited company could employ a lot of people so a clear structure is needed.

Responsibilities of different stakeholders in an organisation

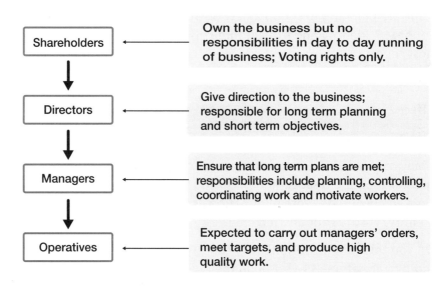

Shareholders — Own the business but no responsibilities in day to day running of business; Voting rights only.

Directors — Give direction to the business; responsible for long term planning and short term objectives.

Managers — Ensure that long term plans are met; responsibilities include planning, controlling, coordinating work and motivate workers.

Operatives — Expected to carry out managers' orders, meet targets, and produce high quality work.

The arrows refer to the direction of authority.

- Every organisation has a structure or 'hierarchy' – these are different levels of management.
- Each level in the structure has different levels of authority (power).
- Roles at the top of the organisation have more authority and responsibilities than those at the bottom.
- The owners are at the top of the chart and the workers at the bottom of the hierarchy.
- The larger an organisation, the more levels of authority there are likely to be.

> Hierarchy simply refers to the way the power in an organisation is arranged.

The main features of an organisation chart

An organisational chart simply shows the internal structure of a company and how authority and management roles are shared out.

- It shows the working relationship between different sections and who is in charge.
- It shows the different departments within an organisation.
- It provides guidance on formal lines of communication as in who to speak to if there is a problem.

By function

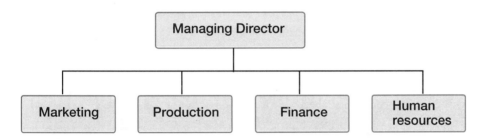

→ Each department is organised by task.
→ It is a common way for limited businesses to be organised.
→ Allows opportunity for people to specialise. This can lead workers to be more productive.
→ Possibility of conflict as departments do not always work together.

By product

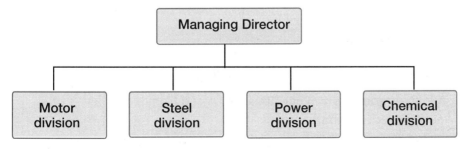

→ All products are likely to have their own production, marketing and finance department.

→ This is helpful if the company makes or sells a wide range of products.

→ Managers make decisions to suit individual products.

→ Can be expensive as each division has many similar functions.

By region

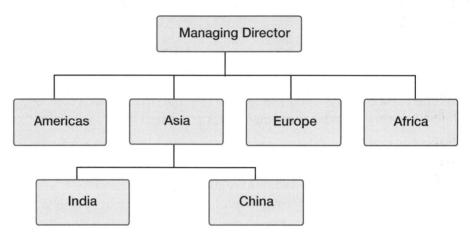

> You could be asked to draw an organisational chart or explain what it shows – in terms of span, hierarchy, how it is organised.

→ Common way for multinationals to be organised.

→ Decentralised structure which means that authority is shared out to the regions.

→ Day to day control is easier as managers focus on own region.

→ Can be expensive as each division has many similar functions.

The concepts of span of control, hierarchy, delegation and chain of command

The main features of an organisation are shown in the above charts.

Organisational structure

Refers to the number of levels of authority in an organisation.

- The main decision makers are at the top of the organisation.
- They have the authority to delegate to others below them in an organisation.

Chain of command

Shows how many levels of authority there are in an organisation.

- The line through which decisions are passed from higher levels of management down the organisation.
- Shows who makes decisions, and who is responsible for whom.
- Can be either short (few levels) or long (many levels) chain.

Span of control

Shows the number of people someone is responsible for.

- Span can be either narrow (few employees) or wide (many employees).

A **wide span** of control means manager is responsible for many workers.

Advantages	Disadvantages
• Delegation helps boost motivation of workers	• May be fewer opportunities for promotion as less supervisory roles
• Faster decision making	• More difficult to control large numbers of workers
• Communication is quicker and more efficient.	• More difficult to know what every subordinate is doing.

A **narrow span** of control means manager is responsible for a few workers.

Advantages	Disadvantages
• Easier to control a small number of workers	• Employees can feel out of touch with decision makers
• Able to maintain better working relationship with workers	• Communication can suffer due to many levels for information to pass through
• More opportunities for workers to be given responsibility or promotion	• Slower decision making as more levels for message to pass through
• More effective feedback.	• Senior management less in touch with what is happening in organisation.

Which is better a wide or narrow span of control?

There is no perfect answer. It depends on many factors including the following.

- **Size of organisation** – a small business with few workers might not need much of a hierarchy.
- **The skills of the employees** – highly skilled employees might need less supervision than unskilled employees.
- **The skill and style of manager** – are they willing or able to delegate?
- **The type of work** – simple tasks need less supervision so wider span possible.

Delegation

Refers to giving authority to carry out tasks and make decisions to someone lower down the organisational structure.

The amount of delegation will depend on the following.

- **Organisational structure:** the more tasks a manager delegates, the broader their span of control.
- **Management style:** an autocratic manager is less likely to delegate tasks compared to a democratic one.

Advantages	Disadvantages
• Saves management time to do other important jobs	• Managers are still responsible for any mistakes made
• Opportunity for workers to learn new skills which could lead to promotion	• Time spent in explaining the task might cause delay
• Work likely to be more interesting for workers improving motivation	• Managers might feel threatened by good workers affecting working relationships
• Can speed up decision making.	• Managers might not know what is happening.

Organisation 1

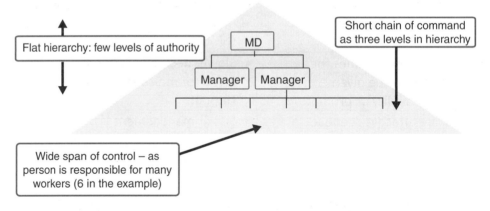

Flat hierarchy: few levels of authority

Short chain of command as three levels in hierarchy

Wide span of control – as person is responsible for many workers (6 in the example)

Usually, a flat hierarchy means a wide span and short chain of command.

Organisation 2

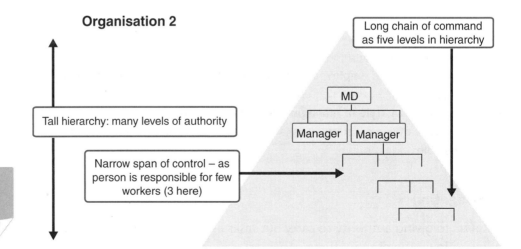

Long chain of command as five levels in hierarchy

Tall hierarchy: many levels of authority

Narrow span of control – as person is responsible for few workers (3 here)

Usually, a tall hierarchy means a narrow span and long chain of command.

There are two other helpful terms to know about when referring to internal organisation.

Centralisation: refers to a structure where most of the decision making takes place at higher levels of management. There is little delegation.

→ Decisions are taken on the basis of entire company.
→ Able to maximise economies of scale as single orders more likely.
→ Slower decision making as need time to receive all information.
→ Slower to respond to local issues so opportunities might be lost.

Decentralisation: refers to a structure where a large amount of the decision making is delegated to lower levels of management.

→ Able to react better and quicker to local issues affecting business.
→ Improves motivation of workers as they feel involved in decision making.
→ Misunderstandings/problems of control and coordination if senior managers are not aware of decisions taken elsewhere in business.
→ More expensive to set up as need due to need to duplicate functions in different locations.

> A decentralised system relies on delegation to work.

The reasons why organisation charts may change as a business grows

- There is no best structure as it depends on the objectives of the business, what they produce, where they sell and the size of the organisation.
- Structure can change as the business grows.
- Most firms start off with a centralised structure. Some might change to a decentralised structure when it becomes too big to manage effectively, if all decisions have to come from the top level.
- It is important for larger businesses to choose the right structure, otherwise control and communication problems could lead to inefficiency and **diseconomies of scale**.

> Useful link:
> Unit 3: Business growth

Progress check

1. Write down definition of the following term, as accurately as you can:
   - Hierarchy
2. Name **one** purpose of an organisational chart.
3. State **two** factors which affect the span of control.
4. Name the **three** main ways to organise a business.
5. Explain **one** benefit of decentralised structure.

Sample question – worked example

Wooden Works make furniture. It started ten years ago, selling its products locally. Today, Wooden Works' products sell across the country. To cope with growing demand, the management wants to reorganise the business by region rather than by function. They have split the company into four regions – north, east, south and west. Each region will have its own departments for human resources, finance and marketing.

1. Do you think it was a good idea for Wooden Works to change the way the business was organised? Justify your answer. [6]

Student's answer:

I think it is a great idea. This means managers will have more responsibility which will be great for motivation. Managers will be able to react more quickly to changes in demand in different parts of the country as they will be able to make decisions that affect their particular area. Customers in different parts of the country are likely to have different tastes. This could help them increase sales if they can give customers what they want. The management might loose some control over the business, but as the business is growing anyway, it's probably worth it.

> **Evaluative statement but needs to be supported by rest of the answer. Explain how 'great for motivation'**

> **The last sentence is not adding anything to opening line. Need to explain this for second evaluation mark.**

> **Do not forget you can also make a case against the change. Just focus on the disadvantages of a regional structure.**

Comment: This is a good answer. Several valid advantages are identified to support the opening statement. The idea of local decisions is developed in context so both analysis marks can be given. There is some attempt at evaluation, but this is not clearly developed. The final line is another knowledge point and a statement rather than evaluation.

Overall mark: 5/6

Key terms to learn

Centralisation: structure where most of the decision making takes place at higher levels of management.

Chain of command: shows how many levels of hierarchy there are in an organisation.

Delegation: giving authority to carry out tasks and make decisions to someone lower down the hierarchy.

Hierarchy: number of levels of authority in organisation.

Span of control: shows the number of people someone is responsible for.

There is a lot to think about in this unit. You need to learn a number of key terms. You could also be asked to describe what an organisational chart shows so practice interpreting diagrams as well.

Examination style questions for you to try

1. What is meant by span of control? [2]

2. Identify and explain **two** disadvantages of a narrow span of command.

   Disadvantage 1:

   Disadvantage 2: [4]

3. Identify and explain **two** advantages and **two** disadvantages of delegation.

   Advantage 1:

   Advantage 2:

   Disadvantage 1:

   Disadvantage 2: [8]

4. Wooden workers plan to use a decentralised structure when they reorganise their business. Do you think there are more advantages than disadvantages for Wooden Works of using decentralisation? Justify your answer. [12]

Learning Summary

By the end of this unit you should understand:
- *The importance of communication in business*
- *The difference between internal and external communication*
- *Barriers to effective communication and ways to overcome them*

The importance of communication in business

- Communication is simply a method of sending message from one person (sender) to another person or group (receiver).
- Purposes of communication are:
  - To pass and receive messages
  - Give instructions
  - Check and receive feedback
  - Method to discuss issues.

- Effective communication ensures that everyone has received and understood the message sent so that orders are taken and sent, the right products are made and correct decisions are taken.
- Effective communication is not just about sending the correct message but using the right method to send it.
- Poor communication is bad for business as it can lead to poor decisions being taken. Wrong decisions could lead to inefficiency, low motivation for workers, and lower profitability.
- Effective communication can help improve motivation leading to better productivity and lower costs.
- Poor communication can affect the image of the business. Customer dissatisfaction could lead to fewer sales.

Types of communication

→ **Vertical:** Up and down the organisation from superiors to subordinates;
→ **Downwards:** Instructions or orders from managers;
→ **Upwards:** Provide information asked for by manager or supervisor;
→ **Formal:** Using channels of communication put in place by business;
→ **Informal:** Using channels of communication set up by the employees themselves outside of formal channels (*grapevine*).

The difference between internal and external communication

Internal communication refers to all communications that take place within an organisation.

- It can be on a single site or between various factories around the world as it is still the same organisation.
- Good communication helps employees do their jobs effectively – orders are met and workers know what to do.

External communication refers to all communication that takes place with people outside the organisation.

- Effective communication is important as a business needs to interact with other people such as customers, suppliers, government and financial lenders.
- Customers want to know an order has been sent and suppliers want to know when materials are needed.

> The type of organisation can affect how effective communication is. A tall hierarchy might mean messages are received too slowly.

> Useful link:
>
> Unit 16: Organisational structure

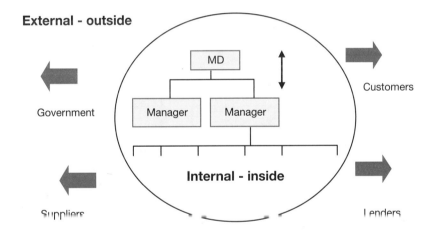

Barriers to effective communication and ways to overcome them

Communication has four parts.

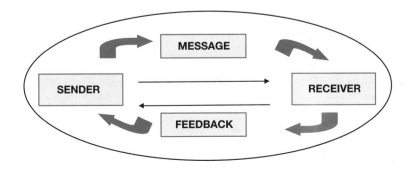

- For communication to be effective, the receiver has to receive and understand the message sent.
- If any part of the process breaks down, this **barrier** will stop the message from getting through as intended. The communication will be ineffective.

> In terms of communication, businesses face the same issues as us. So think about how you would contact people, problems you might face and how you would solve them. They are probably similar to how a business would deal with them.

- Problems can arise at any stage of the communication process.
  - → The sender – wrong message sent, speaking too quickly;
  - → The message itself – too much information, inappropriate language used;
  - → The method of communication used – technical problems;
  - → The receiver – not listening or receives unclear message.
- There are many barriers to effective communication. Below are just some of them and possible steps to overcome them.

If you are asked to identify barriers, remember to look at the type of business (context) it is. Make sure your suggestions are suitable for the size/type of business in question.

Barrier	Problem	Method to overcome it
Language	Receiver does not understand the message	Keep language simple and message short; avoid technical terms. Be aware if message is sent overseas.
Noise	Background sounds so message is not heard clearly	Chose suitable method to communicate. Keep message simple; ask for feedback.
Timing	Wrong channel used so message is not received on time	Chose suitable method that allows for quick response.
Technical breakdown	Message not received due to faulty equipment	Check that method used is reliable; ask for feedback.
Atmosphere	Message not understood as sender and receiver do not trust each other	Ask for feedback. Choose a suitable method where they can see each other.
Location	Message not received due to distance	Chose suitable method for where the receiver is.
Sender does not receive response	Sender unaware of receivers decision	Ask for feedback to check that the message is understood.
Receiver not listening	Receiver might not be paying attention	Make sure message is simple and clear. Ask for feedback to check listening.

Useful link:

Unit 18: Methods of communication

Progress check

1. Write down definitions of the following terms, as accurately as you can:
   - Communication
   - Internal communication
2. State **two** purposes of communication.
3. What is the difference between formal and informal communication?
4. Name **two** barriers to communication.
5. Name **two** external groups of people that a retailer might need to communicate with.

Sample question – worked example

1. What is meant by a 'barrier to communication'?   [2]

   Student's answer:
   A barrier to communication is language problems and noise.

Comment: This answer is wrong. The question asked for a definition, but the answer has just given two examples of possible barriers. Although both are good examples of barriers, this does not answer the question so cannot be rewarded.

Mark 0/2

> Make sure you read the question carefully. If you do not answer the question set, you are unlikely to get any marks.

Key terms to learn

Barriers to communication: any factor which causes a breakdown in communication.

Communication: a method of sending a message from one person (sender) to another person/group (receiver).

External communication: all communications that takes place with people outside the organisation.

Formal communication: using channels of communication put in place by business.

Informal communication: using channels of communication set up by the employees themselves outside of formal channels (*grapevine*).

Internal communication: all communications that take place between people within the same organisation.

You need to understand what communication is, the different types of communication as well as why communication is important. Make sure you understand the problems of poor communication and are able to give suggestions about possible ways to overcome the barriers to communication.

Examination style questions for you to try

Wooden Works make furniture. It started ten years ago, selling its products locally. Today, Wooden Works' products sell across the country. To cope with growing demand, the management wants to reorganise the business by region rather than by function. They have split the company into four regions – north, east, south and west. Each region will have its own departments for human resources, finance, marketing as well as production.

Wooden Works need to use external communication to tell their six suppliers about the change. One supplier was confused by the text message he received. "Is this what you call effective communication?" Figure one is a copy of the text sent.

Figure 1

> Hi All.
>
> We R changing. Don't worry. Pleas endeavour to get all deliveries to u r rendezvous zone at the allocated depot by 8. Any probs – text Jaz.

1. What is meant by 'external communication'? [2]

2. Identify and explain **two** possible barriers to communication shown in Figure 1.

   Barrier 1:

   Barrier 2: [4]

3. Recommend **two** possible changes that Wooden Works could consider to make sure the information reaches all its suppliers. Justify your choices. [8]

18 Effective communication

Learning Summary

By the end of this unit you should understand:
- *The methods of communication*
- *The factors to consider when choosing a method of communication*

The methods of communication

Communication can be either one way or two way.

One way: person receiving message cannot reply to it.

$$Sender \longrightarrow Receiver$$

- A manager gives instruction to workers but workers cannot check that they have understood the message.
- Mistakes are possible as there is no feedback.

Examples: Memos, notice boards, posters.

Two way: person receiving message can give feedback.

$$Sender \longleftrightarrow Receiver$$

- Both sender and receiver is involved in communication
- Feedback allows both to check the message received and whether it has been understood.

Examples: meetings, telephone, video conferencing.

> Useful link:
>
> Unit 17: Communication

> Two-way communication is a better method to ensure effective communication. Effective communication means that the message has reached the receiver and they have also understood the message sent.

- There are three main methods of communication. Each has different uses.
  - Verbal;
  - Written;
  - Visual.
- Most methods could be used for either internal or external communication except memos and notice boards which are usually internal.
- Choosing the right method to use in a given situation is vital if it is to be considered effective communication.

> Make sure you know which methods are useful for different purposes.

Verbal methods

Includes one-to-one conversations, group meetings, telephone calls and video conferencing.

Advantages	Disadvantages
• Information can be quickly sent	• No permanent record of the communication is kept if needed
• Understanding/feedback is easy to obtain as direct contact	• In large meetings, cannot tell if everyone is listening or has understood the message
• Can use body language/ gestures to support message	• Care needed with telephone as one cannot see other person
• Some forms allow you to give same message to many people at same time	• Both sender and receiver needs good communication skills
• Able to gain instant response.	• Face to face meetings are not always possible.

Written communication

Includes letters, emails, faxes, reports, memos and messages on notice boards.

Advantages	Disadvantages
• Permanent record of communication is kept	• Direct feedback is not always possible
• Useful if a lot of detail needs to be sent	• Language might be difficult for some to understand
• Message can be copied for many people to read	• Cannot always check if message has been received
• Emails/text allow for quick and cheap messages to be sent.	• Some forms of written communication can be ignored or seen too late.

Visual methods

Includes posters, charts, PowerPoint presentations and videos.

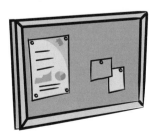

Advantages	Disadvantages
• Allows for attractive and user-friendly forms of presentation	• No feedback
• Diagrams can help in understanding of technical information	• Need to use with other methods of communication
• Summarise information so message is received quickly	• People can interpret information in different way
• Can use pictures to show emotions etc.	• Can be difficult to show some information in visual form.

The factors to consider when choosing a method of communication

Four points to consider are as following.

1. **What is the message** – How much information needs to be sent?
2. **Why is it being sent** – Is it general information or is the information to be kept secret? The business will not make confidential information available to everyone.
3. **Who needs to know** – does the same message need to be sent to one or many people?
4. **How quickly does it need to reach them** – If the message is urgent, then the method used must be quick or the communication will be ineffective. But this is likely to be more expensive to send.

How to choose an appropriate method of communication.

Question	Description	Possible methods
What is the message?	Small amount of information	Written – text, email, memo, notice board; Verbal – phone, face-to-face;
	Detailed information	Written – letter, report; Visual – charts and diagrams;
Why is it being sent?	General information	Written – text, email, memo, notice; Verbal – telephone, meeting; Visual – poster, video;
	Important/confidential information	Written – letter, email; Verbal – face-to-face meeting, telephone call;
Who needs to know?	One person	Written – letter, email; Verbal – face-to-face meeting, telephone call;
	Few people	Written – letter, email; Verbal – face-to-face meeting, telephone call;
	Many people	Written – letter, email, website, press releases; Verbal – general meetings; Visual – poster, video;
How quickly does it need to be sent?	Urgent	Written – email, text, fax; Verbal – telephone call;
	No rush to send	Written – letter, email; Verbal – face-to-face meeting, telephone call.

Technology has an important role to play in communication. It offers many benefits such as speed (email, text), sending detailed information via websites and email attachments for both internal and external purposes. Do not forget the drawbacks though – cost, security concerns and reliability issues etc.

Remember, other more 'traditional' methods are also acceptable answers.

Progress check

1. Write down definitions of the following terms, as accurately as you can:
   - One way communication
   - Verbal communication
2. Give **two** advantages of verbal communication.
3. Give **two** disadvantages of written communication.
4. State **two** factors to consider when choosing a method of communication.
5. Explain the difference between one way and two way communication.

Sample question – worked example

Kape Confection is a large company, that manufactures chocolate. It has agreed to take over Bradbury's, a small independent chocolate maker. Kape wants to tell its shareholders the good news.

> The question says a company; it does not need to apply to Kape.

1. Identify and explain **two** ways used by the management of a company to communicate with shareholders. [6]

   Student's answer:
   Way 1: Have a meeting with shareholders. This is a form of verbal communication which will allow the owners of the company a chance to raise questions so if they do not understand a decision so it's a good opportunity to get direct feedback from the directors.
   Way 2: Annual reports – these will contain detailed financial information about the performance of the business over the past year, and an idea of their future plans. Shareholders will have written copy which they can refer to in future if they have any questions.

> Both points have been developed to show how the ways identified can help company communicate with shareholders.

Comment: This is a good answer. Two methods are identified and clearly explained, so full marks can be awarded.

Overall mark: 6/6

Key terms to learn

One way communication: person receiving message cannot reply to it.

Two way communication: person receiving message can give feedback.

Verbal communication: any communication involving speech.

Visual communication: any communication which involves receiver seeing the information.

Written communication: any communication in a written form.

> You need to understand the main features for each of the method of communication. You will be expected to suggest suitable methods to use in a range of situations, and be able to explain why you think it is a good choice.

Examination style questions for you to try

> Wooden Works make furniture. It started ten years ago, selling its products locally. Today, Wooden Works' products sell across the country. To cope with growing demand, the management wants to reorganise the business by region rather than by function. It will split the company into four regions – north, east, south and west. Each region will have its own departments for human resources, finance, marketing as well as production.
>
> The Director of Human Resources, Sunni, knows she must choose the right method to inform all the employees about this change. Sunni knows that good internal communication is important to the success of the business.

1. Identify **two** methods of one-way communication.

   Method 1:

   Method 2:   [2]

2. What is meant by 'internal communication'?   [2]

3. Identify and explain **two** reasons why Sunni thinks that good internal communication is important to the business.

   Reason 1:

   Reason 2:   [8]

4. The HR Director cannot decide how to inform the workers. Discuss the advantages and disadvantages of each method outlined below. Which method would you recommend Sunni uses? Justify your choice.

   Meeting:

   Letter:

   Telephone:

   Recommendation: [12]

Unit 19 Need for finance

Learning Summary

By the end of this unit you should understand:
- *The reasons why businesses need finance*
- *The importance of working capital*

The reasons why businesses need finance

> Money can refer to cash. Finance is a more general term covering all monetary needs.

- New business needs finance to pay for the start-up costs.
- New business also needs finance to operate i.e., to buy materials before it receives any money from customers for sales.
- All businesses need money to cover day-to-day running costs which is called working capital.
- Some customers will not pay for goods immediately and this can lead to cash flow problems for the business as other costs still need to be.
- Businesses could need finance to expand or replace old capital. This is called capital expenditure.

Start-up costs

It refers to the costs a business must meet before it can start making and selling its goods or services. The main costs a business needs to pay for are the following.

Market research – it helps a business if it knows there is demand for what they are selling. If not, there might be no point in starting the business.

Premises – how much this will cost depends on what the product is and its location. Buying the premises is likely to cost more than renting.

Machinery – equipment will be needed to make the product or vehicles to transport themselves or goods around.

Fixtures and fittings – office furniture, lighting, heating equipment etc. all needs to be paid for.

> Capital should last a long time. Look at long term sources of finance to pay for these costs.

Capital expenditure/expansion costs

- Most businesses will want to expand at some point and will need to buy more capital to make this possible.
- Capital costs are similar to the start up costs for premises, machinery and fixtures and fittings.

- Replacing old equipment, buying extra equipment or moving to a new factory needs finance as well.

Running costs

It refers to the costs involved in making and selling its goods or services. Main costs include the following.

Raw materials – materials and parts needed to make the goods.

Labour costs – these are payments to workers in the form of wages, bonuses who help to make the goods. If they are not paid, they could go on strike, become de-motivated so affecting the quality of work or just leave the business.

Electricity and power – machinery needs power to operate. If the bills are not paid, then the business cannot make the goods.

Marketing and distribution costs – businesses have to make customers aware of the products by marketing and distributing it.

Interest charges – finance borrowed either for start-up, expansion or running costs usually has to be repaid with interest. If a business cannot pay, its creditors can take legal action or force the closure of the business.

> Remember selecting appropriate methods of finance depends on what and how long it is needed for.

If a business does not have enough money to pay all these running costs, it can lead to cash flow problems. Short term sources of finance are most suitable to use to try and avoid cash flow problems.

Useful links:
Unit 20: Sources of funds
Unit 34: Cash flow
Units 35 and 36: Financial accounts. These contain many related issues.

The importance of working capital

Working capital is more than just cash. It also includes debtors and stock. All businesses must have enough working capital so they can pay their short term debts when they are due.

Working Capital = Current assets – Current liabilities

The ability of a firm to meet its short term debts is known as **liquidity**.

➤ If businesses do not have enough working capital to meet day to day expenses they can face cash flow problems.
➤ If a business cannot pay suppliers, they might stop deliveries of materials which could delay or stop production.
➤ If workers are not paid on time, they might become de-motivated, which could affect the quality of work and efficiency.

A business must have enough working capital to ensure its short term survival. Even profitable businesses can fail without enough cash to pay its creditors.

Useful links:
Unit 33: Efficiency
Unit 35: Financial accounts
Units 37–38: Motivation

Progress check

1. Write down definitions of the following terms, as accurately as you can:
   - Start up costs
   - Working capital
2. Explain **two** reasons why a business might need finance.
3. Identify **two** start-up costs for a pottery business.
4. Identify **two** running costs for a printing business.
5. State **one** reason for capital expenditure.

Sample question – worked example

Alejandro is an accountant. He wants to set up his own accountancy business, with his sister, Miranda. They have customers arranged. His sister, Miranda, is a new business advisor in a local bank and knows the problems of running a small business. She has already found them rent free premises to use.

1. Identify **two** start-up costs for a new business. [2]

   Student's answer:
   Cost 1: tables and chairs for the office
   Cost 2: machinery

Comment: Two good examples shown so full marks can be given. Cost one is a practical example and cost two is a general heading. Both are acceptable answers.

Overall mark: 2/2

Key terms to learn

Liquidity: the ability of a firm to meet its short term debts.

Running costs: costs a business must meet so it can continue to make and sell its goods or services.

Start up costs: costs a business must meet before it can start making and selling its goods or services.

Working capital: money to cover day-to-day running costs.

You need to be aware of the different reasons why businesses need money. This will help you understand why they use different sources of finance and why cash flow problems impact on a business

Examination style questions for you to try

Gee is a fruit farmer. He sells his fresh fruit to local shops and markets. He is looking for ways to add value to his products. Gee needs to buy a new tractor and trailer to transport his fruit to market.

1. Gee needs to buy a new tractor and trailer. Explain which type of cost this would be for Gee's business. [2]

2. What is meant by 'working capital'? [2]

3. Explain why working capital is important for a small business like Gee's. [4]

There are not a set number of points that you need to identify for this type of question.

You could either develop one point for this question in detail or explain two points; do not simply list four points – the word explain means you must show some development to gain more than 2 marks.

The sources of internal and external finance

Internal sources of finance

It refers to the money from within the business itself.

Retained profits/reserves

- It refers to the money left over from profit made in previous years that can be put back into the business.
- These are the main source of funds for expansion.

Advantages	Disadvantages
• No interest has to be paid	• Takes time to raise funds
• No need to repay	• Might not raise enough money
• Flexible as can use as required.	• Once spent, lost funds for other uses.

Sell fixed assets

- These are also money left over from profit made in previous years that can be put back into the business.
- Main source of funds for expansion.

Advantages	Disadvantages
• No interest has to be paid	• Can take time to sell assets
• No need to repay	• Might not raise much money
• Better use rather than keeping old assets.	• Loss of business asset – cannot sell everything.

Owners capital

- Money put into business by owners at start-up.
- Main source of funds for sole trader.

Advantages	Disadvantages
• No interest has to be paid	• Risk losing own money
• No need to repay.	• Only raises limited amount of money.

Manage working capital

- By chasing up customers to pay more quickly.
- By reducing amount of stock held.
- By taking longer to pay suppliers for materials.

Advantages	Disadvantages
• No interest has to be paid	• Could upset customers so lose sales
• No need to repay	• Not enough stock to make goods
• Can help improve business efficiency.	• Suppliers might refuse to provide stock if pay too slowly/loss of discounts.

External sources of finance

It refers to money from sources outside the business.

Borrow from friends/family

- People you know might not ask for interest or security.
- This source suits sole trader/small business.

Advantages	Disadvantages
• No interest or security needed	• Only likely to raise small amounts
• Possibly quicker than asking bank for finance.	• Unsure how long one has the money.

Bank overdraft

- Bank allows business to take out more money from account than there is in it.
- Used for short term/cash flow purposes.

Advantages	Disadvantages
• Flexible as only pay interest on amount used	• High rate of interest payable
• If not used, no interest charged.	• Repayable at any time.

Bank loans/mortgage

- It refers to a set amount of money lent for a certain period of time.
- Amount is repayable with interest.
- It can be short, medium or long term.

Advantages	Disadvantages
• Has set time to repay	• Interest payable
• Can be quick to arrange with lender	• Security needed if unable to repay

Trade credit

- Suppliers allow business to buy goods but pay later.
- It is a short term measure that can help cash flow.

Advantages	Disadvantages
• No interest has to be paid	• If payment is late supplier could stop delivery
• Easy to arrange as most suppliers offer it.	• Loss of discounts will raise costs.

Leasing/hire purchase

- Allows business to use expensive assets without paying out large initial costs.
- The business is required to pay monthly amount for use.
- Lease is never own; can own hire purchase (after last payment).

Advantages	Disadvantages
• No large initial payment needed	• Lease never own asset, so cannot sell
• If leasing, lease company cover cost of repair.	• Monthly payments must be made.

Share issue

- Limited companies can issue shares to raise large sums of money.
- Used for capital expenditure.

Advantages	Disadvantages
• No need to repay	• Risk of takeover if too many shares sold
• No interest payable (dividends only if successful).	• Only option for limited companies.

These are the main sources of external finance you should focus on. But there are others such as factoring, government grants and venture capitalists.

The difference between short-term and long term finance

The length of time a business needs the money for is an important factor in the choice of finance. Why and for how long a business needs the money will influence the choice of finance selected. A business will need money for both day to day expenditure (short term) as well as using to fund capital expenditure (long term).

Short term finance	Medium/long term finance
Time: Less than one year	**Time:** More than one year
Main use: Cash flow/meet day to day running costs	**Main use:** Buy capital/fund expansion
Sources to consider: Bank overdraft Short term loan Trade credit Reduce stock held Shorten amount of time customers have to pay	**Sources to consider:** Medium/long term bank loans Mortgages Leasing/Hire purchase Share issue Debentures Government grants Sale of assets

> You must learn which methods are used for which purpose.

> Do not forget short and long term finance includes a mixture of both internal and external methods.

There are many different definitions for short term and long term finance. Do not worry about this just try to focus on what each type is used for. As the table shows, there are a lot of options that you could suggest. Just remember to read the question carefully to make sure you are selecting a suitable method. Always explain why you think it is appropriate.

The difference between loans and shares

Limited companies have more choices than unlimited companies. They can sell shares.

How do they decide between taking out a loan and selling shares?

Loans are debt	Shareholders are owners
Loans mean borrowing money from banks and other financial lenders.	Selling shares mean selling some of the ownership of a business.
– One can retain ownership of the business. – Interest must be paid on it before any profit is paid out to owners. – Lenders can force a business to close down if they cannot meet payments. – Loans are high risk as more loans mean more debt interest must be paid even if the business does not make a profit. If payments are not made, the lender can force the business to sell assets to repay them or even close down the business.	– Shares do not have to be repaid. – Only limited companies can issue shares. – Could lose ownership and control of the business if too many shares sold. – Shareholders will want a share of the profits at some point (dividend).

The factors which affect the method of finance chosen

Not all businesses can or will choose the same method of finance. It depends on several factors.

→ How long is the money needed for – short or long term?
→ What is the money needed for – start-up, working capital or expansion?
→ How much is needed – different sources will raise different amounts.
→ What risk is involved – for example debt or shares? What will happen if the business cannot repay the money?
→ Type and size of business – not all options are available to all businesses.
→ Cost of finance – interest has to be paid on some methods of finance.

Any lender will want to know the following.

• Can they afford to pay the money and interest back?
• How much debt does the company already have? The higher the level of debt, the greater the risk that the business might not be able to pay back the loan.
• How well is the business managed? Do they have the experience and skills to run the business?

Progress check

1. Write down definitions of the following terms, as accurately as you can:
   • Mortgage
   • Overdraft
2. State **two** methods of internal finance.
3. Explain **one** difference between a loan and a share.
4. Name **two** short term sources of finance.
5. State **one** use of long term finance for a limited company.

Sample question – worked example

Gee is a fruit farmer. He sells his fresh fruit to local shops and markets. Gee needs to buy a new tractor and trailer to transport his fruit to market. To buy a new one, will cost $25 000. He has little savings as he has invested everything back into the farm. His current overdraft is $1000. He thinks he has three options – increase his overdraft, bank loan or lease a vehicle.

1. Consider the advantages and disadvantages of the **three** options and advise Gee on which would be the most suitable source of finance to use. Justify your recommendation. [12]

Option 1: (overdraft) an overdraft is a facility arranged with a bank to allow a customer to make payments in excess of the cash in the account up to an agreed limit. Interest is paid on daily basis depending on how much is used. It is not very good if you need a lot of money.

Option 2: (bank loan) A bank loan can be used to raise a large amount of capital and as Gee needs $25 000 to buy a tractor and trailer, it could be an option. The loan can be paid back slowly and spread over a number of years. This is good as Gee will be able to earn some money to pay off the loan by selling his fruit. The only problem is he will have to pay interest on the loan and so the loan will cost Gee more than $25 000.

Option 3: (leasing) leasing is the best option. It lets a business use expensive assets without having to pay out a lot of money to start with. If you have not got much money like Gee, who's invested everything in his farm, it's got to be the best option. If the tractor breaks down, which they always seem to do, Gee will not have to pay anything, because he does not own it. This will save him money in repairs. The only problem is he will not own it, and it could cost him more each month to lease it if they charge a lot.

Recommendation: Leasing is definitely the best option for Gee. He will not have a debt to pay off and he can always upgrade it to a new model whenever he wants.

> **Only knowledge, no explanation or application has been given.**

> **In the recommendation, there is a need to explain why leasing is better than the loan. It could be a lease because he could still be paying for the tractor when the tractor is no longer useful. If he needs another tractor, this would require another loan, which would further increase his costs. Overdraft is not appropriate as capital expenditure.**

Comment: The answer shows good knowledge of advantages and disadvantages of each option. Option 1 can only be given knowledge marks as there is no development or application to Gee.

Both Options 2 and 3 show good knowledge and understanding of the advantages and disadvantages of each method of finance. They are clearly applied to Gee, so the application marks can be awarded.

There is some attempt at evaluation, but in order to score the additional two evaluation marks, there needs to be some comparison between the three methods to support why option 3 is actually better than the other two.

Overall mark: 10/12

Key terms to learn

Dividend: payment made to shareholders from the profits of the business after tax.

External finance: money from sources outside the business.

Internal finance: money from within the business itself.

Mortgage: a loan which is secured (supported by) against an asset. If the loan is not repaid, the asset can be taken.

Overdraft: a facility arranged with a bank to allow a customer to make payments in excess of the cash in the account up to an agreed limit.

Trade credit: arrangement to buy goods or services from suppliers without having to make immediate cash payment.

> You have a lot to learn on sources of finance. You need to understand the different sources of funds available to a business. Can you identify and explain which sources of finance are suitable for different purposes? You could be asked to make and justify decisions on suitable sources in a range of different contexts.

Examination style questions for you to try

> Abraham is a car mechanic. He has always wanted to run his own business. He has saved $15 000 to invest in his own business. He will need to borrow an additional $10 000 for machinery, plus extra money for stock. He is thinking of using trade credit to buy his stock or his overdraft.
>
> Abraham is not sure which method of finance to use for the additional $10 000 for his equipment. There are a number of factors which will influence his choice of finance.

1. Besides trade credit, identify **two** sources of external finance.

   Source 1:

   Source 2: [2]

2. Identify and explain **one** advantage and **one** disadvantage of trade credit for Abraham's business.

   Advantage:

   Disadvantage: [8]

3. Identify and explain **two** factors which influence the choice of finance for a business.

   Factor 1:

   Factor 2: [4]

4. Abraham knows there are a number of factors which will influence his choice of finance. Which do you think are the most important factors that Abraham has to consider? Justify your choice. [6]

   Make sure you make a decision and be clear as to why you think it is the best method.

5. Abraham is not sure whether it is better to use trade credit or his overdraft to buy stock. Which do you think is the best method of finance for Abraham to use? Justify your choice. [6]

Section 3:

Business activity to achieve objectives

Unit 21 Customers, markets and marketing

Learning Summary

By the end of this unit you should understand:

- **The role of marketing**
- **The difference between mass market and niche market**
- **The concept of market segmentation**
- **The difference between market orientation and product orientation**

The role of marketing

A product can refer to either a good or service.

Marketing is all about 'anticipating, identifying and satisfying customer needs – at a profit'. It is more than just advertising and promotion.

It involves the following.

- **Market research** – identifying and anticipating needs;
- **Product** – developing the product to meet the needs;
- **Pricing** – setting a price customers are willing to pay;
- **Place** – making sure the product is available when and where customers want it;
- **Promotion** – making sure customers know the product exists and create interest in it.

Useful links:

Unit 22: Market research;

Units 23–29: Marketing

If a business gets all these elements right, they should sell their products and hopefully make a profit.

Mass market and niche market

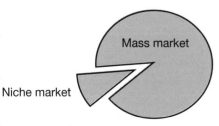

Mass market

Niche market

A market is a place where buyers and sellers meet to trade goods. The size of the market varies with the product being sold.

Mass market

It is a market with large numbers of customers.

- → Usually sells a standardised product.
- → Prices tend to be lower due to more competition.
- → Large volume of sales allows for economies of scale which favour larger businesses.

Niche market

It is a smaller section of a larger market, usually selling a more specialised product.

→ Small level of sales.
→ Prices tend to be higher in niche markets.
→ Suits small businesses who can give time to focus on needs of their customers.
→ Small number of sales can deter large businesses as they are not as profitable.
→ Small market means limited potential for growth.
→ Specialist market – high risk if demand falls.

> If a niche market attracts a lot of customers, it can become a mass market.

The concept of market segmentation

- All businesses in either a mass or niche market will try to identify who their customers are. This allows them to better match their products to suit their customer's needs.
- Splitting up the market into particular groups of people is called **segmentation**.
- Each group will consist of customers with similar characteristics and similar product needs. These are called **segments**.

Markets can be segmented in many ways.

Age – people of a similar age, tend to share similar interests.

Gender – product can be aimed at men, women or children etc.

Income – people earning more money might be able to afford more luxury goods.

Location – different places have different cultures so interests are likely to vary.

Interests – some people like sports, others like music which involves different products.

Size of households – households with families will have different needs to households with only single occupants.

Segmentation is important as it can help businesses to:

➢ Develop products that better match specific customer requirements to increase sales and profits.
➢ Spot gaps in the market that provide opportunities to increase sales.

Market orientation and product orientation

Product orientation

Business makes the product and then tries to find people to buy it.

- Suits products which are necessities such as food.

- Focus for producer is price and quality.
- Few businesses use this approach today.

Market orientation

Business which takes into account customer needs before developing the product.

- Businesses usually carry out market research first to find out customer needs.
- This ensures products made are what customers are willing to buy. This helps increase sales and profit.
- Most businesses use this approach today due to increasing competition in most markets.

Progress check

1. Write down definitions of the following terms, as accurately as you can:
   - Market segment
   - Mass market
2. Identify **two** parts of marketing.
3. State **two** features of a niche market.
4. Explain **one** reason how segmentation can help businesses.
5. State **two** ways that segment a market.

Sample question – worked example

Kape Confection is a large company that manufactures chocolate. They produce and sell their products in several countries around the world. Their policy has always been to sell as many items as they can, cheaply. All products are made by machines. A recent piece of market research has shown that customer tastes are changing towards better quality chocolate. They have recently agreed to take over Bradbury's, a small independent chocolate maker. Their luxury hand made chocolates are very popular with its rich customers. Bradbury's was keen to increase sales, as they only had a small local market for their product. "It's been a good niche market for us" said Joe Bradbury "but we want to grow."

1. What is meant by a 'niche market'? [2]

   Students answer:
   A niche market is a small part of the market. Bradbury only sold to a small local market.

Comment: The answer shows some understanding of a niche market. But as there is also a relevant example to support this, from the text, this is enough to gain the second mark.

Overall mark: 2/2

Key terms to learn

Marketing: anticipating, identifying and satisfying customer needs – at a profit.

Market orientation: a business which takes into account customer needs before developing the product.

Market segment: smaller group of customers with similar characteristics and similar product needs.

Mass market: a market which has a large number of customers for a standard product.

Niche market: a smaller section of a larger market, usually selling a more specialised product.

Product orientation: business makes the product, and then tries to find people to buy it.

Segmentation: splitting up the market into particular groups of people.

> This unit covers many basic concepts that you need to understand. Make sure you can define all the main terms mentioned and be able to provide examples of segmentation and the different market types.

Examination style questions for you to try

> Joe Bradbury is confused. The marketing manager at Kape Confection keeps talking about market segmentation and being market orientated. What is wrong with just making a product and selling it? Last year we had a market share of 37% in a $950 000 market!

1. What is meant by 'market segmentation'? [2]

2. Calculate the value of Bradbury's sales last year. [2]

3. Identify and explain **two** advantages of market segmentation for Kape Confection.

   Advantage 1:

   Advantage 2: [8]

4. The marketing manager at Kape Confection keeps talking about being market orientated. Do you think it is important for Kape's business to be market orientated? Explain your answer. [12]

> Make sure you refer to Kape in your answer. You will lose marks if you do not apply your answer. Read the question carefully.

Market research

The need for market research

Market research involves finding out the needs of customers before developing a product.

Benefits of market research includes the following.

- Ablility to obtain detailed information about a market.
- Ablility to identify needs of current and potential customers.
- By Identifying customer needs to make products which would sell.
- Identifying market trends so as to respond to changing demands in order to remain competitive.
- Helping with the planning of marketing campaigns.
- Providing information to help solve business problems such as reasons for falling sales.

The methods of primary and secondary research

Primary research involves collecting new information that did not exist before. It is also known as field research.

Methods include:

- **Interviews** – face to face or by telephone. Allows for more detailed information but how questions are asked can lead to bias.
- **Questionnaires** – list of set questions used. Easier to compare results but answers will depend on questions asked and can take a long time to collect.
- **Observation** – watching or recording what people do or buy. It's cheap to do but only provides basic information.
- **Consumer panels/focus groups** – a small group of people who often meet to give their views on products or issues. They provide detailed information but can be expensive and time consuming to arrange.

- **Experiments** – new products will be tested to find out customers reactions to the product. Good way to find out customers opinions on a product before it's launched but results depend on who is asked and whether they give their real opinions or say what the business wants to hear.

Advantages	Disadvantages
• First hand information is gathered	• It is expensive to collect as it is new information
• It is specific to requirements of the individual company	• It is time consuming to collect as information did not exist before
• Information is only available to their company.	• It is not always feasible as might not be able to access target customers.

Secondary research involves using information that already exists. It is also known as desk research. It is useful when the business wants general information about the market such as population or size of market.

Sources include:

- **Own sales information** – records of previous years sales.
- **Government statistics** – national governments will provide information on a range of issues such as population, income, and economic data.
- **Articles** – newspapers or the internet can provide general information on markets or general information about the trading conditions/changing tastes in the market.
- **Trade organisations** – can provide information on particular markets or industries for their members.
- **Market research agencies** – carry out research for companies or other organisations. The results are often made available for anyone to see.

Advantages	Disadvantages
• Quick/easy to access as it's already available	• Not much reliable as collected for another purpose
• Cheaper than primary research as the information is either free or available for a small fee	• This data is available to competitors as well
• Can help identify issues before conducting primary research	• Out of date if information is old, may not be relevant for current purposes
• Could include additional helpful information that business had not considered.	• If research is from another country, cultural differences could affect reliability of results.

The choice between primary and secondary research depends on:

- What the business wants to know;
- How quickly they want the information;
- How much money they have to spend.

Points to remember when designing a questionnaire

Good research will try
to use both qualitative
and quantitative
information.

- What information do you want to find out, as this will influence what is asked and the type of questions used.

Quantitative information is based on numbers. It does not provide reasons behind the answers but is easy to present as a graph or chart.	**Qualitative** information is based on opinions and reasons. The information is much more detailed but can be difficult to present in a chart or graph. It can be hard to compare two opinions.

- Identify suitable questions to ask as the questions used must gather the information required.
- Should open or closed questions be used? Open questions give more detailed responses. Closed questions only allow simple answers from a limited range of options.
- The questions asked must be clear and easy to understand.
- Avoid leading questions. Make sure the questions used allow people to give their own opinions without too much guidance from the interviewer. Otherwise, it could lead to bias.
- Try to test the questionnaire before use. This allows a business to identify poorly designed questions or find out whether all the necessary information is available.

The different methods of sampling

It would take too much money and time to ask everyone for their views and opinions. Businesses can only ask a small number of the population. Such a method is called a **sample**.

→ The sample tries to represent the views of all potential customers.
→ The larger the sample size used, the less is the chance of bias.

The limitations of market research

Accurate, up to date information can be very helpful for a business. Being able to identify and meet customer needs could give a business a competitive advantage, leading to increased sales and profits. But both primary and secondary methods can produce information that is unreliable or inaccurate. Biased information can lead to the wrong decisions being made which could cost the business sales and profit.

1. Cost and time issues – gathering information is expensive. The more accurate and relevant, the longer it is likely to take to collect. Does the business have enough time to collect 'perfect' data?

2. Methodology – were the right questions asked? Were they leading questions? Was there interviewer bias? How large was the sample?
3. People's views change over time – what the customers were happy to buy before could be different now. Income, tastes and other factors can affect their opinions.
4. If the product is new – do customers understand what the product is? Will people just say what they think researcher wants to hear?

Bias is all about trying to influence something in an unfair way.

Bias can exist because of:

- Poorly worded questions
- How the interviewer asks the questions
- Questions may not cover all the necessary information
- Have enough people been asked
- Have the right people been asked to have a representative sample.

Progress check

1. Write down definitions of the following terms, as accurately as you can:
   - Consumer panel
   - Primary research
2. State **two** methods of secondary research.
3. State **two** methods of primary research.
4. What is the difference between an open question and a closed question?
5. Outline **three** points to remember when designing a questionnaire.

Sample question – worked example

Kallis Engineering is a small engineering business based in South Africa. It makes farm tools. Kallis is planning to expand overseas by selling their tools in parts of Asia in the next six months. Some managers think there are more disadvantages than advantages to trading overseas.
The Marketing Manager is planning to carry out some market research. He has set aside a small budget to help pay for this.

Always try to link your answer to the context of the question.

1. The Marketing Manager is considering using a questionnaire as part of his market research. Identify and explain **four** suitable questions that the marketing manager could ask. **[8]**

Student's answer:
Question 1: How much do you pay for tools? This would allow Kallis to know how much people pay for tools.
Question 2: What type of tools do you use? This would allow Kallis to know which type of tools customers use.
Question 3: Where do you buy your tools from? This would help Kallis to work out where the best place to sell his tools would be. There would be little point in selling them in places where their potential customers would not be found.
Question 4: How often do you buy tools? This would help Kallis to try to work out the possible level of demand there would be for his tools. He could then plan his production better.

> In questions 1 and 2 explanation is just a repeat of the knowledge points.

Comment: Four suitable questions have been identified so all the knowledge marks would be awarded. But only question three has been developed to show why this is a useful question for Kallis to ask.

The explanations for questions one and two only repeat the question rather than try to explain why these questions are helpful. For question one about pay would help Kallis set his prices, so he does not charge too much or too little. Question two is helpful so Kallis can decide which tools to sell to ensure he gets sufficient sales.

Overall mark: 6/8

Key terms to learn

Market research: finding out the needs of customers before developing a product.

Primary research: involves collecting new information that did not exist before.

Qualitative information: information is based on opinions and reasons.

Quantitative information: information is based on numbers.

Sampling: research based on a small number of the population.

Secondary research: research using information that already exists.

> The key concepts you need to understand are why market research is used; the different method of market research and understanding the limitations of market research.

Examination style questions for you to try

1. What is meant by a 'primary market research'? **[2]**

2. Identify and explain **two** reasons why market research might not be useful to a business.

   Reason 1:

   Reason 2: **[4]**

3. Identify and explain **two** reasons why market research might be important for Kallis engineering.

   Reason 1:

   Reason 2: **[8]**

4. The marketing manager at Kallis Engineering is planning to carry out some market research. Consider the advantages and disadvantages of primary and secondary research. Recommend which method Kallis should use. Justify your choice.

   Option 1 (Primary):

   Option 2 (Secondary):

   Recommendation: **[12]**

23 Presentation and use of data

The different ways of presenting data

How data is presented is important. Many people will be interested in the results of market research or want to see the business accounts. The information must be put into a form that is easy to understand. Presentation is all about trying to make sense of the information collected so that it is:

- Easier to read
- Has a visual impact
- More user friendly for a wide range of people
- Highlights the main findings of any research.

There are many different ways to present data. The main ones are tables, graphs and charts.

Worked example: Cool Clothing

Cool Clothing sells their products all over the world. They are planning to expand the number of outlets they have but cannot decide where to open them. They have carried out some market research to help them.

Table

It is a simple record of facts and figures presented in rows and columns. It is useful if you want to show a lot of detailed information.

- It is easy to construct
- Shows all the data collected
- Able to include a lot of information
- But it is difficult to see trends quickly
- Useful to collate data in organised way.

Location	Value of sales
A	8000
B	5000
C	18000
D	6000
V	12000
W	7000

Cool Clothing – sales value ($000s)

Charts

If you do not simply want to list numbers in a table, charts are useful as they have more visual impact. A chart is a group of related facts presented in some form of diagram. It shows information in a form that is easy and quick to understand. The type of chart used will depend on what information needs to be shown. The three main types are **bar charts**, **pie charts** and **line charts**.

Bar charts

It shows data in bars or columns. The higher the height of the column, the higher is the value. It is very useful for showing trends over time.

- Easy to construct
- Easy to see results quickly
- Clear visual image
- It can only show a small number of simple figures.

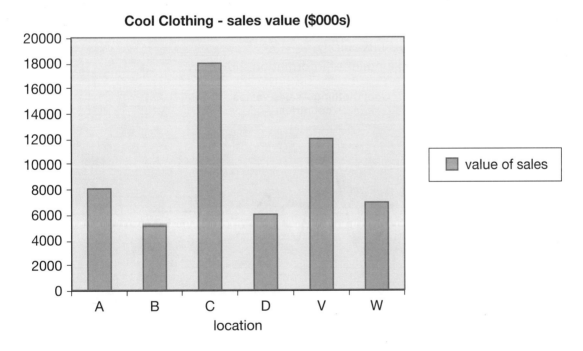

Pie charts

It shows proportions as in how much one part is of the whole. It is very useful when one wants to see simple comparisons between different options for same question.

- Very visual
- Easy to see results quickly
- Can be difficult to draw without computer software
- Does not include actual totals, only percentages.

Cool Clothing – sales values in countries ($000s)

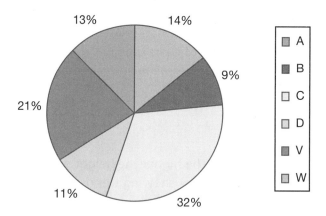

13%   14%

9%

21%

11%   32%

Legend:
- A
- B
- C
- D
- V
- W

Line graphs

It shows the relationship between two sets of numbers. In the figure it shows the relationship between value of sales and each country. It is useful when want to show trends over time.

- Easy to see results quickly
- Only limited amount of information shown.

Cool Clothing – sales values in countries

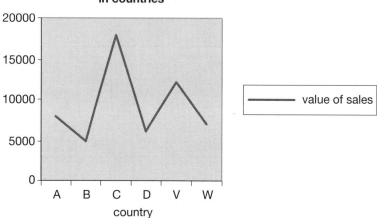

value of sales

There are other ways to present information including pictograms, photographs, maps and diagrams. It's all about choosing the most suitable method for what the business is trying to show.

What is a pictogram?

This is where data is represented by symbols of the item being displayed.

- Can be very attractive and are good for visual impact.
- Very difficult to represent in exact numbers.

The need to draw simple conclusions from data

Drawing a chart or a table to present information is not enough. A business is looking to see what the information will show them. Being able to explain what the results show is just as important.

What you need to say depends on the question, but try to:

- **Identify** what the chart or table shows – which are the highest numbers, which are the lowest? Simple statements are usually fine.
- **Include** numbers to support what you are saying.
- **Say** whether you think the results are good or bad for the business. If the question asks about sales, higher is better. But if you are looking at unemployment figures, lower is better.

 WARNING: The usefulness of any information will depend on how reliable it is. If the market research/data is wrong, good analysis will not help the business make the right decision.

> **Say what you can see. Use numbers to support what you are saying. This shows understanding and application.**

> **Useful links:**
>
> **Units 17 and 18: Communication**

Example: Cool Clothing
All the charts and tables show the same information.

What do the charts show?
The results show that the highest value of sales is in country C with $18 000 000. This is followed by country V which has $12 000 000 in sales. The lowest value of sales is found in Country B, where Cool Clothing sales are only worth $5 000 000.

But how does this information help the business decide where to open more outlets?
Option 1: This means they should open more shops in country C, where sales are the highest. Customers in country C must like their products, so more shops could mean more sales and possibly higher profits.

Option 2: Cool Clothing might not have many shops in country B, D and A so this might be why the value of sales is only $5m, $6m and $8m. If they opened more shops in these countries they might be able to gain more sales.

> **Either option is possible with the amount of data provided.**

The way information is presented is designed to help improve communication.

For communication to be effective, it is important that a business chooses the most suitable method of presentation to help the business get their message across to the right people.

The key points to remember are:

– What information needs to be presented?
– Who is the information for?

Progress check

1. What is a table of information?
2. State **one** advantage of using a pie chart.
3. What is a line graph used for?
4. Name **one** advantage of using a bar chart.
5. Give **one** advantage of presenting information in a table.

Sample question – worked example

Gee is a fruit farmer. He sells his fresh fruit to local shops and markets. Gee wants to increase the range of products he grows. He has been looking at his sales information for the past three years. Figure below shows the results.

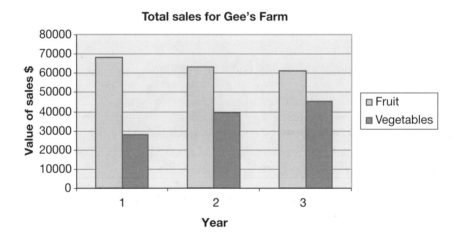

1. Identify **two** changes shown in the figure. Explain how Gee can use this information to help him increase the range of products he plans to sell. **[6]**

   Change 1: Sales of vegetables have increased from just under $30 000 to $45 000 over the years. This shows that Gee should try to sell more vegetables, as this is what his customers are demanding. By selling more vegetables, he could widen his customer base leading to ever more sales.
   Change 2: Sales of fruit have fallen by about $8000 over the same time. No one wants Gee's fruit.

Good development is shown in change 1.

Change 2 is statement only, but not explained how this will help Gee in his decision.

Comment: This is a good answer. The answer has correctly identified two changes shown by the chart, and has provided numerical evidence to support them. Change 1 has been developed to show how the information could help Gee.

Overall mark: 5/6

Key terms to learn

There are not any key terms for this unit. It is more important that you practice looking at some charts, and comment on what they show.

> Presentation and analysis of data is not just about drawing diagrams. You also need to be able to identify what the diagram shows, and explain what this might mean for the user.

Examination style questions for you to try

Fizzed Fruit is a company which produces a wide range of fruit drinks. The company are looking to provide a range of healthy drinks for older people. Rahul, the Chairman of the company told the marketing department to research into what people like to drink. Table 1 shows information that they gathered from a newspaper survey of 2000 people.

Table 1

	Men	Women
Water	10	27
Fruit drinks	23	40
Milk	26	15
Fizzy drinks	23	6
Other	18	12

> If you have to draw a chart or table remember to label the lines and give the chart a title.

1. Identify and explain **one** advantage and **one** disadvantage of using a table to present data.

    Advantage:

    Disadvantage: [4]

2. Using the information, draw a graph or chart to show the results of this question for fruit drinks and fizzy drinks. [4]

3. Identify and explain **two** ways that Fizzed Fruits could use this information to help them in their marketing decisions.

    Way 1:

    Way 2: [8]

Learning Summary

By the end of this unit you should understand:
- *The purpose of the marketing mix*
- *The four parts of the marketing mix*

The purpose of the marketing mix

We know that **marketing** is all about 'anticipating, identifying and satisfying customer needs – at a profit'. **Market research** tries to identify what customers want. The next step is to satisfy those needs.

To market its products profitably, a business has to think about four things **(the 4P's)**.

Product What they sell

Price How much it is sold for

Place (distribution) where it is sold

Promotion How to make people know about it

Useful links:
Units 25–29

- Every business will have to come up with the right combination of these factors for their particular business.
- The combination of product, price, place and promotion is called the marketing mix or the 4P's.
- A business must get all four parts right to be successful, just like pieces of a puzzle. It must sell the right product, at the right price, in the right place to the right people at the right time.
- If one element is wrong, the mix is likely to be wrong so might not meet the customer's needs. The business could lose sales and profit.
- The mix will change over time i.e., a product will need a different mix when it is first launched compared to when it is nearing the end of its life.

The four parts of the marketing mix

A business has plenty to think about if they are to have the right marketing mix. Some of the issues to consider are mentioned below.

Product – What to sell

- Should they produce one product or a range of items?
- What features to include – colour, size, environmentally friendly?
- Which production method to use?
- Is quality important?
- Is after sales service needed?
- How to package the product – to protect or attract?

Price – What price to sell the product at

- Is the market competitive?
- Is the product new or old?
- Should they use promotions to attract customers?
- Is the demand elastic or inelastic?
- What are the objectives of the company?
- Image – luxury and basic items will be priced differently.

The content of this unit is all about identifying links. It covers ideas that any business (and you) need to consider when marketing a product.

Place (distribution) – Where it is sold

- How to sell the product – direct to customers or use retailers?
- Which method of distribution should they use?
- Should the product be widely available or sold in a few places only?
- Which channel of distribution should they use?
- If exporting, what about transport costs and trade barriers?
- How will the type of product affect its distribution?

The issues identified here overlap with many other units from production and finance to all the other marketing units, which follow.

Promotion – Making people know about it

- How much can they afford to spend on promotion?
- How competitive is the market?
- How often to advertise?
- Where to advertise?
- Should they use above or below the line promotion?
- Who are we advertising to?

In Stores Now

22% Off

Promotional Discount Available

Technology has had an impact on marketing. The increasing use of e-commerce has affected where products are sold and advertised.

Useful link:

Unit 7: Technology

More goods and services are being bought and sold on-line. This has many implications for the marketing mix. Businesses have to think about issues such as:

- How to attract customers attention – web site, e-mail shots, text messages, advertising on social network sites.
- How to get products safely and securely to customers anywhere in the world – costs, packaging, time, quality issues.

Progress check

1. Write down definitions of the following term, as accurately as you can:
    *   Marketing mix
2. Name the 4 P's.
3. Which of the four P's includes quality?
4. Should a business focus on only one element of the marketing mix? Explain.
5. What is another name for place?

Sample question – worked example

Kallis Engineering is a small engineering firm in South Africa. It makes a wide range of farm tools. It is planning to expand the business by selling its tools in Asia. Some of the managers are concerned about the idea but can see the benefits of trading overseas.

1. Explain a suitable marketing mix for Kallis Engineering's business before their expansion. **[12]**

    Product – as the tools are used for farming they must be long-lasting and durable so can be used in hard, stony soil. If the tools break easily, people will not trust any of the products that they make, which could damage their reputation and sales. After sales support would be helpful for farmers, so that repairs could be done quickly. Farmers will need to be able to have tools available at all times as they never know when they might need their equipment.

    Price – this will depend on the quality and cost of the tools. The safest price to set would be cost plus pricing as it would ensure some profit is made. But if there are many other rival businesses selling similar tools, competitive pricing might be necessary to ensure sufficient sales.

    Promotion – as a small company they might not be able to afford TV advertising. Specialist magazines or flyers handed out around local markets to attract suitable customers would be a good idea. Promotions such as buy a plough get a free pitchfork or shovel might encourage sales.

Good application has been used in the answer.

Place – They could consider selling products directly to customers by visiting farms. For smaller equipment, mail order or the internet might be suitable to widen their potential market. They could attend trade fairs or farmers markets so they are targeting their specific customer base.

Comment: This is a good answer. Knowledge of all four elements of the marketing mix has been shown along with good application to the scenario.

Overall mark: 12 /12

Key terms to learn

Marketing mix: the combination of product, price, place and promotion used to sell goods and services to consumers.

This is an introductory section for the units that follow. Be aware of the issues that have been outlined here. Remember – for a successful product all elements of the marketing mix must be right.

Examination style questions for you to try

1. What is meant by a marketing mix? [2]

2. Identify **two** elements of the marketing mix.

   Element 1:

   Element 2: [2]

   Splash Active specialises in providing activity holidays for families. All its holidays are sold through local travel agents or booked at one of the four sites. Leaflets and posters are their main forms of promotion. There are a lot of companies selling the same type of holidays.

   Splash Active prides itself on its good reputation and competitive prices. The Marketing Director is looking at ways to increase sales outside of the main holiday season.

3. Identify and explain **two** changes to the marketing mix that might be used to increase Splash Active's sales of holidays?

   Change 1:

   Change 2: [8]

By the end of this unit you should understand:
- *The importance of product*
- *The product life cycle*
- *The role of package*
- *The importance of branding*

The importance of product

Getting the product right is the basis for a good marketing mix.

- It is the main reason why people buy something. If people do not want or like the product, they will not buy it.
- Does the product do what it is designed for? It has to be fit for purpose.
- The quality must match the price charged.
- Design is important as people will want a product that works and increasingly looks good as well.
- Research and development is time consuming and expensive but it is important to ensure the product is what consumers want.

The product life cycle

The **product life cycle** refers to the stages a product will pass through from its introduction to growth to the end of the products' time in the market.

→ All products go through the same stages. It is only how long each stage lasts that is different.
→ A business with many products will have many different product life cycles to manage.

Features of each stage

- **Introduction/launch** – the product is made available for customers to buy. Promotion is important to inform and interest the potential customers.
- **Growth** – sales and profits rise slowly as customers become aware of the product. Market share will rise. Brand loyalty might happen.
- **Maturity** – product reaches the peak of its sales and profits. Market share is at its highest level. Costs are likely to be low due to economies of scale.

Useful link:
Unit 3: Size of firm

- **Saturation** – increased competition means there are too many similar products. Sales and profits begin to fall.
- **Decline** – demand falls as people switch to other products or tastes change. Market share falls as well. A decision is needed whether to use an extension strategy or to stop production altogether.

Extension strategies

As a product nears or reaches the decline stage, the business might try to keep the product in the market for longer i.e., '*extend its life cycle*' by trying to boost the sales of the product to slow its rate of decline.

To encourage sales, they could use a number of strategies such as:

- Sell the product to a new market
- Target a different market segment
- Add new features to 'improve' the product
- Change the packages to change its image
- Encourage customers to use the product more often.

> You could be asked to draw or label a product life cycle. Make sure you know the order of each stage.

> Do not confuse these strategies with general promotions techniques such as lower prices or more advertising.

> You must be able to identify what will happen to sales and profits at each stage of the product life cycle.

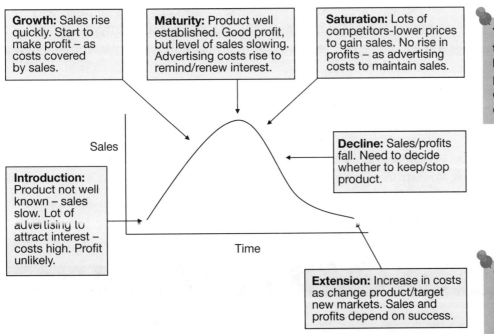

Growth: Sales rise quickly. Start to make profit – as costs covered by sales.

Maturity: Product well established. Good profit, but level of sales slowing. Advertising costs rise to remind/renew interest.

Saturation: Lots of competitors-lower prices to gain sales. No rise in profits – as advertising costs to maintain sales.

Decline: Sales/profits fall. Need to decide whether to keep/stop product.

Sales

Introduction: Product not well known – sales slow. Lot of advertising to attract interest – costs high. Profit unlikely.

Time

Extension: Increase in costs as change product/target new markets. Sales and profits depend on success.

> The marketing mix will change as a product goes through its life cycle.

The role of packaging

Packaging serves many functions as it is more than just a container.

- Protect the product so that it reaches the customer in perfect condition.
- Provide information so that the customer knows how to use the product.
- Contain safety information, required by law to inform or protect customers.
- Means to attract customers as the use of colour and shape can help a product stand out against competition.

- Help create unique identity as distinctive packaging can add to the products image to attract customers.
- Quality of packaging can help boost brand image. Customers expect luxury products to have expensive packaging.
- Help extend the life of the product as re-packaging can be used to remind/attract customers.

The importance of branding

Businesses want to make their products stand out from the competition. This will hopefully encourage people to buy their products rather than competitor's products.

Branding involves giving a product a special name to create a unique identity. This is called a **brand name**.

- Branding is designed to increase sales of a product and to extend the products' useful life.
- The brand name helps customers identify with a particular product. Businesses hope that the name sticks to the customer's mind, so they continue to buy their product. This is called **brand loyalty**.
- A brand name can be either a product (example, i-pod) or the company's name (such as Nike).

Other ways to create a unique identity for a product includes the following.

- **Product differentiation** – adding features to make the product different to similar products in the market. This is called a **Unique Selling Point**.
- **Packaging** – how a product is presented can raise customer awareness.
- **Advertising** – associating a product with an individual who portrays a certain image.
- **Place** – only selling the product in a limited range of outlets to suggest exclusive.

> The product is important. It is the main reason why people buy something. Without a good product, promotion, price and place have less value.

Progress check

1. Write down definitions of the following terms, as accurately as you can:
   - Branding
   - Extension strategy
2. What do you understand by the term 'fit for purpose'?
3. Name **two** roles of packaging.
4. Name **two** stages of the product life cycle.
5. Identify **two** extension strategies.

Sample question – worked example

Fizzed Fruits produce a wide range of fruit based drinks. It is a very competitive market. All their products are sold in distinctive fruit shaped cartons. The cartons are expensive to make but it is all part of the brand. The Marketing Manager believes packaging is important to a successful product.

Fizzed Fruits have recently launched a new citrus drink called 'full on fruit'. It has targeted the product at the mass market. The drink is sold in the popular Fizzed Fruits cartons and advertised locally on radio and through in store promotions. The Finance Manager, Faros, is very disappointed with initial sales, but understands it is at the introduction stage of its product life cycle. Faros thinks it's better than just trying to extend the life of existing products. The Marketing Manager is not so sure.

1. Identify and explain **two** benefits of branding for Fizzed Fruits. **[8]**

Benefit 1: Fizzed Fruits operate in a very competitive market. As there are a lot of other drinks available, a brand name is unique so will help the product stand out against rival products. This should help Fizzed Fruits compete against other businesses to maintain their sales.

Benefit 2: If the brand is good, people it will encourage loyalty as customers know what to expect and continue to buy this drink over rival drinks so boosting sales. The distinctive packaging is likely to catch the attention of potential customers, so they are more likely to try the product and if they like it, should continue to buy it.

> The answer shows good application and development of points.

Comment: This is a good answer. Both points are valid and are well explained to show how branding is a benefit for Fizzed Fruits.

Overall mark: 8/8

Key terms to learn

Branding: involves giving a product a special name to create a unique identity.

Brand name: the special name by which the product or company is known.

Product differentiation: adding features to make the product different from similar products in the market.

Product life cycle: the stages a product will pass through from its introduction to growth to the end of the product's time in the market.

Unique selling point: a feature that makes a product different to similar products in the market.

You must learn the concepts of product life cycle, packaging and branding. You will be expected to understand the importance of branding and packaging for a business. Make sure you understand the significance of each stage of the product life cycle and what each stage means in terms of costs, sales and profit.

Examination style questions for you to try

1. Identify **two** features of the introduction stage, in the product life cycle.

    Feature 1:

    Feature 2: [2]

2. Identify **four** functions of packaging. Explain the importance of each of these functions for a business.

    Function 1:

    Function 2:

    Function 3:

    Function 4: [8]

3. Do you think that packaging is important to the success of Fizzed Fruits? Justify your answer. [12]

4. The Finance Manager thinks it is better to develop new products rather than extend the life of existing ones. Do you agree with this view? Justify your answer. [6]

Learning Summary

By the end of this unit you should understand:
- *The significance of price elasticity of demand*
- *The main methods of pricing*

The significance of price elasticity of demand

- Demand is what people are willing and able to buy.
- People only buy products if they can afford to pay for them and think the price represents good value for money.
- The most important factor affecting demand is the price of the product.
- Demand is also influenced by income, taste, price of other goods etc.

How much demand is affected by a change in price of the good is called price elasticity of demand.

Demand is classed as either elastic or inelastic.

> **Useful link:**
> **Unit 8: Demand**

Price elastic	Price inelastic
• Change in price leads to a larger % change in demand	• Change in price leads to a smaller % change in demand
• Demand is responsive to change in price	• Demand is less responsive to change in price
• If prices rise:	• If prices rise:
• Sales will fall by more than percentage change in price	• Sales will fall by less than percentage change in price
• Profits likely to fall	• Profits likely to rise
• If prices fall:	• If prices fall:
• Sales will fall by more than percentage change in price	• Sales will rise by less than percentage change in price
• Profits likely to rise	• Profits likely to fall

→ Demand for most goods is elastic because there are many alternative products for them.
→ Demand for products with few substitutes such as luxury and branded items are usually inelastic.

Significance of elasticity

If costs rise, a business might increase the price to maintain profits.

- If demand is elastic, sales will fall by more than extra raised by price rise – so profits likely to fall more.
- So it could be better to have a lower profit margin to maintain current level of sales.

> You only need to understand why this concept is important. Learn how elasticity can affect the demand for products.

The main methods of pricing

> Do not confuse mark up with profit margin. Mark up is based on cost. Profit margin is based on selling price.

Cost plus

– Price covers cost of production plus set amount for profit (mark-up).

– Useful to guarantee a certain amount of profit.

– Not suitable for highly competitive market as might lose sales to cheaper competitors.

Advantages	Disadvantages
• Quick and simple to use. • Ensures costs covered. • Guarantees some profit on each unit sold.	• How much mark up to charge? • Sales could be affected if price set is too high for market.

Competitive pricing

– Price set based on what competitors are charging.

– Useful for most situations; if many rivals likely to be a lot of choice.

– But if have dominant position, or unique product might want to charge higher prices.

Advantages	Disadvantages
• Price similar to rivals so sales are maintained. • Realistic pricing encourages high sales.	• How to attract customers to product? • Actions of competitors likely to have major impact on marketing strategy. • No guarantee of profit.

Penetration pricing

– Setting a very low price to enter a new market.

– Prices might be increased later to increase profits.

– Useful strategy when entering new market to attract interest in product.

– Not suitable for long term as company unlikely to cover cost of products.

Advantages	Disadvantages
• Attracts customers to low prices. • Useful way to increase market share quickly. • Can also credit interest in other products that business might sell, further increasing sales.	• Possible loss of revenue as prices set lower. • Price might not cover costs. • Takes long time to recover development costs of new product. • If business tries to increase price customers might buy from rivals.

Price skimming

- Setting a high price for a new product.

- Customer is willing to pay more to have latest product. Prices can be lowered later to maintain level of sales.

- Useful strategy when high demand likely for a new product.

- When rivals enter market, they could undercut business so lose sales.

Advantages	Disadvantages
• Able to recover development costs quicker due to high price. • Reinforces quality image for product.	• Not everyone can afford initial high price so could lose possible sales. • Room for competitors to enter market with lower prices.

Psychological pricing

- Price is used to influence the perception of customers.

- To make product appear cheaper than it is; example, $1.99 not $2.

- Set a high price to create image of quality.

Advantages	Disadvantages
• Used to attract certain type of customer to buy product. • Can increase sales without having to alter price significantly.	• Perception could reduce sales if product seen as too expensive or too cheap.

> **Useful link:**
> **Unit 28: Promotion**

> These are the main methods of pricing. Another important method is promotional pricing - but this is only used for limited periods of time.

Progress check

1. Write down definitions of the following terms, as accurately as you can:
   - Price elasticity
   - Penetration pricing
2. If price was lowered for a price inelastic product, would sales rise or fall?
3. State **one** situation when cost plus pricing is useful.
4. Explain **one** advantage of price skimming.
5. Explain **one** problem of using penetration pricing.

Sample question – worked example

Splash Active specialises in providing activity holidays for families. There are a lot of companies selling the same type of holidays. All its holidays are sold through local travel agents, or booked at one of the four sites. Leaflets and posters are the main form of promotion.

Splash Active prides itself on a good reputation and competitive prices. The Marketing Director believes that demand is price elastic.

1. What is meant by 'demand is price elastic'? [2]

Students answer:
Demand will rise if the price of the product falls.

Comment: This answer shows some understanding of demand but does not explain the concept of price elasticity. To gain both marks there must be a clearer understanding of the link to the amount of change in demand.

Overall mark: 1/2

Key terms to learn

Competitive pricing: product is priced at or just below a competitor's price to try to gain more of the market.

Cost plus pricing: price covers cost of production plus set amount for profit.

Penetration pricing: setting a very low price to enter a new market.

Price elastic: a change in price leading to a larger change in demand.

Price elasticity of demand: the responsiveness of demand for a product as a result of a change in the price.

Price inelastic: a change in price leading to a smaller change in demand.

Price skimming: setting a high price for a new product.

Psychological pricing: price is used to influence the perception of customers.

You need to know and understand the difference between the various types of pricing. You could be asked to use this information to make decisions about what methods of pricing are suitable in certain situations. Be aware that different situations are likely to require different pricing strategies.

Price elasticity confuses many people. You will not be asked to calculate it, but you need to understand the basics. Just make sure you know the impact of price elasticity on the demand for a product – will it lead to sales going up or down? How will this effect profits?

Examination style questions for you to try

1. What is meant by 'competitive pricing'? **[2]**

2. Identify and explain **two** effects of price elasticity on demand for a product.

    Effect 1:

    Effect 2: **[4]**

Fizzed Fruits produces a wide range of fruit based drinks. It is a very competitive market. All their products are sold in distinctive fruit shaped cartons. The cartons are expensive to make but it is all part of the brand. The marketing manager believes packaging is important to a successful product.

Fizzed fruits have recently launched a new citrus drink called 'full on fruit'. They have targeted the product at the mass market. The drink is sold in the popular Fizzed fruits cartons, and advertised locally on radio and through in store promotions.

---

3. The Marketing Manager is trying to decide on a pricing strategy for the new citrus drink. Describe **three** suitable pricing strategies the company might use. Recommend which you think is the best strategy for Fizzed Fruits to use. Justify your choice.

    Strategy 1:

    Strategy 2:

    Strategy 3:

    Recommendation: **[12]**

Unit

27 Place

Learning Summary

By the end of this unit you should understand:
- *The channels of distribution*
- *The difference between a wholesaler and agent*
- *The factors to consider when choosing a method of distribution*

The channels of distribution

Place refers to 'where the product is sold and the methods used to get the product there'.

Two key decisions need to be taken:

1. How do producers get their products to the consumer?
2. Where will the product be sold?

How do producers get their products to the consumer?

How goods reach consumers is called a channel of distribution. There are four main channels.

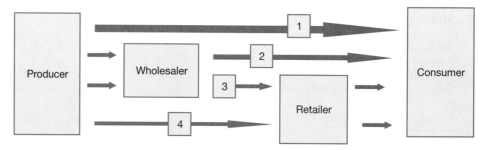

Method 1: Producer to consumer

- This is the most direct channel as the producer sells the goods directly to the customer.
- This cuts out need for both retailers and wholesalers.
- This is increasingly turning into a popular channel due to global nature of many markets.
- Examples – farmer selling goods from farm, factory shops, mail order and internet selling etc.

Useful link:
Unit 7: Impact of technology

140

Advantages	Disadvantages
• This is the fastest channel. • Producer receives direct feedback from consumers. • Goods are cheaper as they do not include costs of wholesaler and retailer.	• Can be difficult for consumers to find products. • Not everyone has access to internet. • Smaller potential market as fewer people aware of products. • Additional time and costs of distribution such as transport, staff etc.

Method 2: Producer to wholesaler to consumer

• Producer sells products to wholesaler who then sells the items to the customer.
• Wholesaler buys products in bulk at a discounted price. He 'breaks bulk' by reselling smaller quantities onto the consumer.
• Example – cash and carry stores etc.

Advantages	Disadvantages
• Wholesaler carries risk of not selling product rather than producer. • Producer has time to focus on production. • Producer has fewer people to deal with.	• Prices higher than if bought directly. • Lower levels of customer service as no direct contact with producer. • Limits potential market as sold in few outlets. • Producer makes less profit as sells at discount to wholesaler.

Method 3: Producer to wholesaler to retailer to consumer

• Similar to method two with the addition that the wholesaler sells products to retailers. The retailer then sells the items on to the consumer.
• This is a traditional route used by many small/medium businesses.

Advantages	Disadvantages
• Risk of not selling product with wholesaler not producer.	• Prices likely to be more expensive for consumers. Both retailer and wholesalers need to make profit.
• Producer has time to focus on production. • Producer does not have to deal with lots of retailers. • Wholesaler holds a range of stock so retailers have more choice. • Retailers able to buy amount needed as wholesaler breaks bulk this means lower storage costs.	• Can take longer for goods to be available as more stages. • Producer makes less profit as sells at discount to wholesaler. • Producer does not gain first hand information as no direct contact with customers. • Producer likely to make less profit as many links in distribution channel.

Advantages	Disadvantages
• Retailer only buys amount needed so lower overall cost. • Goods made available to many shops increasing potential market. • Consumers benefit from wider choice in local shops.	• Problems with communication could have significant impact on effectiveness as more people involved. • For perishable products, the extra time required to pass through all stages could result in poorer quality goods being available. This could damage reputation of producer, wholesaler and retailer.

Benefits of wholesalers

For producers:

• bulk buying as only having to deal with few large orders;
• storage costs reduced as held by wholesaler;
• any promotions help sales of the producer;
• offer advice to producer as they get feedback from many retailers.

For retailers:

• breaking bulk so only buy what need;
• reduced storage costs;
• offer credit terms helping cash flow;
• delivery from wholesaler so lower transport costs.

> **Channels of distribution refer to how products reach the consumer.**

Method 4: Producer to retailer to consumer

• Larger retailers can act as their own wholesalers. They buy goods directly from the producer and sell them to consumers.

Advantages	Disadvantages
• Faster for retailer as does not need to deal with wholesalers. • Cheaper prices as discounts given to retailer to lower costs. • Producer does not have to deal with lots of retailers. • Producer gets better feedback as link to retailers.	• Retailers must have space to store large quantities of goods. • Retailers have to pay transport costs themselves. • Producer might have to employ extra employees to manage retailers orders. • Retailer might want additional influence over what products are produced.

Where will the product be sold?

• A business can choose to sell products direct to customers or through wholesalers and retailers.
• Retailers include specialist shops, general stores, street vendors, individual or chain stores etc.
• Place will affect the other elements of the mix. Where it is sold can affect the image of the product as luxury items are not sold on market stalls.

Using the internet or a shop means different methods of promotion to inform and create interest.

The difference between a wholesaler and agent

A wholesaler is someone who buys products in large quantities from the producer. They resell smaller quantities of the goods onto retailers or consumers. This is called **breaking bulk**. They receive a discount from producers for bulk buying.

An agent does not buy the goods. They are paid for every sale they help arrange. Agents are often used by businesses who want to sell abroad. They can provide local knowledge of laws, customs and markets.

> **Useful link:**
> **Unit 10: Problems of trading overseas**

The factors to consider when choosing a channel of distribution

Cost

- Transport and administrative costs can be expensive. Faster delivery costs more as well.

Nature of the product

- Perishable and fragile goods need direct channels of distribution.
- Specialist items might not need to be widely available so shorter channels can be used.

The market

- Is the market for the goods large or small?
- Is it sold locally or internationally?
- Which market segment is the product aimed at?

Size of business

- Large organisations might be able to cut out wholesaler whereas small business cannot.

Progress check

1. Write down definitions of the following terms, as accurately as you can:
   - Place
   - Retailer
2. Which is the most direct channel of distribution?
3. In which situation is an agent most likely to be used?
4. State **two** channels of distribution.
5. Name **two** factors to consider when choosing a channel of distribution.

Sample question – worked example

Splash Active specialises in providing activity holidays for families. There are a lot of companies selling the same type of holidays. Most of their holidays are sold through local travel agents. Leaflets and posters are their main form of promotion.

Splash Active prides themselves on their good reputation and competitive prices. The Marketing Director believes that demand is price elastic. He is looking at ways to increase the level of sales. They are thinking of creating a website to boost sales.

1. Identify **one** advantage and **one** disadvantage for customers of Splash Active of having to use travel agents [8]

> Advantage: Customers will have a wider choice of holidays to choose from. Agents will have detailed knowledge of prices and variety of holidays available.
> Disadvantage: Customers might have to pay more for their activity holiday if they book through a travel agent.

Need to explain how wider choice will help customers to find best option and how more cost is a disadvantage.

Comment: This answer shows some knowledge of relevant factors, which have been both applied to Splash Active's business. However neither point has been developed.

The explanation of the advantage is actually another knowledge point rather than analysis of the first point.

Overall mark: 4/8

2. Splash Active is looking for ways to increase sales rather than just using travel agents. They are thinking of creating a website to sell their holidays. Do you think a website would be a better channel for Splash Active to sell their holiday? Justify your answer. [6]

> I think this is a great idea. Websites are cheap to create as they do not need to waste money on printing lots of holiday brochures as all information is online so less costs for the business to pay. They will not have to employ many sales staff as the customer types in all the details. It also never shuts, unlike a travel agent's shop so it's open for business 24 hours a day, seven days a week. They can also attract customers from anywhere in the world as more people will have access to the internet so they will not be limited to local travel agents. Travel agents might be good for some people as not everyone will have access to a computer, but they will have fewer people to target as they only use local agents. But the internet gives them a wider audience to advertise to, so there is more chance to attract more customers. It has to be a better way.

Judgement at the beginning is supported by answer.

Point against website gives balance to the answer.

Comment: This is an excellent answer. A number of valid points are identified and explained. The answer includes more points than are necessary for a six mark question. The question does not ask for both advantages and disadvantages, so a one sided answer on the benefits (or disadvantages) of the internet would be acceptable. However, it is always better if you can make at least one point both for and against the statement. The answer is applied to Splash Active, so full marks can be awarded.

Overall mark: 6/6

For this question, you could also decide that travel agents are still the best 'place' to sell holidays.

Key terms to learn

Channel of distribution: how goods and services get from the producer to the consumer.

Place: refers to where the product is sold and the methods used to get the product there.

Wholesaler: a middleman who buys goods from a producer to sell on to the retailer or customer.

> Make sure you understand the main differences for each channel of distribution. You could be asked to suggest a suitable channel for a product. Remember to discuss the advantages and disadvantages of each channel to help you decide which one to choose.

Examination style questions for you to try

> ABC own five small supermarkets. It sells top of the range products from a wide number of producers. ABC buys all its products from a wholesaler but is thinking of changing this. ABC has been struggling to get all the products it needs, "It's great that we get free delivery but is that enough? Think of the cost savings we could gain."

1. What is meant by a 'wholesaler'? [2]

2. Identify and explain **three** advantages for retailers of using a wholesaler.

   Advantage 1:

   Advantage 2:

   Advantage 3 [6]

3. Do you think ABC should change their channel of distribution? Justify your answer. [12]

28 Promotion

By the end of this unit you should understand:
- *The aims of promotion*
- *The different methods of promotion*
- *The factors to consider when choosing which method to use*

The aims of promotion

Promotion is all about increasing sales.

Promotion refers to all activities that are designed to make customers aware of their products to encourage them to buy. Its' aims are the following.

→ To inform customers about their products
→ To make customers aware of new products
→ To persuade customers to buy their product
→ To remind customers about existing products
→ To improve company image.

Methods can change as the product moves through its life cycle.

The different methods of promotion

Promotion is more than just advertising.

Advertising

- **Informative advertising** giving people information about the product.
- **Persuasive advertising** to convince people that they need or want the product.
- Factors to consider when the choosing methods include the following.
  → **Cost** – amount available to spend and the different cost of each method.
  → **Target audience** (which market segment) – who is the advertising aimed at and what do you want to say.
  → **Size of market** – size and what is being sold.
  → **Stage in product life cycle** – new products will need different strategy to those at growth or maturity stages.

Main methods of advertising

Television

- Useful for mass market products
- Able to reach large and varied number of people
- Visual appeal as colour, images and sound can attract attention
- Expensive so not all can afford to use
- Cost varies depending on the time shown
- No guarantee everyone will see or remember.

Cinema

- Visual appeal as colour, images and sound can attract attention
- Can use to target certain segments
- Smaller audience as not everyone will go to cinema
- Can be expensive as only small audience.

Radio (local and national)

- Able to target advertisement depending on channel/program
- Not as expensive as television but can vary with time played
- Cheaper but reaches fewer people
- Sound based method of advertising
- Local radio is suitable for advertising local events or businesses.

Newspapers/Magazines

- Can keep copy for future reference
- Can include more detailed information
- Cheaper than some methods
- Able to target segments by deciding where to advertise, example local or specialist
- No guarantee people will read.

Leaflets

- Relatively cheap to produce and distribute
- Can be kept as reference
- Can inform as well as persuade
- Often seen as 'junk mail' hence ignored
- Can use to target segments or general.

Posters and billboards

- Visual impact
- Can be seen by many people as they pass by
- Cheap form of advertising
- Difficult to target audience
- Cannot contain much information.

Useful links:

Unit 7: Technology (overlap with E-commerce)

Unit 41: The role of government

Internet

- Increasingly used for advertising
- Relatively cheap as no printing or distribution costs
- Visual and informative
- Can target customers via emails or links to other website
- Plenty of competition so customers actually may not see it.

Consumer protection laws will cover issues such as advertising and competition rules. All businesses will have to be careful about what they claim or offer.

Summary

- Television, radio and cinema are very visual so can have more impact attracting attention and interest. They can be expensive so more suitable for larger businesses and mass market products.
- Newspapers, magazines, posters and leaflets are useful for reference. As they are relatively cheap, they are good options for small businesses.
- Local products think about local radio, posters and leaflets as they do not need to advertise nationally.
- Specialist products tend to have a small market. Business will need to target audience so specialist magazines are a good option.

You will be expected to explain suitable methods in a given context. So learn what each method is useful for. Remember any sensible suggestion is usually allowed.

Sales promotion

- Tries to increase sales from existing customers and encourages others to switch from rival products.

Price reductions

- Promotional pricing i.e., reduce price for limited period of time to boost sales. Customers are attracted by cheaper prices and may continue to buy.

Special offers

- Range of options including Buy One Get One Free (BOGOF), discount coupons or extra added to product
- Only available for limited period. Customers attracted as they think product represents better value for money.

Free samples

- Smaller versions of product given to customers to allow them to try before buy. Tempts people to try product, and if liked, will encourage people to buy.

Point of sale

- Displays where products are sold. Highlight product so stands out from rivals
- At the place of selling, consumer can buy straight away.

Competitions

- Offer customers chance to win a prize usually for nothing
- Customers tempted to buy product so have chance to win something.

Free gifts

- Items given away with product either as one off or collection
- Collections encourage people to continue buying product to complete set.

After sales

- Offer guarantees or help line to reassure customers
- Often used for technology and electrical goods.

Direct marketing

- Includes any activity that involves direct approaches to the customer.
- → **Mail order** – customers select what they want from catalogues and goods sent to them.
- → **Email** – targeted messages/offers sent to individuals via their computer.
- → **Direct mail** – leaflets or letters posted to individuals. These are often ignored as 'junk mail'.

Other forms of promotion

Public relations

- Any activity designed to bring attention to business or product.

- Try to create good image by getting stories in press, sponsorship endorsements or sending information to customers via magazines.
- Entails free publicity.

Sponsorship

- Business gives money or support to an event, project or people.
- Business/product name linked to sponsorship to increase attention.
- Can be used to target market segments or promote certain image.

Celebrity endorsements

- Associating the name of a product or business with a well known person or celebrity.
- Interest in the well known person can boost image and sales of business.
- But if person receives negative publicity this can also damage product and business.

Do not just think about advertising when discussing types of promotion. Remember these other methods. Learn which methods are useful in different situations.

The factors to consider when choosing which method to use

Cost

- How much can a business afford to spend?
- Opportunity cost – money spent on promotion is not available for other purposes such as product development.
- Increases expenses so higher costs could increase price.

Type of product

- Products aimed at producers will use different methods than to consumer goods.
- Specialist products will use different methods to mass market items.

Size of market

- Mass market or niche markets need different approaches.

Progress check

1. Write down definitions of the following terms, as accurately as you can:
   - Above the line
   - Sponsorship
2. Identify **two** methods of sales promotion.
3. State **two** methods of advertising.
4. Name **two** aims of promotion.
5. Outline **two** factors to consider when deciding on a method of promotion.

Sample question – worked example

Nikita is the Marketing Manager at Any Baked. The company makes a range of products from cakes to breads. It sells the products in a variety of shops and supermarkets across the country. Nikita is looking at different methods of promotion in order to increase sales of bread.

1. Explain **three** methods of promotion that Any baked could use to help increase its sales. Recommend which one you think would be the best method for Any Baked to use. Justify your choice. **[12]**

Method 1: Free samples. They could let people try the bread, and if they liked the taste of it, they might buy it. Without knowing what food tastes like, it can be difficult to persuade people to buy it as flavour and taste is important. They could always use less popular breads, which people do not know as well, this is a good way to increase interest. Also it's not too expensive which is important as if the bread is not liked it might be thrown away anyway.

Method 2: Have a display. They could put a lot of the different types of bread on display in the shops, where people will see it. As they walk past, it might remind them about Any Baked's products. If they are left hidden away on a shelf somewhere, people might not see the cakes. If they cannot see what they want, they are not likely to buy it. The only problem is there might not be enough room for a display in all the shops they use to sell their products so not everyone would be made aware so sales might not increase everywhere.

Method 3: Use promotional pricing. By lowering the prices of bread for a short period of time, more customers might be attracted by cheaper prices and buy their products rather than other brands. If they like it, they might continue to buy it after the price has gone back to its usual price. It's easy to do, and shops would be happy as lower prices might bring in more customers.

Recommendation: I would recommend free samples – as people like to try things before they buy it.

> **Good application – taste and flavour are important for food.**

> **Choice made, but not said why it is better than the other two options.**

Comment: This is a good answer. Three appropriate methods have been identified and developed to show how they could be used to help increase sales. This answer does not include advertising in its suggestions, but they would be equally acceptable. There is some attempt at evaluation as a clear choice has been made. For the other evaluation marks, need to explain why this is a better option for Any Baked compared to the other two.

Overall mark: 10/12

Try to answer this question again with three different options.

Remember to explain which option you would recommend.

Why is it better than the other methods?

Key terms to learn

Informative advertising: giving people information about a product.

Persuasive advertising: any advertising which tries to convince people that they need or want the product.

Promotion: refers to all activities that are designed to make customers aware of their products so that they are encouraged at buying them.

Promotional pricing: strategy of reducing price of product for a limited period of time to boost sales.

Sponsorship: business gives money or support to an event, project or people.

You need to know and understand the difference between the various types of promotion.

You could be asked to use this information to make decisions about what methods of promotion are suitable in certain situations. Remember different situations are likely to require different promotion strategies.

Examination style questions for you to try

Splash Active specialises in providing activity holidays for families. There are a lot of companies selling the same type of holidays. All its holidays are sold through local travel agents or booked at one of the four sites. Customers stay in low cost wooden beach houses and have free use of the swimming pools. Leaflets and posters are the main type of promotion.

Splash Active prides itself on its good reputation and competitive prices. It has won many awards for health and safety. The Marketing Director believes that demand is price elastic.

1. What is meant by 'promotion'? [2]

2. Design a new poster for Splash Active to use to promote their business. Use the information in the question to help you decide on the advertising messages to use to sell their holidays. [8]

3. Identify and explain **two** other suitable forms of promotion that would be useful for this company. [6]

4. Do you think that leaflets and posters are the most suitable types of promotion for Splash Active to use? Justify your answer. [6]

Learning Summary

By the end of this unit you should understand:
- **The role of a marketing plan**
- **The importance of a marketing budget**

The role of a marketing plan

A **marketing plan** is a statement of actions a business will take to achieve its marketing objectives. These objectives are based on the business objectives.

Planning objectives

- To allow business to remain competitive
- To allow for better use of resources, time and money
- To help decision making by identifying right marketing mix to use
- To allow business to anticipate changes in market and customer needs
  Able to take advantage of new opportunities and minimise threats
- To help monitor progress towards overall business objectives.

Stages in planning process

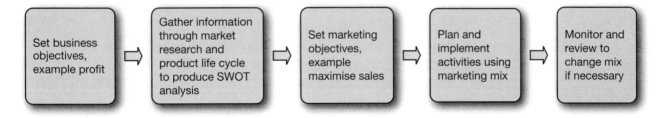

→ **Market research** involves finding out the needs of customers before developing a product (*see unit 22*).

→ **Product life cycle** is the need to know what stage product is at in its lifecycle (*see unit 25*).

→ **Swot analysis**

- Used to work out the strengths, weaknesses, opportunities and threats facing businesses' products.
- Strengths and weaknesses are internal as they refer to the product itself.

- Opportunities and threats are external factors (such as political, economic, social and technology).

Strengths	Weaknesses
• Market leader	• Technology old
Opportunities	**Threats**
• Could benefit from grants	• Overseas competition

- Useful to assess current market conditions and whether current strategy and resources are suitable.
- Can plan what, if any, changes to make.

→ **Marketing objectives** are usually short term and are reviewed regularly. Typical objectives include the following.

- Market penetration by increasing market share or sales.
- Market development by entering new markets or segments.
- Product development by introducing new products/extend life of existing products.

→ Plan and implement activities using **marketing mix**.

- The marketing mix is simply the combination of price, product, promotion and place used by a business (*see units 24–28*).
- The mix can change over time.
- The mix used depends on many things such as the product, its stage in the product life cycle and the current state of the market.
- New products will need a lot of promotion to create interest in a product; whereas products entering maturity might need promotion to remind customers about the product. If a product is in decline, might be better not to waste more money on it.
- Prices can be set either high, low or competitively depending on whether it is new or established. Luxury or basic item? Is the objective market penetration or development?
- Products will change and new features will be added to create an image, extend its life or as a means to enter new markets.
- Place will depend on factors such as the size and location of the market and the product itself.

→ Monitoring and reviewing should happen regularly as it is a useful tool to assess effectiveness of marketing strategy and the marketing budget.

The importance of a marketing budget

- A marketing budget is a financial plan for the marketing of a product for a set period of time.

- Nearly all marketing costs time and money so it is important to make best use of resources.
- Estimate of projected costs to market a business' products (or services).
- Typical costs might include cost of adverts, free gifts, salaries for marketing managers, cost of office space.
- Budgets help a business to monitor the success of marketing activities.
- Helpful in decision making to make best use of resources.
- It is based on forecasts and estimates, therefore cannot guarantee sales.

> A marketing budget is similar to any budget but only focusing on the marketing of a product.

Progress check

1. Write down definitions of the following terms, as accurately as you can:
   - Marketing budget
   - SWOT analysis
2. State **two** stages of the planning process.
3. Explain **two** reasons why planning is helpful for a business.
4. Identify **two** marketing objectives that a business might have.

Sample question – worked example

1. What is meant by a 'marketing budget'?   **[2]**

Students answer: A budget is a financial plan for a set period of time.

Comment: This is a good general definition of a budget which is worth 1 mark. The answer does not refer to the marketing element of the question is which is needed for the second mark.

Overall Mark: 1/2

Key terms to learn

Marketing budget: a financial plan for the marketing of a product for a set period of time.

Marketing plan: statement of the actions a business will take in order to achieve its marketing objectives.

SWOT analysis: looking at the strengths, weaknesses, opportunities and threats facing a business or product.

This unit looks at the process and issues that a business needs to consider when working out its marketing strategy.

You need to be able to analyse strategies used and be able to make judgements about how suitable they are. Be prepared to suggest and explain possible changes that might be needed in a given situation.

Examination style questions for you to try

Bradbury's is a small independent chocolate maker. Its luxury hand made chocolates are very popular with its rich customers. Bradbury's wants to increase sales, as it only has a small local market for its products. The owner, Joe Bradbury does not believe in marketing plans. "What is wrong with just making a product and selling it? Last year we had a market share of 37% in a $950,000 market."

1. What is a 'marketing plan'? [2]

2. Joe Bradbury believes that good products sell themselves. Do you agree with this view? Justify your answer. [6]

3. Explain a suitable marketing mix that Bradbury could use to sell these high quality chocolates to customers. Justify your choices. [12]

Unit
30 How are goods produced

The role of production

Production is the process of converting raw materials into finished goods. This is done by combining together the four factors of production – land, labour, capital and enterprise.

How goods are produced matters because of the following.

- Business will want to ensure that enough products are available when required to meet customer needs.
- The method used will affect both the fixed and variable costs of the business.
- The cost will influence the price they, want and can, afford to charge.
- Efficient production is more cost effective (financial return gained is worth the expenditure).
- The quality of the product must match what customers expect and the image the business wants to convey.

Production can be either of the below.

Capital intensive	Labour intensive
• When production uses high proportion of capital (machinery) to make goods.	• When production uses a high proportion of labour to make goods.

How production is carried out depends on several things.

- What product is produced
- Amount needed to be produced
- The factors of production available
- Method of production chosen.

> Useful links:
> Unit 26: Price
> Unit 25: Product
> Unit 33: Improving efficiency and quality

> The product is probably the most important factor to consider.

The different methods of production

Job production

It refers to making individual products to meet customer requirements. One product is made at a time.

Features

- Each product is unique as made to specific requirements;
- Uses highly skilled workers;
- Labour intensive;
- High set up costs;
- Flexible as approach changes to suit each order;
- Expensive to make;
- Can take a long time to make.

Job production is used for one off items such as bridges, ships, individually made clothing etc.

> **Learn the main methods. You could be asked to recommend a method to use in a given situation.**

Advantages	Disadvantages
• Unique products • High quality products • Production is very flexible • High level of job satisfaction for workers.	• Few if any economies of scale • Expensive to make • Management can be difficult as every job different.

Batch production

It refers to producing a number of similar items in groups or sets.

Features

- Limited amounts made;
- No variety is each batch;
- Machines must be reset after each batch;
- Less skilled workers used;
- Can benefit from some economies of scale;
- Allows for some division of labour.

Batch production is used for any products with range of designs and colours such as types of shoes, clothing etc.

> **Useful link:**
> **Unit 3: Business growth**

Advantages	Disadvantages
• Some flexibility as different variety of product can be made • Cheaper than job production as some economies of scale • Lower wages as less skilled workers used.	• Takes time to reset machinery so slows down production • Lower job satisfaction for worker so motivation can be an issue • Storage costs of unfinished goods.

Flow production

It refers to production of large numbers of same products continually. It is also known as mass production as it is used for mass market products.

- Products being made pass straight from one stage of production to the next.
- Flow involves a lot of machinery as the business aims to keep production going all the time.
- How the factory is set out is important, as flow production tries to reduce the movement of workers and materials between stages. This should help efficiency.

Features

- Large volumes;
- Continuous production;
- Identical products made;
- Capital intensive;
- Work is repetitive so motivation issues;
- Inflexible;
- Expensive to set up;
- Benefit from economies of scale;
- Allows for division of labour.

Flow production is used for any mass market item that is in constant demand such as cars etc.

Advantages	Disadvantages
• Economies of scale so lower unit cost • Lowest labour costs as unskilled workers paid less; less training likely • Continuous production allows for more product availability.	• Inflexible as difficult to change products made • Expensive to set up and maintain • If machines break down all production stops • Worker motivation can be a big problem.

Useful links:
Units 37–38: Motivation

Division of labour refers to breaking a job into smaller, repetitive tasks. This allows work to be done quickly with less skilled workers so business is able to reduce labour costs. As workers specialise (focus) on one task, motivation and boredom can become an issue.

Difference between batch and flow production

Amount produced:	Batch is limited volume	Flow is high volume
Type of production:	Batch stops and starts	Flow is continuous
Variety of product:	Batch has some variety	Flow is one product

Progress check

1. Write down definitions of the following terms, as accurately as you can:
   - Batch production
   - Labour intensive
2. Identify **two** features of job production.
3. What is the purpose of production?
4. Which method of production is likely produce the most output?
5. Which method of production is most likely to lead to problems with motivation?

There are plenty of concepts mentioned here that overlap with other concepts in the book. Some of the main themes to focus on are the following.

Unit 3 – Economies of scale: the advantages of larger scale production;
Unit 20 – Sources of finance: different methods to pay for capital required;
Unit 33 – Improving efficiency;
Unit 37 – The issue of motivation and methods to overcome motivational problems.

Sample question – worked example

Bradbury's is a small independent chocolate maker. Its luxury hand made chocolates are very popular with its rich customers. Bradbury's wants to increase sales, as it only has a small local market for its products. The owner, Joe Bradbury does not believe in marketing plans. "What is wrong with just making a product and selling it? Last year we had a market share of 37% in a $950 000 market."

Question refers to a business so answer does not need to apply to Bradbury.

1. Bradbury's use job production. identify and explain **one** advantage and **one** disadvantage of job production for a business. **[4]**

   Advantage: As the products tend to be unique the business is able to charge higher prices for the products.
   Disadvantage: Workers tend to have higher job satisfaction as the work is more varied. They are therefore less likely to leave.

Comment: This answer shows good knowledge of two advantages of job production, which have both been explained. However only one can be rewarded as the question asked for a disadvantage as well.

Overall mark: 2/4

Key terms to learn

Batch production: producing a number of similar items in groups or sets.

Capital intensive: when production uses high proportion of capital (machinery) to make goods.

Flow production: producing large numbers of the same product continually.

Job production: making individual products as per customer requirements.

Labour intensive: when production uses a high proportion of labour to make goods.

Production: the process of converting raw materials or components into finished goods.

> The method of production used will mainly depend on what is produced. Do not forget to use the links in your answers. There are many overlaps; finance is important as capital equipment is expensive. The role of worker and what each method means in terms of pay and motivation. Do not forget the benefits of economies of scale.

Examination style questions for you to try

> Kape Confection is a large company that manufactures chocolate. It produces and sells its products around the world. Kape Confection aims to sell as many items as it can at low prices. All products are made by machines, using batch production. The management are thinking of using flow production.

1. What is meant by 'flow production'?   [2]

2. Identify and explain **three** problems a business might face when using flow production.

    Problem 1:

    Problem 2:

    Problem 3:   [6]

3. Kape Confection uses batch production. Do you think this is the best method for them to use? Justify your answer.   [6]

4. Discuss the advantages and disadvantages of different methods of production to decide whether batch production is the best method for Kape Confection to use. Justify your answer.   [12]

31 Costs

Learning Summary

By the end of this unit you should understand:
- *The different classification of costs*
- *The role of break even analysis in decision making*
- *The benefits and limitations of break even*

The different classification of costs

Useful links:

Unit 34: Cash flow

Unit 35: Financial accounts

- All resources cost money, from rent and materials to printing posters.
- Businesses need to work out how much it costs to produce all their goods. This is called the **cost of production**.
- Costs are usually shown in financial statements as either:
  - Cash outflows in cash flow forecast;
  - Cost of goods sold or expenses in **profit and loss account**.

Costs are classed on the basis of what they are used for.

Fixed costs and variable costs

The most common way of classifying costs is based on how they are used in production. This classification is used for break even analysis.

Be careful with wages. If worker pay changes depending on what they do; example, time or piece rate – they are variable. If employees or managers get a set amount every month, it's a fixed cost.

Fixed costs	Variable costs
• It refers to costs that do not vary with the level of production.	• It refers to costs that vary with the level of production.
• These costs will remain the same whether a business produces anything or not.	• These costs will increase or decrease with the level of production. – Higher output means higher variable costs. – Lower output means lower variable cost.
• Examples include rent, interest on loans, salaries etc.	• Examples include wages, raw materials etc.

TOTAL COSTS (TC) = FC + VC

Total costs equals the total of fixed costs and variable costs

---

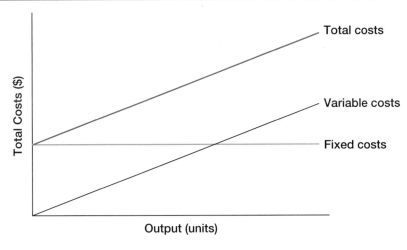

Indirect and direct costs

Indirect costs

- It refers to costs that are **not** directly linked to the production of a particular product.
- They are also known as overheads and is similar to fixed costs.
- Items are similar to expenses in a profit and loss account.
- Examples include management salaries, rent, marketing and telephone etc.

Direct costs

- It refers to costs that are directly linked to the production of a particular product.
- They are similar to variable costs.
- Items included as direct cost are closely related to cost of goods sold.
- Examples include wages, raw materials etc.

The role of break even analysis in decision making

Break even analysis is a technique used to help management work out how much to produce. It is based on identifying the fixed costs and variable costs of producing a certain product.

Managers can then draw diagrams (break even charts) to work out the costs, and possible profit (or loss) at different levels of production and sales.

Break even point is where the level of sales revenue equals the costs of production.

Total costs (TC) = Total revenue (TR)

- If sales revenue is less than total cost, the business makes a loss.
- At break even point, the business is making neither a profit nor a loss.
- If sales revenue is more than total cost, the business makes a profit.

Businesses use break even analysis to help them decide what level of output and sales to produce.

Break even can be calculated by table or chart.

Example:
A product has a selling price of $25. The variable costs are $15 and fixed costs are $6000.

What level of output is needed to cover all its costs?

The table shows the information in a table.

Break even output: **600** units
Break even revenue: $15 000

If they sell more than 600 units, they will make a profit.

output	FC	VC	TC	sales	profit
0	6000	0	6000	0	-6000
100	6000	1500	7500	2500	-5000
200	6000	3000	9000	5000	-4000
300	6000	4500	10500	7500	-3000
400	6000	6000	12000	10000	-2000
500	6000	7500	13500	12500	-1000
600	6000	9000	15000	15000	0
700	6000	10500	16500	17500	1000
800	6000	12000	18000	20000	2000
900	6000	13500	19500	22500	3000
1000	6000	15000	21000	25000	4000
1100	6000	16500	22500	27500	5000

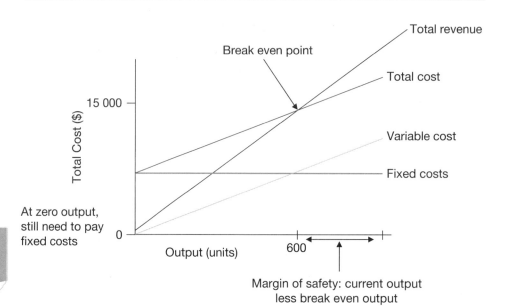

If asked to draw a break even chart remember to label all the lines.

Break even formula

You do not need a chart to work out break even. There is a formula. This can be written two ways but it is the same calculation.

Per unit in the formula is important.

$$\frac{\text{Fixed costs}}{\text{Selling price} - \text{Variable cost per unit}}$$

$$\frac{\text{Fixed costs}}{\text{Contribution per unit}}$$

→ **Contribution** is selling price – variable cost per unit

It shows the amount of revenue left from each sale that is available to go towards fixed cost.

Using the example: $\dfrac{6000}{25-15} = 600\,units$

This is the same as shown in the chart.

Remember that any change in fixed costs, variable cost or selling price will mean a new break even output. This will change the amount of profit or loss made.

– If costs increase or prices decrease:

→ The break even point will increase;
→ The business will need to sell more to make a profit.

– If costs decrease or price increase:

→ The break even point will decrease;
→ The business will need to sell less to make a profit.

The benefits and limitations of break even

Benefits

- Used to decide what level of output and sales are needed when starting business.
- Helps support loan applications as shows good business planning.
- Able to see effect of any changes in price or costs to help better decision making.
- Simple and quick to use.

Limitations

- Based on assumption that everything made will be sold, which is not always true. Some products are seasonal and tastes change.
- Costs or prices could change suddenly so results can be misleading.
- Only a forecast, the figures used may not be accurate enough for decision making.

Progress check

1. Write down definitions of the following terms , as accurately as you can:
   - Break even output
   - Average cost
2. Give **two** examples of fixed costs.
3. What is another term for indirect costs?
4. Explain **one** problem of break even analysis.
5. Would higher costs increase or decrease break even point?

Sample question – worked example

Wooden Works is a successful and growing company who makes furniture. Its most successful product is chairs, which are sold to businesses. The Finance Manager has been looking at costs. Each office chair is sold for $25. He has calculated the fixed costs at $150000 and variable costs at $15 per chair. He is trying to calculate the contribution per chair.

1. Calculate Wooden Works contribution per chair. [2]

   Students answer:
   Selling price per unit – variable cost = $11

Comment: The answer is incorrect as the contribution is $10. However as the correct formula has been shown, the method mark can still be given.

Overall mark: 1/2

Key terms to learn

Average cost: the total cost of production divided by total output.

Break even point: the level of output where total costs equals total revenue.

Contribution: the selling price of the product less the amount of variable costs used to make it.

Direct cost: costs that are directly linked to the production of a particular product.

Fixed cost: costs that do not vary with the level of production.

Indirect cost: costs that are not directly linked to the production of a particular product.

Margin of safety: difference between current level of output and the break even output.

Overheads: a cost which is unrelated to the level of output of a business but is one that is incurred by the existence of the business.

Total cost: equals the sum of fixed cost and variable costs added together.

Variable cost: costs that vary with the level of production.

You must understand the different costs and be able to give appropriate examples of each. You could be asked calculations, so make sure you know the various formulas for the different costs.
You will also need to be able to explain, interpret and use a simple break even chart. Make sure you can correctly label a break even chart and are able to work out break even output from it. You only need to be able to make simple comments about what you see.

Examination style questions for you to try

1. Give an example of **one** variable cost and **one** fixed cost that Wooden Works might have.

   Variable cost:

   Fixed cost: [2]

2. The Finance Manager is trying to work out how many chairs he will need to break even. Using the information provided, construct a simple break even chart for Wooden Works. [6]

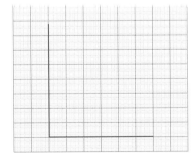

3. Identify and explain **one** advantage and **one** disadvantage for Wooden Works of using break even analysis.

   Advantage:

   Disadvantage: [4]

4. The Finance Manager believes that a break even chart is important to the successful financial management of Wooden Works. Do you agree with this view? Justify your answer. [6]

32 Location

Learning Summary

By the end of this unit you should understand:
- *The factors affecting location decisions for a business*
- *Choosing the best location for different types of business*

The factors affecting location decisions for a business

- All businesses, whether they produce goods or services have to be based somewhere.
- Finding the right location involves identifying which factors are the most important for a particular business.
- Similar factors apply whether the business is relocating or setting up a new factory.
- A business chooses its location for many reasons. The main ones are discussed below.

Raw materials

- Businesses using a lot of raw materials to make products are better located near the materials to keep transport costs low.
- If materials are easy to access and transport, a business might decide to locate nearer the customer.

Tradition

- Some industries are associated with particular places such as mining or cotton. This is usually the place where the raw materials are found.
- Areas can develops specialist skills leading other similar businesses to locate there as well.

Customers

- If finished goods are expensive or bulky to move, it can be better to locate near the customers to keep transport costs lower.
- Service providers are often located near customers so it is easier for customers to reach them.

Environment

- Physical factors such as amount of space needed and access to natural resources affect the location as well.
- Climate is important as certain foodstuffs need particular weather conditions to grow.
- Proximity of natural features will affect some businesses. A sailing club, for example, will need access to water etc.

Infrastructure

- Many businesses need access to power and electricity to operate equipment.
- Transport links are important for importers, exporters and distribution businesses. A wholesaler will want good transport links to ensure that supplies can be moved easily between producers and consumers.
- Communication is increasingly important. Remote or mountainous areas might have difficulty accessing telephone/internet networks.

Availability of workers

- Some businesses need specialist workers who might only be found in some areas.
- A business looking to keep wages low might chose an area with high unemployment or a low cost country.
- A remote location for a mine might require a business to bring in workers which will increase their costs.

> **Useful link:**
> **Unit 21: Markets**

Location of competitors

- Being near competitors can be good. Lots of similar businesses in an area can lead to suppliers setting up nearby so lowering transport costs
- The local workforce might already have the right skills which could reduce training costs.
- Too much competition could affect the demand for their products, reducing sales.

> **Useful link:**
> **Unit 6: Role of Government**

Government

Can influence location decisions in a number of ways.

- Legislation might restrict where a business can locate and how it is allowed to operate.
- Grants and other incentives can be offered if a business locates in particular locations. This can help lower their costs.
- Different countries have different laws. Lower health and safety standards could help reduce training or operating costs.
- Minimum wage laws will determine how much the business must pay its workers.

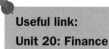

Useful link:

Unit 20: Finance

Cost

- The best locations are often expensive.
- Building a new factory is expensive in terms of cost of land and installing the necessary equipment etc.
- Additional costs of local taxes and insurance should not be forgotten.

Personal reasons

- Owners or managers might want to locate in particular places. Small businesses, in particular sole traders, might want to locate near their home so that they do not have to travel far.

Most questions on location will require you to use these factors in a given situation. Read the question carefully to make sure you know what type of business it is, so you work out which factors to discuss.

Choosing the best location for different types of business

Different factors will be important depending on the following.

- The type of business sector operated in – primary, secondary or tertiary which will affect the type of product sold.
- Where is the market located – domestic or international business.

Primary sector

Some points to consider in this sector.

- Access to raw materials are important as a mine will only be located where minerals are found.
- Transport links are important as they are needed to send out materials and bring in machinery and workers.
- Climate is important as certain places are better for growing different agricultural products.
- Access to workers is important as enough suitable workers are required from nearby.
- Traditions matter also as fishermen are always found near water etc.

Secondary sector

Some points to consider in this sector.

- If the materials used are bulky, it is better to be close to the supplier.
- Transport links are important as they will need access to markets and suppliers.

- If buying or selling overseas, Government policies could affect what or how much is sold.
- Factories need power and space.
- Labour intensive business need suitable workers from nearby.
- Government laws could affect location.

Tertiary sector

Some points to consider in this sector.

- Most service providers will try to be close to their customers for ease of access.
- Communication links are important particularly with the growth of e-commerce, and providing a good customer service.
- Access to skilled workers. Think about what type of business it is. An architect will need more specialist workers than a retail shop.
- A central location in a city will cost more than an out of town site.
- Personal reasons such as where do they want to set up the business are also a consideration.

For some larger businesses, including **multinational companies**, the issue is:

Which country to locate in?

Some points to consider:

- Access to raw materials as might need to locate near resources to ensure enough supply.
- Access to market depending on where are the products sold. The country needs to be nearer to or where the demand is rising.
- Infrastructure as low cost countries for workers might not have the right transport or communication links in place.
- Access to workers as enough suitable workers required from nearby.
- Role of Government as different countries could have different rules and laws. This could impact on how and what can be made. Grants/assistance could reduce expenses for business.

> **Useful link:**
>
> **Unit 15:**
> **Multinationals**

> There is usually no right answer to location questions. Just make sure you explain why the factors you have chosen are important.

Progress check

1. Identify **three** location factors that any business will need to consider.
2. What does infrastructure refer to?
3. Identify **two** factors that might be important to retailer.
4. Why is climate an issue for some businesses?
5. Identify **two** factors that a manufacturing business would need to consider.

Sample question – worked example

Kape Confection is a large company that manufactures chocolate. It produces and sells its products around the world. Kape Confection aims to sell as many items as it can at low prices. All products are made by machines. Kape are looking to expand into more countries. It wants to open another distribution centre, which will create 300 new jobs.

The question does not state the number of factors so work on 3 or 4.

There is good application in this answer, as it refers to 'melt' and the '300 employees'.

1. Advise Kape Confection on which factors will be most important in the decision about where to locate the new distribution centre. Justify your answer. [12]

Student's answer:

As it is a distribution centre, it needs to be near roads, so that the chocolate can be easily brought in and out. It is no good putting it somewhere remote, that lorries cannot get to, as this will delay deliveries. The availability of power is also important. Chocolate would have to be kept at the right temperature, if it is too hot it would melt, so they will need electricity to that they can store the chocolate in the correct conditions while it is in the warehouse. A third factor is the availability of workers as the warehouse will require a large number of employees, about 300 people to work on the there. The government could also be an important factor. They might offer grants to help a business set up in certain locations. A large company like Kape is creating 300 jobs so the Government might want to encourage them to set up in their country. Kape sells chocolate all over the world, so they could locate the centre in many countries. If Kape can get access to a grant to lower their costs, that could be a good reason to locate in one place rather than another.

Do not use the same explanation for all reasons as this is repetition, and unless the point is clearly different, it will only be rewarded once.

Comment: This is a good answer. Four relevant location factors have been identified. Each one has been explained to show why the factor is important to the location of the distribution centre, so full marks can be awarded. The question does not ask for the most important so no final decision is needed.

Overall mark: 12/12

Key terms to learn

There are no new terms to learn for this unit. Make sure you know which factors are important for different types of business.

> Learn the main factors. The important thing to remember is only to talk about factors which are relevant to the business in the question. Do not just list all the factors – if you do, you will only be able to gain knowledge marks.

Examination style questions for you to try

1. Identify **two** ways a Government might try to influence the location of a firm.

    Way 1:

    Way 2:   [2]

2. Identify and explain **two** possible reasons why a Government might try to influence the location of a business.

    Reason 1:

    Reason 2:

    > Razzaq is a sole trader. He owns two small bread shops in the same part of the city. He wants to open another shop, but is not sure where the best location for a new shop would be?

3. Identify and explain **three** factors that Razzaq should take into account when setting up a new shop.

    Factor 1:

    Factor 2:

    Factor 3:   [6]

> When explaining why a factor is important try to avoid simply statements like 'it's cheaper'. Try to explain how or why it might be cheaper.

By the end of this unit you should understand:

- **The concept of productivity**
- **The difference between efficiency and productivity**
- **The methods of improving efficiency**
- **The different methods of lean production**
- **The importance of quality control**

The concept of productivity

Useful links:

Unit 3: Economies of scale

Unit 30: Methods of production

Productivity is one measure of efficiency. It measures the amount of output produced against inputs used to make it.

There are many ways to calculate this. The main ones are as mentioned here.

By labour	By machine	By hours
$\dfrac{\text{Total output}}{\text{Number of employees}}$	$\dfrac{\text{Total output}}{\text{Number of machines}}$	$\dfrac{\text{Total output}}{\text{Number of hours}}$

The formula for each one is similar: $\dfrac{\text{Output}}{\text{Input used}}$

Calculation questions are common. Remember to include the formula in your answer.

Example,
A factory employs 50 workers. Annual output is 8250 units in 2010.
What is the productivity per worker?

$$\frac{8250}{50} = 165 \text{ units per worker}$$

Each worker produced 165 units in the year 2010.

- Shows how many units each worker produces in a set period of time (usually one year).
- Shows how well resources are being used.
- The higher the figure, the higher the level of productivity.

- A lower figure could indicate a lower level of productivity.
- A business will aim for lower **average costs** and **higher productivity**.
- Larger businesses tend to have lower average costs. This is because they can benefit more from **economies of scale**.

A business uses productivity information to compare performance over time or against similar businesses. This shows if (or where) changes need to be made.

Productivity is affected by many factors including the following.

→ Sickness
→ Machine breakdown
→ Industrial action
→ Skill level of workers
→ Level of worker motivation
→ Capital or labour intensive business.

Useful link:
Unit 3: Business growth

Useful links
Units 37–39: motivation and training

The difference between efficiency and productivity

• Efficiency refers to how well a business uses its resources. • An efficient business makes good use of its resources. • An inefficient business does not make the best use of resources.	• Productivity is only one measure of efficiency. • Measures amount of output produced against inputs used to make it. • Higher productivity is better.

The methods of improving efficiency

- **Work study** – examines how work is carried out to identify ways to improve how each task is done. Could result in redesign of layout or job done.
- **Training** – having staff with better skills could mean fewer mistakes are made. This might improve productivity so that the cost of training is covered by increased output or increased profits.
- **Develop methods of team working** – workers are split into groups who are responsible for making either a specific part or the whole product.
- **Update old technology** – new technology can help improve efficiency. Machines do not need breaks or wages like people. It can help produce more products in less time.

Good communication can also help improve efficiency (see units 17 and 18).

The different methods of lean production

Lean production involves using techniques to cut down waste in a business to improve efficiency.

→ Aims to use as few resources as possible.

→ Many methods involve more employees in the decision making process which should help increase levels of motivation.

Methods of lean production are discussed below.

Just in time

- Production is carefully planned so materials arrive when needed so stock costs are kept to a minimum.
- Stock control is very important if a system is to work.
- Must have suppliers who can provide stock when required or the production stops and orders might not be met.
- This reduces the amount of space needed for stock.
- It reduces the cost of holding stock to help improve cash flow.

Kaizen

- It is also known as continuous improvement.
- Everyone is encouraged to think of ways to improve how they work.
- This is based on idea that 'many small changes' made can have a large impact on efficiency.
- Workers often work in groups to identify and discuss ideas.
- Good way to increase motivation through worker involvement.

Total quality management

- It entails an approach to quality based on the idea that everyone in the business is responsible for quality.
- So administration and delivery to customer is just as important as checking the standard of products throughout production.
- **Quality circles** i.e., groups of workers from many departments meet regularly to discuss ways to improve quality.

Team working

- Groups of workers are given responsibility for making either parts or the whole product.
- Increased motivation as workers arrange how the work is organised.
- Efficiency could be improved as workers should understand production process better than managers.

The importance of quality control

Quality control is all about trying to ensure that set standards of quality are maintained throughout the production process. Good quality control starts at the design stage and continues even after the customer has bought the product.

Quality control is important for many reasons.

- To ensure customer satisfaction. Customers expect good quality products. If the goods or services produced are of poor quality, customers will go elsewhere.

- Products need to be checked throughout production for safety, appearance and mistakes.
- If errors are spotted early and corrected this can reduce costs and wastage helping the business become more efficient.
- If products do not meet minimum legal standards, the business could face a fine or legal action.
- Poor quality products could damage the businesses' reputation leading to lower sales.

> **Useful link:**
> **Unit 25: Product**

Progress check

1. Write down definitions of the following terms , as accurately as you can:
   - Lean production
   - Just in time
2. Are lower average costs a sign of higher or lower efficiency? Explain your answer.
3. What is the connection between economies of scale and efficiency?
4. What is team working?
5. Outline **two** reasons for why quality control is important.

Sample question – worked example

Homer is the Production Manager at Any Baked. He wants to make the factory more efficient. Homer has gathered data about the workers productivity. This is shown in the table. All workers work a 40 hour week in both years.

> **Always read the question carefully. Make sure you have identified the right trend by looking at the right year.**

Year	Total labour-hours worked per week	Output per week [units]	Output per employee per week [units]
2009	80 000	230 000	115
2010	100 000	270 000	108

1. Identify and explain **two** possible reasons why the productivity of the workforce changed in 2010. **[4]**

   Students Answer:

   Reason 1: Homer might have got new machines that can make more than old machines so productivity has increased.

   Reason 2: Homer has taken on new workers who are better bakers so they are able to produce more products.

Comment: This answer is incorrect. Output per employee has fallen by seven units per worker, not increased. So although the points identified are valid reasons for an improvement in productivity this does not answer the question set, so no marks can be given.

Overall mark: 0/4

Key terms to learn

Efficiency: refers to how well a business uses its resources.

Just in time: production is carefully planned to ensure materials arrive at the right time in the production process, so stock is kept to a minimum.

Kaizen: everyone is encouraged to think of ways to improve how they work rather than just investing in new technology.

Lean production: involves using techniques to cut down waste in a business thereby improving efficiency.

Productivity: measures amount of output produced against inputs used to make it.

Quality control: ensure set standards of quality are maintained throughout the production process.

Total quality management: approach to quality based on the idea that everyone in the business is responsible for quality.

> You need to understand the concepts of efficiency, productivity and quality. They overlap with many other topics. Efficiency overlaps with economies of scale (unit 3), technology (7), costs (31), efficiency ratios (36) motivation (37 and 38) in particular. Remember you can usually use any of this information to help you answer questions on efficiency.

Examination style questions for you to try

> Any Baked makes a range of products from cakes to breads. Sales have grown steadily over the last five years. It needs to increase production again. A number of their old machines keep breaking down. Homer, the Production Manager, wants to introduce new technology into the business as he thinks it will improve productivity. He wants to make the factory more efficient. The Finance Director is worried about buying new equipment, as the business has a lot of loans. Renting is not an option. The older workers are worried about what the change will mean for their jobs.

1. What is meant by 'improve productivity'? [2]

2. Besides new technology, identify and explain **three** other methods that Homer could use to improve efficiency.

   Method 1:

   Method 2:

   Method 3: [6]

3. Discuss the possible advantages and disadvantages of introducing new technology for Any Baked. Do you think it is a good idea for the business to introduce new technology? Justify your answer. [12]

Unit 34 Cash and cash flow forecasts

Learning Summary

By the end of this unit you should understand:

- *The importance of cash*
- *The benefits of using a cash flow forecast*
- *The role of a budget*

The importance of cash

- **Cash** is a liquid asset. It can be used straightaway to buy stock or to pay debts.
- Managing cash is important. Without enough cash, even a profitable business will fail as they need to pay debts as and when due.
- **Cash flow** is the flow of all money in and out of the business.
- The amount of money flowing in and out of the business is shown in a cash flow forecast.

The cash flow forecast

- A cash flow forecast tries to show the timings of cash inflows and outflows.
- If the cash outflows are more than the cash inflows, the business will have a shortfall in their day to day finance.
- A business can survive without profit for a short time, but without money for materials and wages, it is unlikely to survive for long.
- This will show when a business can expect cash flow problems, so that they have time to take steps to avoid them.
- **Cash inflows** refer to money coming into the business. This includes cash from sales, proceeds from sale of assets and money from loans and grants.
- **Cash outflows** refer to money going out of the business. This includes wages, rent, material costs, advertising and interest payments.

Example: Business			
In $000	**Month 1**	**Month 2**	**Month 3**
Opening balance (A)	0	(150)	(90)
Cash in			
Cash sales	550	550	550
Total cash inflow (B)	550	550	550
Cash out			
Wages	180	180	180
Raw materials	220	220	120
Rent	250	0	0
Other costs	50	90	90
Total cash outflow (C)	700	490	390
Net cash flow (D) = (B) – (C)	(150)	60	160
Closing balance (A) + (D)	(150)	(90)	70

Opening balance – amount of cash at the beginning of period

Net cash flow – the difference between cash inflows and outflows over the period

Closing balance – amount of cash left at the end of period

Shows
- negative cash flows in months 1 and 2
- positive cash flow of $70 000 in month 3

Do not forget that the closing balance for one month becomes the opening balance for next month.

Sales are shown only when money is received. This is not always the same time as when goods are sold as customers might buy goods on credit.

Problems caused by poor cash flow

Poor cash flow means there is not enough cash to pay day to day expenses.

- Suppliers could stop supplying materials to make goods or discounts.
- Unpaid workers could become de-motivated.
- Lenders might want higher interest rates on loans as business is seen as more risky.

Cash flow is a short term problem so use short term finance to solve them.

Ways to solve cash flow problems

Choice will depend on the cause of problem.

Options include the following.

- Increase cash sales
- Short term loan
- Overdraft
- Reduce amount of stock held

- Ask debtors to pay quicker
- Ask creditors for more time
- Trade credit

The benefits of using a cash flow forecast

- It shows any gaps, or shortfalls, between cash receipts and payments.
- If temporary shortfalls are forecast, the business has time to arrange extra funds to cover the shortfall.
- It helps loan applications as banks are more likely to lend them money if a business can show they have funds to pay them back.
- It helps business planning as able to see when problems are likely.

The most important thing to remember about cash flow is timing.

> **Useful link:**
>
> **Unit 20: Ways to overcome cash flow problems**

- If a business does not have the money at the right time, it can cause financial problems to any size of business. Remember the problems are not just financial.
- Workers need their wages to meet their basic needs. If late, they might become de-motivated or could even threaten to stop work.
- Suppliers might refuse to provide materials. This could affect production. Delays will impact on their efficiency.
- Unfulfilled orders could lead to customer complaints. This could damage their reputation, and lead to a loss of sales.

Cash flow forecasts simply allow businesses to see what money is coming in and going out at any time. It's just a tool to help them manage their money.

The role of a budget

A **budget** is a financial plan for a future period of time.

Budgets are useful to:

→ Help plan and coordinate activities.
→ Enable business to set targets to help achieve business objectives.
→ Motivate workers by setting targets to work towards.
→ Help highlight differences between planned and actual costs. Business can then take action to solve problems.
→ Review previous activities.
→ Control costs.
→ Monitor different departments spending.

Budgets are based on estimates so they can be wrong. The more reliable the information, the more accurate the forecast and the more useful a budget can be.

Progress check

1. Write down definitions of the following terms, as accurately as you can:
   - Net cash flow
   - Budget
2. What is the purpose of a cash flow forecast?
3. State **two** cash outflows that a small business might have.
4. State **two** methods a business could use to overcome a cash flow problem.
5. Identify **two** reasons for using budgets.

Sample question – worked example

Sylvia and her brother own a market stall selling local fruits and vegetables. Sales have fallen since a new supermarket opened two kilometres away. The supermarket offers low prices and more products. The supermarket benefits from economies of scale. Sylvia is worried about her cash flow problem. "We are throwing away food that I still have to pay for. The rent is due for review in January. Everyone else's rent has doubled; will we have enough cash to pay for it?" She is going to produce a cash flow forecast.

1. What is meant by a 'cash flow problem'? **[2]**

   Student's answer:
   The movement of all money in and out of the business.

Comment: The answer shows good understanding of what cash flow is, but has not fully answered the question set. The answer has only focused on the term cash flow and not why it is a problem.

Overall Mark: 1/2

> **Always remember to read the question carefully to ensure you have covered all parts of the question.**

2. Why might a cash flow forecast help Sylvia to run her business? **[4]**

   Student's answer:
   Cash flow forecast tries to show where how and when cash will enter and leave a business. It can help Sylvia as it shows her when she needs more cash, and how much she might need to

> **A good definition has been provided.**

pay all her bills such as rent which is due for review in March. If she knows when she might have a problem, she can ask for help before she needs it. If she can show she has a plan, banks are more likely to give her what she needs as it shows that she knows what she is doing.

Comment: This is a good answer. There is clear understanding of what a cash flow forecast is and the answer explains how it can help Sylvia to plan better.

Overall mark: 4/4

This style of question does not ask for a certain number of points to be explained. You could develop one point well, like this answer or develop two points for the four marks.

Key terms to learn

Budget: a financial plan for a future period of time.

Closing balance: amount of cash left at end of the period.

Cash flow: the movement of all money in and out of the business.

Cash flow forecast: shows the amount of money coming into and going out of a business over a period of time, usually one year.

Net Cash flow: the difference between cash inflows and outflows over the period.

Opening Balance: amount of cash at beginning of period.

You only need to understand the basic rules of cash flow forecasts. Remember, you could be asked to complete a simple cash flow forecast so make sure you know which numbers go where.

You must understand as well why cash flow is important and explain how a business can use forecasts to help avoid financial problems.

Examination style questions for you to try

Sylvia has produced the following cash flow forecast for next year.

	Jan.	Feb.	March
Opening balance	0	70	110
Cash in			
Sales	800	770	850
Cash out			
Bought fruit	450	450	550
Rent	50	50	50
Wages	200	200	200
Other	30	30	50
Cash left at end of month	70	?	50
Closing balance	?	110	160

1. Sylvia's cash flow forecast is incomplete. Calculate the figures for:

   Closing balance:

   Net cash flow: [2]

2. Identify and explain **two** reasons why cash flow might be a problem for Sylvia's business.

   Reason 1:

   Reason 2: [8]

3. Identify and explain **four** measures a business could take to improve their cash flow.

   Method 1:

   Method 2:

   Method 3:

   Method 4: [8]

4. Do you think Sylvia should be concerned about her cash flow position? Justify your answer. [12]

35 Financial accounts

The reason why profit matters to businesses

Profit is simply what is left over from revenue after all costs have been paid. It can be written as 'total revenue minus total cost'. It is a key objective, as it's a:

- Reward for enterprise
- Reward for risk taking by investors
- Source of internal funds for emergency
- Source of internal funds for reinvestment.

A business can survive in the short term without profit. But if a business continues to make a loss it will have to close down.

The difference between cash and profit

Profit is not the same as cash. Profit is the surplus of revenue after all costs have been paid. Cash is money that is immediately available to spend. They refer to different things.

- If goods are sold on credit, they are classed as sales. They are included in the profit and loss account for profit purposes. But the business does not have any cash until the customers actually pay for the goods.
- Materials bought on credit can be used, but no cash has been spent until the payment is made. Only when payments are made is the cash affected.
- A profitable business can fail because it runs out of cash. This means they are unable to pay their debts when they fall due.
- Profit might be important in the long term, but cash is important in the short term.

The main features of a profit and loss account

- **Profit and loss** account shows the income and expenditure of business over a given period of time.
- It is helpful as it shows the value of sales that has been made, and how and where money has been spent to make them.
- It shows how the business has made its profit.
- The profit and loss is split into three sections:
  → Trading account
  → Profit and loss account
  → Appropriation account.

You could be asked to fill in missing figures from a profit and loss account. Make sure you know how each profit figure is calculated, and which figures to add or subtract to work profit out.

> The whole document is called the profit and loss account even though it only refers to one part of the document.

The layout of a profit and loss account

Profit and loss account for Z foods for period year ending Dec 2010 ($m)

Trading account

Shows how the gross profit of business has been made

- Sales revenue: Value of all goods sold (credit and cash)
- Cost of sales: How much spent on direct cost to make goods
- Gross profit is amount of profit left after paying for direct costs. Can be written as revenue minus cost of goods sold

Sales revenue	150
Less Cost of sales	(70)
Gross Profit	80

Profit and loss account

Shows amount of sales revenue left after paying for all other costs

- Expenses: Includes all indirect costs of making goods such as rent, interest and other overheads
- Net profit: Sales revenue minus total costs

Less Expenses	(55)
Net profit	25

Appropriation account

Shows how much profit spent on tax and dividends

- Tax: The amount of profit paid to the government
- Dividends: Share of profit given to shareholders
- Retained profit: Amount of profit left over for the business to use

Less tax	(12)
Profit after tax	13
Dividends	(7)
Retained profit	6

How do profit and loss accounts help a business in decision making?

Using the example of Z Foods, many simple observations can be made.

- Value of sales is $150m
- Gross profit was $80m
- Net profit was $25m
- Retained profit was $5m

What does this show?
Sales of $150m might seem good but the business only had $5m left, after all other costs, to reinvest in the business.

What can Z foods do?
Z Foods can look to see where costs could be lowered to increase the amount of profit made.

The main features of a balance sheet

Useful links:
Unit 34: Cash flow
Unit 36: Ratios

- Balance sheet is a record of what a business owns, what it owes and the value of the capital invested in a business.
- It reflects the value of a business at a particular point in time.
- Items the business owns are called **assets**.
- Payments owed to other people are called **liabilities**.

Z Foods Balance sheet as at December 2010

Assets		($000)
Fixed assets		120
Current assets		
Stock	45	
Debtors	25	
Cash	20	
	90	
Less Current liabilities		
Creditors	55	
Net current assets	35	
Net assets		**145**
Financed by:		
Shareholders funds:		
Share capital		65
Retained profit /reserves		25
Long term liabilities		55
Capital Employed		**145**

Assets

What does the business own?

- **Fixed assets:** These are long lasting items that can be used repeatedly. Example land, machinery etc.
- **Current assets:** are short term assets. They can easily be turned into cash. Example stock, debtors etc.
- **Current liabilities:** Debts which have to be paid back in less than one year. Example bank overdraft, suppliers etc.
- **Net current assets:** It is also known as working capital. It equals to current assets less current liabilities.
- **Net assets:** Shows net value of all assets owned by business. It is fixed assets plus net current assets.

Where does the money come from to fund these net assets?

There are two main internal sources of finance – shareholders funds and debt.

Shareholders funds: It refers to the total of all money invested by business owners; they are of two types.

- **Share capital:** Money put into business when shares were originally issued.
- **Retained profit:** Profit left over from other years.

Debt: They are as followed.

- **Long term liabilities:** Money owed, to be paid back after one year. Example long term loans, debentures etc.
- **Capital employed:** The total of all long term and permanent capital of a business.

> Net assets should always equal to capital employed.

> You will not be asked to construct a balance sheet in the exam, but make sure you know where each item appears in the document and what it shows.

Progress check

1. Write down definitions of the following terms , as accurately as you can:
   - Current liability
   - Cost of sales
2. Name the sections of a profit and loss account for a sole trader.
3. State **two** headings in a balance sheet.
4. What is another name for net current assets?
5. What should capital employed balance with?

Sample question – worked example

Ronaldo and his brother are partners in a small but successful glass making business. Ronaldo has been looking at the accounts. The table shows an incomplete profit and loss account.

Profit/Loss account	($000's)
Glass Brothers for year ending 31 December 2010	
Sales	?
Cost of sales	140
Gross profit	100
Overheads	?
Net profit	20

Always check you have the right number of zeros from the units.

1. Calculate the value of sales and overheads for Ronaldo's business. **[2]**

   Student's answer:
   Sales: 240000
   Overheads: 6000

Comment: The value for sales is correct, but overheads are wrong. The value has two zeros missing which makes the units incorrect. The correct answer should read 60000.

Overall mark: 1/2

2. Ronaldo thinks that as he has $20 000 in net profit, he should have the same amount of cash. Explain why this might not be the case. **[4]**

   Student's answer:
   Profit is not the same as cash. He could actually have no cash in the bank because Ronaldo might have sold some glass products to someone who has not paid him yet. He would have recorded this as sales, but it is not cash until he receives the money. Or he could have bought some materials to make the glass, so he has spent it before he makes any sales. It's all about timing.

Comment: There is clear understanding of the difference between profit and cash, which is supported by an example.

The materials example is sufficiently explained for full marks.

Overall mark: 4/4

Key terms to learn

Appropriation account: shows how much profit is spent on tax and dividends by a limited company.

Assets: any item that the business owns.

Balance sheet: a record of what a business owns, what it owes and the value of the capital invested in a business.

Cost of sales: shows how much the direct costs of making items are.

Current assets: short term assets that can easily be turned into cash.

Current liabilities: debts which have to be paid back in less than one year.

Dividends: share of profit given to shareholders.

Fixed assets: long lasting items that can be used again and again.

Gross profit: amount of sales revenue left after paying for cost of making goods.

Liabilities: payments owed to others.

Long term liabilities: money owed which only has to be paid back after one year.

Net current assets: amount of current assets less current liabilities.

Net profit: sales revenue minus total costs.

Profit: amount left over from revenue after all costs have been paid.

Profit and loss account: shows amount of sales revenue left after paying for all other costs.

Retained profit: amount of profit left over for the business to use.

Share capital: money put into business when shares originally issued.

Shareholders funds: the total of all the money invested by the owners of the business.

Trading account: shows how the gross profit of business has been made.

> There are a lot of terms to learn for this unit. Make sure you know what items are recorded in which document. Remember each document is looking at different things. The profit and loss account focuses on how a business makes and spends its money over the year. The balance sheet shows the value of a business at a particular point in time.

Examination style questions for you to try

Kape Confection is public limited company, based in country T. It produces and sells a wide range of chocolates across the world. Profits have risen from $15m to $126m over last five years. Kape Confection aims to sell as many items as it can at low prices. All products are made by machine. Kape are planning to buy a specialist chocolate company to enter the luxury chocolate market. Companies such as Kape have to produce financial statements each year including balance sheets and profit and loss accounts.

1. Give an example of each of the following that would be found in the balance sheet of Kape Confection.

    (i) Current asset

    (ii) Fixed asset   [2]

2. The balance sheet of Kape Confection also showed that the business had creditors valued at $15m. Explain what this means.   [2]

3. Kape Confection made a net profit of $126m last year. Identify and explain **two** reasons why profit is important to a business like Kape Confection.

    Reason 1:

    Reason 2:   [8]

3. Financial accounts are important to all businesses. Explain why producing a cash flow forecast, a profit and loss account and a break even chart is important to the successful financial management of Kape Confection? Justify your answers.   [12]

36 Interpreting financial accounts

Learning Summary

By the end of this unit you should understand:
- **The main ratios used to interpret accounts**
- **The different users of accounts**
- **The limitations of ratio analysis**

The main ratios used to interpret accounts

Ratios are used to:

- Help judge business results
- Allow comparisons with previous years
- Identify trends in performance
- Allows comparisons with similar companies.

Ratios can be split into two main groups as stated below.

> You will only be expected to make simple statements about what the ratios show.

Profitability ratios

→ Measures how much profit has been made.
→ Higher the value, the more profitable the company.

Gross profit margin

- Measures amount of gross profit for every $1 of sales.
- The bigger the percentage, the greater the profit:

$$\frac{\text{Gross profit}}{\text{Sales}} = 100 = \%$$

Ways to improve gross profit margin:

- Increase sales but maintain cost of sales;
- Cut cost of sales by lowering wages or material costs.

Example: Z FOODS

2010: Sales $150m and Gross profit $80m

2009: 49%

$$\frac{80}{150} \times 100 = 53\%$$

Shows the business made 53c in gross profit for every $ of sales in 2010.

It has improved by 4% over the year, which is good.

Net profit margin

- Measures amount of net profit for every $1 of sales.
- Shows how well doing in controlling overheads.
- The bigger the percentage, the greater the profit:

$$\frac{\text{Net profit}}{\text{Sales}} \times 100 = \%$$

Ways to improve net profit margin:

- Increasing sales revenue more than expenses;
- Reducing expenses whilst maintaining level of sales.

Example: Z FOODS

2010: Sales $25m and Gross profit $80m

2009: 18%

$$\frac{25}{150} \times 100 = 16.6\%$$

The business made just over 16c in net profit for every $ of sales in 2010.

This is worse than 2009, as it has fallen by 1.4%.

Useful links:

Unit 33: Ways to improve efficiency

Return on capital employed (ROCE)

- Measures amount of profit made for each $1 invested in the business.
- The bigger the percentage, the more efficiently the business is using its capital employed.
- Very useful for investors:

$$\frac{\text{Net profit}}{\text{Capital employed}} \times 100 = \%$$

Ways to improve ROCE:

- Making better use of capital without reducing profit;
- Increase profit made with the same amount of capital employed.

Example: Z FOODS

2010: Net profit $25m
Capital employed $145m

2009: 19.1%

$$\frac{25}{145} \times 100 = 17.2\%$$

Shows the business made 17.2c for every $1 invested in the business.

This is worse than 2009 as it has fallen by 1.9%. They have not used their resources as well as last year.

Liquidity ratios

→ Liquidity refers to how easily a business can repay its short term debts.
→ Liquid assets are cash or any assets that can be turned into cash quickly.
→ Focuses on whether a business has enough working capital to meet day to day running costs.
→ But too many liquid assets could mean that the resources are not being well used.

Current ratio

- Shows whether the business can pay its current liabilities out of current assets.
- Ideal ratio is 1.5 times as it means that business can easily pay debts as due:

$$\frac{\text{Current asset}}{\text{Current liabilities}}$$

- If figure too low, could indicate cash flow problems.
- If too high, they could have too much cash. Might be better invested in equipment.

Example: Z FOODS

2010: Current assets $90m, current liabilities $55m

2009: 1.6 times

$$90 : 55 = 1.64 \text{ times}$$

Shows have 1.64 current assets for every current liability

It is slightly better than 2009 as it has risen by 0.04 times

Acid test ratio

- Shows whether the business can pay its current liabilities out of current assets without stock.
- Stock can be difficult to sell quickly to obtain cash.
- Target is in between 0.5 – 1:

$$\frac{\text{Current asset} - \text{stock}}{\text{Current liabilities}}$$

- If too low, business faces cash flow problems as unable to sell stock quickly to meet debts.
- Too high then business is not making best use of resources so less efficient.

Example: Z FOODS

2010: Current assets (less – stock) $45m, current liabilities $55m

2009: 0.62 times

$$45 : 55 = 0.82 \text{ times}$$

Shows business has 0.82 current assets for every current liability

This has improved on 2009 by 0.2 times

Useful links

Units 19–20: Finance;

Unit 34: Managing cash flow

There are other ratios but these are the ones you need to know for this exam.

The different users of accounts

- Most stakeholders will be interested in the performance of the business.
- Ratio analysis will be more useful to groups such as lenders and shareholders than customers and employees.
- Accounts will not include all the information they will want to see, but it still contains a lot of useful information.
- For example, it can help investors decide whether to buy shares in the business, hold on or sell the shares they already own. They also want to assess the ability of the business to pay dividends.

Useful link:

Unit 5: Stakeholders

Stakeholder	Why interested	Useful ratios/information
Shareholders	• To see how well business is doing • To see whether value of investment up or down • To decide future investment in the company	Profitability ratios Gross profit Net profit Return on capital employed Profit figures Dividend paid
Lenders	• Whether loans will be repaid – how risky is the business • Whether interest will be repaid on time	Profitability ratios Liquidity ratios Cash flow forecast
Creditors	• How secure is their money • Will company be able to repay them on time	Profitability ratios Liquidity ratios
Employees	• Level of profits decide the bonus they receive • How secure are their jobs	Profit figures Future objectives
Managers	• See how well business is doing so spot problems • Level of profits decide the bonus they receive • How secure are their jobs	Profitability ratios Liquidity ratios Profit figures Future objectives
Customers	• Will business continue to supply goods	Profit figures Future objectives
Government	• Profitable businesses pay more tax • How secure are jobs for local community	Profit figures Future objectives

Accounts refer to the profit and loss, balance sheet and cash flow forecasts. Unless the question states a particular one, you can refer to any in your answers.

Example: Z FOODS

Why would a lender look at the accounts?

Profitability ratios: Gross profit margin has improved by 4%. Both net profit margin ($\downarrow$1.4%) and return on capital employed ($\downarrow$1.9%) has decreased. This is worrying as it indicates overheads are too high so profitability is falling.

Liquidity ratios: Both measures have improved. Good news as Z Foods is more likely to be able to meet its debts as they become due and could afford to pay the interest on any loans given.

The limitations of ratio analysis

Ratios only act as a guide to help decision making.

- They are based on past results so not always the best guide to what will happen in the future.
- Ratios are no good on their own; they must be compared to something. Either previous years to identify trends or against similar businesses to assess competitiveness.
- Different types of businesses could use different ways of measuring items such as stock and value of assets; this will affect the results.
- Different businesses might have different liquidity requirements depending on what they sell.
- Some ratios do not work if the business has made a loss.
- 'Ideal' ratios is only ever a guideline, as it depends on other factors such as type and size of business.
- Ratios only consider financial data. Other factors can also affect performance.

> Always remember to include the formula for ratios used. Check that you have used the figures for the right year.

Summary: Which figures come from which documents?

Liquidity ratios:

    Acid test and current ratio: Balance sheet

Performance ratios:

    Gross profit and net profit margin: Profit and loss account

    Return on capital employed: Both balance sheet and profit and loss account

---

Progress check

1. Write down definitions of the following terms, as accurately as you can:
   - Liquidity
   - Return on capital employed
2. State **two** liquidity ratios.
3. Write out the formula for **two** performance ratios.
4. What is the purpose of ratio analysis?
5. Identify any **two** stakeholder groups who would be interested in looking at the accounts.

Sample question – worked example

Solid Metal Mining (SMM) extracts copper, nickel and other minerals from various locations around the world. Its main objective is profit. Last year SMM made net profits of $36m on sales of $1 440m.

Appendix 1: Extract from accounts

Balance sheet as at 31 December 2010 ($m)

Fixed assets		320
Current assets	60	
Debtors	30	
Stock	30	
Current liabilities		
Overdraft	40	
Creditors	40	
		80
Net assets		300
Financed by:		
Share capital	120	
Retained profit	105	
Long term liabilities	80	
Capital employed		300

1. Do you think Solid Metal Mining is in a strong financial position? Explain your answer using information from Appendix 1 and other information provided. **[12]**

Net Profit margin = 36/1440 = 2.5%
Current ratio = 60/80 = 0.75 times
Acid test ratio = 30/80 = 0.375 times
Return on capital employed = 1440/300 * 100 = 480 %

I think SMM are doing okay. They made a net profit of $36m in 2010, which is a lot of money. The net profit margin was 2.5% but ROCE was even better at 480% so this shows they are using the money invested very well.

Liquidity is a problem as they have more liabilities than assets, so if everyone wanted payment they would not be able to pay them back. They do not seem to have any cash which is a worry. But they might not need much cash as they are a mining business. The ROCE figure is so good, this do not really matter so that's why I think they are doing okay.

> **ROCE is calculated using profit figure not sales; therefore, the calculation here is wrong.**

> **Correct analysis of ROCE ratio but based on wrong calculation so it can not be rewarded.**

Comment: This answer shows some understanding of ratios. Three ratios have been correctly calculated, and there is a good observation about the lack of cash. Good understanding of liquidity is shown which can be rewarded.

However, the return on capital employed figure is wrong, so no analysis marks can be awarded based on an incorrect calculation. There is only a general statement on how strong Solid Metal Mining's financial position is, which is not clearly supported by what has been written so no evaluation marks would be credited.

Overall mark: 8/12

Key terms to learn

Acid test: ability of a business to pay its short term debts, excluding the value of stock.

Current ratio: ability of a business to pay its short term debts from its current assets.

Gross profit margin: amount of profit made for every $1 of sales.

Liquidity: ability of a business to meet its short term debts.

Net profit margin: amount of profit made for every $1 of sales after allowing for expenses.

Return on capital employed (ROCE): measures how efficiently a business uses its capital to make a profit.

Stakeholder: any person or group who has an interest in the activities and performance of a business.

Working capital: amount available for the day-to-day running of the business and to settle short-term debts.

> You must learn the key liquidity and performance ratios. Make sure you understand what each ratio shows. You could be asked to calculate or explain the significance of any of these ratios, so practice is important. Try to look at as many examples as you can. It's the only way to master ratio analysis.

The five ratios to learn		
Ratio	Type of ratio	Formula
Current ratio	Liquidity	Current assets/current liabilities

Acid test ratio	Liquidity	Current assets – stock /current liabilities
Gross profit	Performance	Gross profit/sales *100 = %
Net profit	Performance	Net profit/sales *100 = %
Return on capital employed	Performance	Net profit/capital employed *100 = %

Examination style questions for you to try

Irfan is the Finance Director at Fizzed Fruits. He has been looking at its accounts. He wants to know whether 2010 has been a successful year. In 2010, its sales increased by $140m and net profit by $10m from 2009. A summary is shown in the table.

Profit/Loss Account for Fizzed Fruits for the year ending Dec 2010	
	$m
Sales	500
Cost of sales	350
Gross profit	150
Overheads	110
Net profit	40

1. Calculate the net profit margin for 2010. **[2]**

2. Explain what the net profit margin tells you about Fizzed Fruit's financial position. **[4]**

3. In 2010 sales of the business rose by $140m and net profit by $10m compared to 2009. Do these figures suggest that Fizzed Fruits was successful in 2010? **[6]**

4. Identify and explain how **two** stakeholder groups might find the Fizzed Fruits' profit and loss account useful.

    Stakeholder 1:

    Stakeholder 2: **[8]**

Section 4:

People in business

Unit 37 Why people work

Learning Summary

By the end of this unit you should understand:
- *The role of work in satisfying human needs*
- *The concept of motivation*
- *The methods of financial rewards*
- *The methods of non-financial rewards*

The role of work in satisfying human needs

People work for many reasons.

- **Money** – people need money to pay for their needs and wants.
- **Security** – having a job that will be there for many years.
- **Job satisfaction** – enjoying what they do.
- **Self-esteem** – feeling important as have something to contribute to society.
- **Social** – to feel part of a group.

The concept of motivation

- **Motivation** is 'something that makes people want to work'.
- Different people will be motivated by different things. What works for one person might not work for everyone.
- To motivate people, a business must try to offer the right rewards to suit each individual.
- Motivation theories are ideas that try to explain what motivates different people. This should help the business choose the right reward to increase workers' motivation.
- Motivation is important as motivated workers will work harder than unmotivated workers which can help the businesses' efficiency.

Useful link:
Unit 33: Efficiency

The organisation must offer the following to motivate workers.

→ Must offer the right rewards to suit each worker.
→ Workers must know how to achieve the rewards.
→ Workers must believe reward is achievable.
→ Workers must believe rewards are fair.

Motivated workers are likely to be:	This could help the business achieve:
– More productive – Produce better quality work – Contribute more ideas.	– More sales – More efficient production – Lower costs – More profit.

There are many theories of motivation. You will not be asked to explain any of them in detail. It is more important you understand why motivation is important. The theories are just trying to explain why different methods of reward are used.

The three main motivation theories

5. **Self fulfilment** – feel achieved own goals

4. **Self esteem** – feel recognised for efforts

3. **Social needs** – working with others

2. **Safety needs** – feel secure in job

1. **Physical needs** – water, food, shelter

Does this match with how you or your family would rank your needs?

Maslow's hierarchy of needs

Basic idea is that all people are motivated by the same things (needs). These are ranked in order of importance from basic needs to complex needs.

To motivate people each set of needs must be satisfied in the right order. Once each set of needs have been satisfied they no longer act as a motivator to people.

McGregor's theory X and Y

McGregor's ideas focused on how managers look at workers. He concluded that all workers could be split into two groups.

Theory X	Theory Y
• Workers are only motivated by money. • Workers are lazy, do not like work and have no ambitions.	• Workers are motivated by many needs. • Workers enjoy work, have ambitions.
This means:	This means:
• Workers must always be supervised. • Pay is the best motivator.	• Sharing responsibility and consulting workers are good ways to motivate. • Pay alone will not motivate workers.

Herzberg's hygiene factors

Herzberg believed that all workers' needs could be simply split into two groups.

Hygiene factors	Motivating factors
• Factors which are necessary for people to work, but do not make people work harder.	• Factors which encourage people to work harder.
This means	This means
• Workers expect basic needs to be provided for them such as safe working conditions, fair pay etc. • These rewards do not motivate workers.	• Adding variety/tasks to make work more interesting. • Sharing responsibility, consulting and praising workers.

The methods of financial rewards

Payment methods

> The key point about wages is that they are variable. The amount paid can change from week to week.

1. **Time rate** – system of pay where workers are paid a set amount for each hour worked. The more hours worked, the higher the amount worker earns. This encourages people to work longer periods to earn more pay. But this can lead to slow rate of work as people take longer than needed so paid for more hours. This is useful when it is difficult to measure output.

2. **Piece rate** – workers paid by amount of output they produce. The more a worker makes, the higher the amount that person earns.

It encourages workers to produce more to earn more pay. But can lead to poor quality as workers rush to complete work.

Performance related pay

It refers to when pay is based on an assessment of how well someone is carrying out their job. Below are the forms mentioned.

- **Bonuses** – is a sum of money paid to workers, in addition to their basic pay if they reach certain performance targets. Workers are encouraged to work harder to meet targets to earn the extra money.
- **Commission** – people earn a certain percentage of sales they have made. They have an incentive to sell more to earn more money. This is usually paid to sales staff.
- **Profit sharing** – all workers receive an additional payment based on the level of profits made by the business. All workers will try to help business increase its profits as higher profits mean more money for all the workers.
- **Share ownership** – some limited companies offer employees a chance to buy shares in business. Workers should work harder as they are part owners in the business.
- **Fringe benefits** – extra incentives given to employees; example discounts, insurance or company car. These are given in addition to wages.

> You need to know the difference between each method and how they can help motivate workers.

The methods of non–financial rewards

Maslow, Herzberg and McGregor's theory Y all suggest that money is not the only motivator. A business cannot afford to pay employees as much as some want. Some employees have other reasons for working such as social or esteem needs. Good communication and involving employees can be just as effective as paying people more money. There are also the following methods to consider.

Job enrichment

- Employee is given more difficult tasks to do.
- Employees are encouraged to take part in the decision-making and consultation process.
- Workers are motivated as work is more challenging and they feel valued.

Advantages	Disadvantages
• Less supervision needed • Reduces boredom • Develops workers skills	• Workers might need training which adds to costs • Workers might want pay rise

Job rotation

- Employees are able to do other jobs at different times.
- Workers do one simple job for a period, then move to another simple job.
- Workers' boredom is reduced as they do not have to repeat the same job all the time.

Advantages	Disadvantages
• Flexible work force as able to cover other jobs • Reduces boredom as more variety of tasks • Develops workers skills.	• The range of tasks given are similar so boredom can return • Some workers might be better at certain tasks than others. This means quality and productivity might vary.

Job enlargement

- Employee is given a wider range of similar tasks to do as part of their usual job.
- Extra tasks are added to their job description to make their duties more interesting.

Advantages	Disadvantages
• Reduces boredom as more variety of tasks • Develops workers skills.	• If just more of same, the employee could feel being overworked.

Team working

- Employees are given responsibility for parts of the production process.
- Employees are encouraged to take part in the decision-making and consultation process.
- Workers are motivated as work is more challenging and they feel valued.
- Often used as part of lean production.

Advantages	Disadvantages
• Less supervision needed • Reduces boredom as involvement is encouraged • Develops workers skills.	• Workers might need training which adds to costs • Workers might want pay rise as have more responsibility.

All methods of reward can cost money. A business will hope the extra output or efficiency gained will be enough to cover the costs of using the method.

Progress check

1. Write down definitions of the following terms , as accurately as you can:
   • Piece rate
   • Motivation
2. Name **two** hygiene factors.
3. Name the **five** levels in Maslow's hierarchy of needs.
4. What is the difference between theory X and theory Y workers?
5. True or false – only financial methods of reward increase the costs for a business.

Sample question – worked example

Splash Active specialises in providing activity holidays for families. Splash Active prides itself on its good reputation and competitive prices. Employees are seen as an important factor in its success. Splash Active has won awards for its good customer service and health and safety. All employees, apart from the managers, are paid by time rate. The Managing Director feels that praising people is the best way to reward employees. The Managing Director likes to know everyone, as he wants everyone to be part of a team, "I want to know if my workers are lacking motivation!"

1. Identify and explain **one** advantage and **one** disadvantage for Splash Active of using time rate. [8]

   Student's answer:
   Advantage: Time rate is good because you only have to pay workers for the amount of hours that they work. If they are not working you do not have to pay them, so this will save them money in lower labour costs.
   Disadvantage: If a business has a lot of slow workers, they might end up paying more money than using piece rate. Slow workers will take longer to produce something. More hours spent working will increase the costs for the business.

   General points have been raised which could apply to any business.

Comment: This answer has clearly developed two valid points about time rate explaining why they are either an advantage or disadvantage. But neither point has been applied to Splash Active so no application marks can be given. Possible application marks could have focused on holidays tend to be seasonal, or the awards for customer service.

To provide good service employees might have to spend more time with customers so more hours would be worked.

Overall mark: 6/8

Key terms to learn

Bonus: a sum of money paid to workers, in addition to their basic pay if they reach certain performance targets.

Commission: people earn a certain percentage of any sales they have made.

Fringe benefits: extra incentives given to employees in addition to wages.

Hygiene factor: any factors which are necessary for people to work, but do not make people work harder.

Job enlargement: employee is given a wider range of similar tasks to do as part of their usual job.

Job enrichment: employee is given a wider range of more complex tasks and encouraged to take part in the decision-making and consultation process.

Job rotation: employees are able to do other jobs at different times.

Motivation: something that makes people want to work.

Piece rate: system of pay where workers paid by amount of output they produce.

Profit sharing: workers receive an additional payment based on the level of profits made by the business.

Time rate: system of pay where workers are paid a set amount for each hour worked.

> You need to learn the different methods of motivation and ways of rewarding workers. Can you explain how the different methods can help increase workers motivation?
>
> You could be asked to select suitable methods in a given context, so you need to know which methods are useful in different situations.

Examination style questions for you to try

1. What is meant by 'time rate'? [2]

2. Identify and explain **two** reasons why workers might lack motivation at Splash Active.

Reason 1:

Reason 2: **[4]**

3. Do you think that praise is the best way to reward employees? Justify your answer. **[6]**

4. The management of Splash Active is thinking of changing the method used to reward employees. Discuss the advantages and disadvantages of each of the following options. Which method would you recommend? Justify your choice.

   Option 1 (bonuses):

   Option 2 (job enrichment):

   Option 3 (fringe benefits):

   Recommendation: **[12]**

The role of management in motivating workers

Managers have many responsibilities. They have to plan, make decisions, solve problems as well as deal with people.

Choosing the right incentive depends on the following.

- **Cost** – the business needs to be able to afford to give bonuses or pay rises.
- **Type of business** – piece rate might not be suitable for all businesses.
- **Employees** – everyone is an individual. What works for one person might not work for all.
- **Manager** – their skills and choices will affect the success of any method.

Managers need to ensure their workers are motivated

Motivation refers to how people approach their work. If workers are motivated, they will be enthusiastic and interested in their work and are likely to work harder. This should lead to less mistakes, better performances and hopefully higher productivity for the business.

To do this, managers have to:

- Persuade workers that what they are being asked to do is best for both the business and the workers.
- Maintain workers morale as if morale is high, workers are likely to be happy and more committed to the business. Low morale could lead to poor performance and lower productivity.
- Look after workers welfare as if workers do not feel safe at work, this can affect their motivation.
- Be an effective leader because the management style used can have a big influence on workers motivation.

The different styles of management

There are three main styles – **autocratic, democratic** and **laissez faire**. Most managers will use only one approach. Some will change their style to suit different situations.

Autocratic

Managers make all the decisions without any discussion with workers.

- Tells workers what to do at all times.
- Manager has total control.
- No delegation.
- Communication is one way, from the top downwards.
- Used when workers are unskilled (or not trusted).

Advantages	Disadvantages
• Manager feels in control of all situations • Quick decision making • Workers have clear direction and they know what to do and expect.	• Motivation can be an issue as workers do not feel involved in decisions • Too dependent on the manager • No scope for individuals to develop skills.

Democratic

Managers make decisions after consultation with workers.

- Workers are encouraged to take part in decision making.
- Manager needs to be a good communicator and willing to delegate.
- Employee centred style.
- Useful when workers are skilled and experienced.

Advantages	Disadvantages
• Manager can feel decisions have support of workers • Workers are likely to be motivated as views are listened to • Encourages loyalty as gives responsibility to worker.	• Decision making can be slow • Do workers have enough knowledge or experience to make decisions • Manager might not agree with decision but has to accept it • Can lead to conflict if views differ.

Laissez faire

Manager leaves the workers to make day to day decisions.

- Managers have little influence in the actions of the workers.
- Workers are free to take own decisions.

– Manager only involved to resolve disagreements.
– Good for small, highly motivated teams.

Advantages	Disadvantages
• People can be more motivated as free to do that they think best • Encourages loyalty as gives responsibility to the worker • Workers can use all their skills for benefit of business.	• No real direction as all do what they think is right • Poor coordination can lead to inefficiency • Can lead to conflicts between team members.

Factors to consider when deciding on the right management style are as following.

- **Manager's own characteristics** – is the manager naturally autocratic or democratic?
- **Characteristics of the group** – does the team respond better to being given clear instructions or to decide what to do on their own?
- **The task** – is it straightforward or complex?
- **Type of business** – a design business is likely to have a different approach to a large factory making standard products.

The problem of high labour turnover

Labour turnover refers to the number of employees joining or leaving an organisation over a given period of time or simply 'how long workers stay.' A business usually wants to keep a stable work force, so will aim to have a low turnover rate.

A high level of labour turnover could be caused by many factors.

- Low wage levels so employees leave to find jobs elsewhere.
- Poor or unsafe working conditions.
- Poor morale and low levels of motivation amongst workers.
- Recruiting and selecting the wrong employees in the first place so unsuitable workers have to (or choose to) leave.
- Growing economy so more or better jobs opportunities available.

Unmotivated workers tend to leave the business. This could mean the following.

➤ Production can suffer as not enough workers to complete all the work required.
➤ Lower efficiency as it takes time to train up new workers, so output per new worker will fall or more mistakes will lead to higher wastage rates.
➤ Lower quality as if skilled workers leave, there will not be enough skilled workers left to maintain standards.
➤ Poorer quality output could affect reputation of the business.
➤ Poorer quality or lower output could lead to lower sales.

➤ Higher costs of recruitment as time and money are spent advertising and interviewing new workers.

➤ Higher costs of training results in more expenses, which could negatively affect profits.

Keeping workers motivated by using the right rewards and management style is therefore very important if a business is to be successful.

Progress check

1. Write down definitions of the following terms , as accurately as you can:
   - Democratic
   - Laissez faire
2. State **two** features of democratic style.
3. Identify **two** functions of management.
4. State **one** situation when laissez faire is a good approach to use.
5. Explain which style of manager you would like to work for.

You could be asked to select a suitable management style to use in a given situation. Make sure you know the advantages and disadvantages of each approach. If a question asks for a decision, remember to make a decision which your answer can support.

Sample question – worked example

Wooden Works makes hand finished furniture, which it sells nationally in country T. To cope with growing demand, the management wants to reorganise the business by region rather than by function.

Wooden Works are having problems recruiting the skilled carpenters needed to complete some of the orders. It employs 160 skilled workers but the number of workers leaving each year is 40. The Human Resources Manager, Rico is worried. Other local businesses offer piece-rate, longer holidays, pensions and safe working conditions that the business cannot afford to match.

The management style at Wooden Works is autocratic. Workers have not been told about the reorganisation, "Workers only have to work. They do not need to know what we are planning. It's a manager's job to make decisions" said Rico "It's easier for everyone that way."

There is good application in this answer. The reference to 'growing too quickly' and 'problems recruiting workers' shows they have understood the context of the question.

1. Identify and explain **two** possible advantages of an autocratic management style for Wooden Works. [8]

   Advantage 1: Manager feels in control of all situations as they are the ones who make the decisions. As they are growing so quickly, it could be better to have only a few people involved in the decision making.

   Advantage 2: Workers know exactly what to do, so there is less likely to be any misunderstandings. It's the manager's job to make decisions and for workers to follow them. Clear direction should help avoid duplication of orders so less wasted resources. If they are having problems recruiting workers, they need everyone to focus on their job so that they can meet the growing demand.

Comment: This is a good answer. Two reasons have been identified and explained. The first point could be expanded to explain why it is a benefit to Wooden Works to only have a few people involved in the decision making for the final mark. A simple line such as 'otherwise messages could become confused leading to wrong decisions being made'. The answer is relevant to the company so the application marks can be given.

Overall mark: 7/8

Key terms to learn

Autocratic: style of management where managers make all the decisions without any discussion with workers.

Democratic: style of management where managers make decisions after consultation with workers.

Labour turnover: refers to the number of people leaving a business in relation to the total number of employees over a set period of time.

Laissez faire: style of management where manager gives workers the freedom to make all day to day decisions, with few guidelines and little direction.

Remember, you need not explain the management styles in great detail. You could be asked to recommend or comment on the style being used so be aware of different situations which might need a different leadership style.

Examination style questions for you to try

> You can be asked a range of different questions on the same topic. Always check to make sure you have the right focus.

1. What is meant by 'management style is autocratic'? [2]

2. Identify and explain **two** possible consequences of a high labour turnover for Homer's business.

   Consequence 1:

   Consequence 2: [8]

3. Do you think it is important for Wooden Works to reduce the number of employees leaving each year? Explain your answer. [6]

4. Wooden Works wants to reduce this level of labour turnover. Discuss possible options that Wooden Works could use to reduce the number of staff leaving. Explain your choices. [12]

> There is a lot of overlap between the ideas covered in units 37 and 38. You can usually use concepts from either unit to answer questions on motivation and labour turnover.

Unit 39 Recruiting, training and terminating employees

The stages in the recruitment and selection process

1 Job vacancy arises

⬇

2 Draw up job description

⬇

3 Write a job specification

⬇

4 Advertise the vacancy

⬇

5 Applications and short listing

⬇

6 Interview and selection

⬇

7 Issue contract of employment

⬇

8 Vacancy filled

1. A job becomes available due to someone leaving or a new position being created due to expansion.

2. **Job description** is a written explanation of what the job is. It states what employee needs to do (roles and responsibilities), who to report to and the main purpose of the job.

3. **Job specification** describes the type of person needed for the job. It lists the qualifications, skills and personal qualities of the ideal candidate. It is also known as a **person specification**. It is used only by management and not seen by employee.

4. Advertising the vacancy refers to advertisement of the post so the potential employees know there is a vacancy. Companies use internal or external methods depending on job.

5. Applications and short listing is a process in which applicants can be asked to complete standard forms or submit letter and CV for job. Business selects suitable candidates from a short list to interview.

6. Interview and selection can be one-to-one or group based; tests or tasks might be set to assess candidates' ability. Based on this, the most appropriate candidate will be selected.

7. Issue of contract of employment which is a legal document setting out the terms of the job and what to do if there are any problems.

    - Includes details such as hours, rate of pay and benefits, start and end dates, details of grievance and disciplinary procedures etc.
    - Contracts help employer and employee if there are any disputes as it sets out what is expected from each of them.

Internal and external recruitment

Internal recruitment

Looks to recruit new person from existing employees.

Methods include the following.

- Newsletters
- Notice boards
- Emails
- Word of mouth from other employees.

Advantages	Disadvantages
• Improves motivation of workers as these are seen as opportunities for promotion • This is cheaper than some external methods • Employees already know how the organisation works • It speeds up the recruitment process.	• It limits potential number of candidates • Reduces the amount of new skills and ideas in business • Creates another vacancy which will need to be filled • Existing employees might always think they have a right to a promotion.

External recruitment

Where business looks outside the organisation to attract workers.

Methods include the following.

- **Local newspapers** – suitable for clerical or manual jobs. Also an option if a lot of skilled workers are available locally, or only need unskilled workers.
- **National newspapers** – used for senior positions, or where few skilled workers are available locally.
- **Specialist magazines** – useful for technical/skilled jobs.
- **Recruitment agencies** – often used for new jobs if the business has little experience in recruiting. Also helpful if the business wants to hide activities from competitors.
- **Government run centres** – provide services to employers and employees to help match workers to jobs. Helps government reduce unemployment levels.

Advantages	Disadvantages
• This brings in new ideas and skills • Brings in experience gained from other businesses • Existing workforce might not have right skills for the job.	• Takes time for new people to become familiar with how the business works • Cost of induction training is to be considered • It is likely to be more expensive to recruit.

Factors to consider when recruiting workers

→ What is the actual job being filled?
→ How much time have they got to find the right person?
→ The cost of different methods?
→ What is the level of employment in the country?

The different methods of training

Training is important as it:

* Increases workers' skills in current job to increase productivity.
* Develops skills for future jobs.
* Can motivate workers who feel valued.
* Makes business more flexible if workers can do more than one job.
* Can reduce mistakes to improve profitably.

There are three main types of training.

> Training is not free. It will cost time, money and even output as workers are learning new skills.

Induction training

– Introduces new people to the business and other workers.
– Helps new workers settle into new working environment.
– Might include health and safety information or a tour of building etc.

On the job

– Employees learn job specific skills whilst they are working.
– Trainer shows learner what to do.
– Quality of training depends on the skills of the person doing the training.
– Cost effective as all workers are still making things.
– It slows down the person who is training.
– Lower product quality as still learning and mistakes are more likely.

Internal

→ Training away from actual place of work but organised by business.
→ Need to employ own staff so only suits large businesses.
→ Specific to the needs of the business.

Off the job

– Training away from the work place.
– Often used to develop more general skills and knowledge.
– Use of specialist trainers so quality of training likely to be higher.
– More expensive than on the job training.
– As away from actual workplace less likely to disrupt production.
– Can be either internally or externally based training.

External

→ Training done outside of the business by third party.
→ Less likely to apply to specific business situation.
→ Courses can be expensive.

The difference between dismissal and redundancy

Redundancy occurs when the employer has to release workers to reduce costs or the job they did is no longer needed.

- Worker has not done anything wrong.
- Worker is often entitled to some compensation.

Reasons for redundancy are as following.

- Closure of a factory due to failure of the business – all workers would be released.
- Relocation to another location – so some jobs are created elsewhere.
- Automation of the work – so workers are no longer needed.

Dismissal occurs when the employee is told to leave as the behaviour is considered unreasonable or the employee has broken the terms of contract.

> **Useful link:**
>
> **Unit 41: Role of trade unions**

Progress check

1. Write down definitions of the following terms, as accurately as you can:
   - Off the job
   - Induction training
2. What is another name for a job specification?
3. True or false – is internal training free? Explain.
4. State **one** advantage of on the job training.
5. State **one** advantage of off the job training.

Sample question – worked example

Kape Confection is a large company that manufactures chocolate. It produces and sells its products in several countries around the world. Kape Confection aims to sell as many items as it can at low prices. All products are made by machines.

Kape are planning to buy Bradbury's, a small hand made chocolate producer. Several of Bradbury's workers are expected to be made redundant, as the work will become more automated.

1. Bradbury's workers are expected to be made redundant rather than dismissed. Explain the difference between the two terms. **[4]**

   Student's answer:
   Bradbury's workers will have no job because it will be done by machines. The job does not exist anymore. If they had done something wrong, like stolen chocolate they could be dismissed. But they have not, it's just that the job has gone.

Comment: This is a good answer. Both terms have been covered and the difference between them has been explained in relation to Bradbury's business.

Overall mark: 4/4

Key terms to learn

Dismissal: ending of an employees contract due to unreasonable behaviour or poor performance by worker.

Induction training: training aimed at introducing new employees to the business and its procedures.

Job description: written description of what the job involves.

Job specification: describes the type of person needed for the job.

Off the job: training that happens away from the actual workplace.

On the job: employees learn job specific skills whilst they are working.

Redundancy: employee is released because the job they did is no longer needed.

There are again a lot of concepts to learn here. Make sure you understand the main stages of the recruitment process, and can explain the purpose of each part.

Examination style questions for you to try

Wooden Works makes hand finished furniture, which it sells nationally in country T. To cope with growing demand, the management wants to reorganise the business by region rather than by function.

Wooden Works are having problems recruiting the skilled carpenters needed to complete some of the orders. It employs 160 skilled workers but the number of workers leaving each year is 40.

The Human Resources Manager, Rico, is worried. "The company's growing reputation is based on quality products. What are we to do? Other local businesses offer piece-rate, longer holidays, pensions and safe working conditions that the business cannot afford to match. I need to recruit another five skilled carpenters. All I seem to do is issue contracts to new workers. I've just been told we also need a new Finance Director."

1. Identify **two** pieces of information found in the contract for new workers.

    Feature 1:

    Feature 2: [2]

2. Identify and explain **two** reasons why it might be important for Wooden Works to recruit skilled workers.

    Reason 1:

    Reason 2: [8]

3. Wooden Works also needs a new Finance Director. Human Resources Manager, Rico cannot decide whether to recruit someone within the company or externally. Which option do you think Rico should choose? Justify your choice. [6]

4. The recruitment process involves many stages, including job description, job specification, advertisement and interviews. Why is each of these stages of the recruitment and selection process important to Wooden Works when choosing suitable employees? Justify your answer for each stage.

    Job description:

    Job specification:

    Advertisement:

    Interviews: [12]

Regulating and controlling business activity

The impact of business decisions

Learning Summary

By the end of this unit you should understand:

- *The reasons for government intervention*
- *The methods of government intervention*
- *The difference between nationalisation and privatisation*
- *The role of competition policy*
- *The impact of international trade*

The reasons for government intervention

Remember that most countries are mixed economies. This means that the Government will try to influence business activity in the interests of the people, the economy and the environment.

> Much of this information has already been covered in other units. See how much you can remember.

Government have many objectives and uses four main tools to help them achieve their aims.

Monetary policy		Possible government objectives include:		Legislation

Possible government objectives include:
1. Ensure essential goods and services are available at reasonable cost
2. Ban/control the supply of harmful products
3. Protect interests of customers
4. Reduce level of unemployment
5. Control level of inflation
6. Encourage economic growth
7. Encourage domestic and international trade
8. Control negative effects of business activity on environment

> Useful link:
> Unit 9: Types of economy

Fiscal policy				Competition and trade policies

The methods of government intervention

Useful links:

Unit 6: Government influence

Unit 41: Government regulation

- **Monetary policy:** is about controlling the amount of money in economy through interest rates to help manage rate of inflation.
- **Fiscal policies:** refers to how the Government raises and spends its money through taxation and expenditure.
- **Legislation:** on issues such as consumer protection, employee protection etc. These aim to set minimum standards to prevent exploitation of certain stakeholder groups in businesses.
- **Policies on nationalisation, competition and international trade:** aims to promote competition and the effective use of resources by the country.

The difference between nationalisation and privatisation

- When all business activity is controlled by the Government, it is called a **command economy.** All businesses are part of the **public sector.**
- When all business activity is controlled by private individuals, it is called a **market economy.** All businesses are part of the **private sector.**
- When there are both businesses owned by the Government and private individuals, it is called a **mixed economy.** All businesses are either part of the **public sector or private sector.**
- This is all a question of who is in control of business activity.

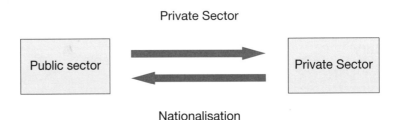

Nationalisation	Privatisation
• Involves transfer of business from private to public sector • Government takes over the running of certain industries themselves.	• Involves transfer of business from public to private sector • Usually happens as business becomes too large and inefficient.

Reasons for nationalisation	Reasons for privatisation
• Ensures provision of essential services such as health • Ensures prices charged are affordable • Protects jobs if a company is a large employer • Control of some industries is part of wider government objectives.	• Private sector firms are believed to be more efficient because of the need to make a profit • Public sector businesses can become too large to manage effectively. This could lead to diseconomies of scale.

Some types of business will move between the public and private sector many times. This can depend on factors such as Government policies and how important the goods and services are to the economy.

Activity

Try to find examples of businesses in your country which have moved between the public and private sectors. Can you explain the reasons for it?

The role of competition policy

Some business activities need to be controlled. Competition can lead some businesses to do unacceptable things as they try to increase profits. Governments want to stop bad practices but still encourage competition and protect consumers.

Some points to remember are as following.

* Most governments are keen to encourage competition.
* Competition laws set minimum standards or rules that all businesses should follow. These are designed to protect customers against dangerous products and misleading advertising. Customers have legal rights should the laws be broken.
* Competition means consumers should benefit from lower prices, better quality and more choices.
* Governments try to restrict or control monopolies who try to limit the choice and increase prices for consumers.
* Businesses can benefit as all businesses must comply with rules or face legal action. It should help avoid unfair competition.

Useful links:

Unit 8: Markets

Unit 9: Competition

Useful link:

Unit 10: International trade

The impact of international trade

International trade creates both opportunities and threats for a country. Governments mainly try to encourage trade as it creates:

* An opportunity to sell more goods (exports) so domestic businesses could make more profit which might lead to more tax paid.
* Helps balance of payments so improving the countries' international standing with other countries.

- A wider choice of products for consumers.
- More competition so possibly lower prices for consumers.
- Need for extra output could mean more jobs created so lower unemployment levels in the country.

However, the increased competition can have negative effects.

- Wider choice could lead to less sales for domestic businesses if goods made overseas (imports) are of better quality or cheaper.
- Loss of jobs if local businesses cannot compete.
- People could obtain goods that the government wants to restrict.

Government will try to support exports and limit imports if they want to encourage economic growth.

Methods to support exports include:	Methods to restrict imports include:
<ul><li>Offer guarantees to export businesses so less risk</li><li>Subsidies so prices charged are cheaper in export markets</li><li>Advice</li><li>Organising trade fairs to promote country or goods</li><li>Provide suitable transport infrastructure</li><li>Improve the communication infrastructure to make international communication cheaper, easier, and faster</li><li>Try to avoid/discourage rises in currency</li></ul>	<ul><li>Tariffs – an import tax on imports increases the price at which they can be profitably sold in the country, reducing demand</li><li>Quotas – limit the amount that a business can import from other countries</li><li>Impose restrictions on what can be sold</li><li>Set minimum standards that products must meet</li><li>If possible, try to influence exchange rate value of currency</li><li>Depreciation will make imports more expensive</li><li>Ban products</li></ul>

Exchange rates also affect businesses that buy and sell goods from abroad.

→ Rising exchange rates mean exports are more expensive but imports are cheaper.
→ This helps importers but could mean fewer sales for exporters.

> Rise in exchange rates: Helps importer but bad for exporter

→ Falling exchange rates mean exports are cheaper for other countries to buy so more sales for exporters.
→ However, businesses who import materials and goods will face higher costs.

> Fall in exchange rates: Helps exporter but bad for importer

Progress check

1. Write down definitions of the following terms, as accurately as you can:
   * Nationalisation
   * Monetary policy
2. List **two** reasons a government might give for nationalising a business.
3. State **two** government objectives.
4. Why do governments want to control monopolies?
5. Give **two** reasons why a Government might want to increase the amount of international trade.

Sample question – worked example

Denzel imports sugar from the West Indies for use in his sweet factory, based in Europe.

1. Explain how an appreciation in the exchange rate and the introduction of a quota on imported sugar might affect his business. **[8]**

   Student's answer:

   Appreciation in the exchange rate: An appreciation in the exchange rate is good for Denzel. It will reduce import prices, making it cheaper for Denzel to buy sugar so he could lower costs. He could either lower the price he charges for his sweets or increase his profit margin.

   Introduction of a quota: It depends on whether he can get sugar from Europe. He will be limited to how much sugar he can buy from other countries. It might not be as good but if he can get from his own country, it should not be a problem.

> Clear development showing effect on business.

Comment: The explanation of the effect of the appreciation is clearly developed in context, so can be given full marks.

There is some understanding of the impact of a quota. However, the effect on the business needs to be developed to score more than two marks. For example, if the sugar he buys is not as good, it could affect the quality of the sweets that he can make, which could have a negative impact on possible sales.

Overall mark: 6/8

Key terms to learn

Nationalisation: involves the transfer of a business from the private to public sector.

Privatisation: involves the transfer of a business from the public to private sector.

> There is a lot of cross over with other units here. Make a note of the many links shown so you have a fuller understanding of the role of government on business activity.

Examination style questions for you to try

> T&U Partners is owned by two brothers. The business produces building blocks made by recycling waste plastic. The blocks are very cheap to make. The brothers believe the blocks are ideal for low cost housing.
>
> Despite having no business experience, the brothers set up their own business making 'green blocks'. Funded by a government grant, they rented an old factory near the city centre. Rubbish was delivered to the site, twice a week. Demand has grown quickly from 1000 to 15 000 blocks per week.
>
> The business has received a new order for 10 000 more blocks per week. Usman, one of the owners is concerned that they might have to relocate. "We will need to triple the number of deliveries, and take on extra staff. The government are planning new pollution laws? We have to cope with rules for everything – workers, the quality of the bricks. When is it going to end? It all costs us more money."

1. Governments will try to control business activity. Give **two** examples of how a Government controls business activity.

   Example 1:

   Example 2: [2]

2. Identify and explain **two** reasons why a Government might want to help a business set up.

   Reason 1:

   Reason 2: [4]

3. The Government wants to introduce new competition laws. Do you think competition laws always help consumers? Justify your answer. [6]

4. Discuss how T&U Partners might be affected by government controls on its business. [12]

Government regulation

Learning Summary

By the end of this unit you should understand:
- *The role of trade unions*
- *The forms of industrial action*
- *The importance of health and safety*
- *The concept of ethics in business*

The role of trade unions

A **trade union** is a group that tries to protect the interest of workers.

- Employees who belong to a union are called **members**.
- Two main functions of a trade union are to represent their members and to negotiate with employers.
- **Collective bargaining** – the union represents all members in negotiations, rather than individual workers asking employers. This should give the union more influence and help members get a better deal.

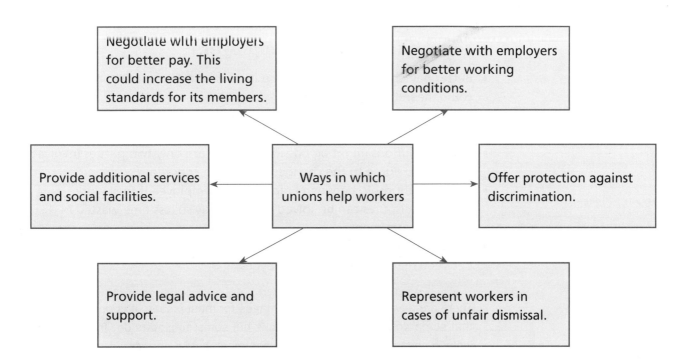

Negotiate with employers for better pay. This could increase the living standards for its members.

Negotiate with employers for better working conditions.

Provide additional services and social facilities.

Ways in which unions help workers

Offer protection against discrimination.

Provide legal advice and support.

Represent workers in cases of unfair dismissal.

How does the work of unions affect the business

A good relationship between employers and employees is important if a business wants to be successful. But employers and employees want different things. It's a balancing act.

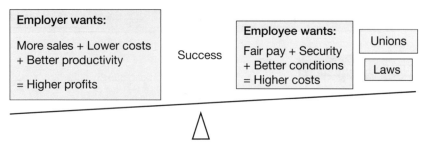

Unions help represent individual workers to stop employers trying to exploit them. Government pass laws to protect workers. There are four main areas covered by employment laws:

→ Health and safety
→ Wages
→ Contracts terms and conditions of employment
→ Protection against discrimination.

What are the possible problems for businesses

• Businesses want lower costs and higher profits. Extra costs for training or pay will lead to higher costs.
• Large unions can have more influence over a business. They can alter decisions that the business wants to take.
• Time spent in long negotiations can distract management from other management responsibilities.

Unions can also help employers

• Better pay and conditions can help increase workers motivation. This could mean better productivity.
• Can save time as only have to negotiate with one organisation rather than lots of individuals.
• Clearer solutions might be possible as there are only two parties involved so easier to agree to the changes in working conditions.
• Better relationship between employer and employee if they work together; disputes can be solved more quickly so less time wasted in individual arguments.
• Could lead to fewer industrial disputes if there is a better relationship between management and employees.

There are advantages and disadvantages for most issues. It is possible that some workers do not want unions but some employers do. Try to include points for both sides of the argument in your answer.

The forms of industrial action

If unions and employers cannot agree, workers might threaten employers with industrial action. Unions might organise industrial action to put pressure on employers if negotiation does not work.

These include the following.

- **Work to rule** – only do tasks that are included in job description. Could lead to less output or some jobs not done.
- **Go slow** – workers do tasks very slowly so reducing productivity.
- **Overtime bans** – refuse to work any longer than contracted hours. Output could be lost at busy times.
- **Strike** – refuse to do any work. This is meant to stop production. The business loses output and workers are not paid.

Businesses will want to avoid this. Industrial action can damage its reputation.

→ Could lead to fewer sales as customers are worried about where goods will be available.
→ Could damage relationship with workers leading to lower motivation and less productivity.
→ Could have problems attracting new employees if seen as unfair employer.

> Most employers know that employees are important. If a worker is unhappy with their pay and conditions, they are likely to be less motivated.
>
> - This can affect their productivity and can lead to workers leaving.
> - Lower output and additional recruitment costs could cost more than meeting workers' demands.

Useful link:

Units 37 and 38: Management styles and motivation

The importance of health and safety

Laws exist to ensure fair treatment of workers. Areas covered include the following.

- **Laws on minimum wages** – this guarantees all workers a basic amount for each hour worked or output produced.
- **Employment contracts** – state the terms of the job and what to do if there are any problems. Employers and workers can use this to help resolve disagreements.
- **Protection against discrimination** – ensures that workers are not unfairly treated because of their gender, race or any physical disabilities.
- **Minimum standards for working conditions** – workplaces should be safe. This could include protective clothing, breaks and good ventilation.

Different countries have different laws. You do not need to learn any but be aware of what the laws are trying to do.

Useful link:

Unit 39: Recruitment

Example of health and safety law	How law might affect business
Maximum hours of work	– Might need to recruit more workers to ensure that production is finished – Offer overtime payments – Introduce breaks
Protection from dangerous machinery	– Adding guards to equipment or providing extra training
Provision of safety equipment and clothing	– Providing harnesses, goggles, safety helmets or clothing etc.
Lighting and heating	– Install extra heaters or fans, or extra lighting into building
Basic hygiene facilities	– Install extra toilets or washing facilities

Many businesses provide their workers with better pay and conditions than the law requires.

Businesses might try to ignore trade unions, but they cannot avoid laws. If they ignore the law they could face legal action or in extreme cases be closed down.

Do laws always help workers?

- Not necessarily. To reduce costs, a business might look to relocate to another country or make changes to methods of production. Jobs might be at risk.
- Workers could be restricted by the number of hours they can work. This limits the amount they can earn.

The concept of ethics in business

- **Ethics** is all about behaving in a way which is right and fair.
- The aim of most private sector businesses is **profit**. Ethics and profits can clash. Ethical behaviour costs money. This increases business costs. Higher costs mean lower profits.

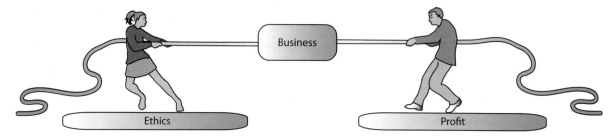

- People and businesses have different standards for behaviour. Most businesses will try to treat their workers and customers fairly. But others could mistreat workers and try to sell poor quality goods.

- Legislation exists to protect people against businesses who try to exploit others for their own gain.
- Ethics are becoming more important. The number of *fair trade schemes* which guarantee a fair price to suppliers is growing. Pressure groups will campaign against businesses that employ workers in unsafe conditions for very low wages.
- There is a growing market for ethically made goods. Many businesses operate and promote themselves as socially responsible to increase their appeal to customers.
- By treating workers fairly a business can be seen as good employers. More people might want to work for them.

> There is usually no right answer to questions about ethics. Remember to discuss both sides of the argument before you make a decision.

Progress check

1. Write down definitions of the following terms, as accurately as you can:
   - Ethics
   - Collective bargaining
2. What are people who join a union called?
3. True or false: unions can make laws.
4. State **two** forms of industrial action.
5. Explain **one** way that an ethical approach can help businesses.

Sample question – worked example

Snappers is a shoe manufacturer based in country A. Due to falling sales, the directors are thinking of shutting down factory B, as this will result in fewer job losses. More workers there are thinking of joining the trade union.

Comparison Information on factory A and factory B

	Factory A	Factory B
Output per week (pairs of shoes)	145 000	120 000
Number of employees	1000	800
Labour cost per hour	$3	$4
Average hourly wage in country	$2.75	$3.95
Hours worked per week	40	40
Union membership	502	140
Accidents last year	31	79

1. Identify and explain **two** reasons why employees at Snappers might want to join the trade union. [8]

Student's answer:

Reason 1: To gain an increase in wages because they can bargain on behalf of the workers. The workers would find it difficult to individually ask for a pay rise and there is strength in numbers. They are more likely to be successful than if they asked for a pay rise individually.

Reason 2: To ask for better working conditions. There are 48 more accidents in factory B than factory A. This might be due to lower standards as they have less union members. If more workers join the union, it is more difficult for the managers to ignore their campaign as they would have strength in numbers.

> There is no application to snappers in reason 1.

Comment: This is a good answer. Both are valid reasons why workers would want to join a union. Unfortunately reason one, could apply to any business so no application mark can be given. The answer only needed to refer to the current wage rate for the extra mark to be given.

Overall mark: 7/8

Key terms to learn

Collective bargaining: the union represents all members in negotiations with management rather than each individual workers representing themselves.

Ethics: is concerned about behaving in a way which is right and fair.

Industrial action: action taken by workers, usually at the suggestion of a union, to put pressure on the employer.

Trade union: an organisation set up to protect the interest of its members.

> This unit also looks at the role of government, and people in business. Be aware of the overlaps between topics, and use the links to help you answer questions.
>
> The new material covered here is all about employee protection. Make sure you understand the impact of laws and trade union action on businesses.

Examination style questions for you to try

1. Identify **two** dangers to the health and safety of workers that might arise in Snappers factory.

   Danger 1:

   Danger 2: **[2]**

2. Identify and explain **two** measures that a company could introduce to improve the health and safety of its workers.

   Measure 1:

   Measure 2: **[4]**

3. Do you think that Snappers should spend money on improving health and safety in its factory? Justify your answer. **[6]**

   > The Government of country A has announced new employment laws to encourage multinational businesses to set up in the country. A number of companies want to locate here as the Government plans to reduce the minimum wage and to give workers less job security. Businesses will be able to dismiss workers more easily. Trade unions are not happy about these changes.

4. Do you think trade union should be unhappy about these new laws? Justify your answer. **[12]**

42 Other influences on business activity

By the end of this unit you should understand:

- *The role of pressure groups*
- *The different stages of the business cycle*

The success of a business is influenced by many external factors.

- A business needs to take account of these influences or they risk losing business.
- Taking account of environmental issues can even help give businesses a competitive advantage. Green issues are popular. If a business is seen as 'green' they could attract more customers and increase sales.
- But change costs money. If sales do not cover the additional expense, the business will make less profit or even a loss.

'Green' refers to environmentally friendly behaviour.

The main influences on a business are discussed below.

Can be a threat if offer lower prices, better quality or new products
Competitors
New products could boost sales for all

Factors affecting demand can change leading to more or less sales
Customers
Can remain loyal to some brands

Legislation can impact on what and how products are made or where business locates
Government
Help set minimum standards for all to follow
Use of fiscal and montary policy affecting growth and demand

Trade unions
Will campaign to improve pay and working conditions for its members

Action of other countries can increase or restrict trade
Global economy
Changes in business cycle can lead to fall or rise in sales

Can be a threat to what business plans to do
Pressure groups
Able to use a range of options to influence business behaviour

The role of pressure groups

- Businesses can not ignore what people think. Changing tastes or opinions on environmental matters will affect how and what it produces.
- A **pressure group** is a group of people who come together with a common aim to try to influence the activities and decisions of businesses or government. Usually focus on a *narrow* or *single* issue. (example, oppose a planned factory).
- Pressure groups can campaign for any issue. Typical issues include environmental, health and the location of businesses.
- The aim is to create enough awareness about an issue to make the business change what they do.
- Businesses will try to resist making changes as it could lead to higher costs.
- The difference between Government and pressure groups is that businesses **must** do what the Governments say or face legal action.
- Pressure groups only try to influence the behaviour of others. They will influence decisions rather than to attempt to win or exercise government power.
- Pressure groups do not have the power to make laws but businesses often have to listen to pressure groups or risk losing sales and customers.

Some of the methods used by pressure groups to influence business activity are listed below.

Methods used		Effect of actions on business
Hold public meetings Lobby companies Write letters Organise demonstrations		Will try to create bad publicity for business → negative effect on reputation of business → can reduce level of sales. Business will try to avoid bad reputation by altering plans.
Stop buying products of the business		Aims to have direct impact on level of sales → could lead to lower levels of profits as well as impact on reputation. Business will need to alter plans if it wants to retain sales.
Lobby Government or authorities		Raise awareness of issues with policy makers' → Government could introduce new rules or laws. Business have to follow laws otherwise face legal action or even closure.

Remember pressure groups do not have the power to make laws.

The different stages of the business cycle

> **Do not confuse business cycle with product life cycle.**

Government tries to manage the economy to provide stable conditions for business to operate in.

- **Business cycle** refers to changes in the level of economic growth over time.
- It records the ups and downs in Gross Domestic Product (value of goods and services produced) of the country.
- It is also known as the **trade cycle**.
- The business cycle affects all businesses in an economy.

> **You need to understand how changes in the business cycle affect businesses.**

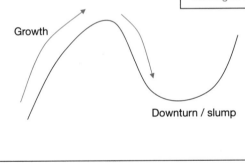

Boom – the peak of the cycle
- Demand high and rising as business and consumer confidence high
- High employment levels
- High demand leads to higher prices
- Risk of inflation
- Higher wage demands could lead to higher costs

Recession
- GDP falling
- Falling demand leads to fewer sales and falling profits
- Fixed costs still need to be paid
- Some redundancies likely leading to higher unemployment

Growth
- GDP rising
- Sales and profits should rise
- Levels of output rises
- Costs rise to meet growing demand

Downturn /slump – when economy at the bottom of cycle
- Fixed costs still need to be paid
- Few sales and low profits
- Many businesses could fail
- Rising unemployment

Progress check

1. Write down definitions of the following terms, as accurately as you can:
   - Boycott
   - Slump
2. Which of the following is another name for the business cycle – trade cycle or product life cycle?
3. Name **two** external influences on a business.
4. What does GDP stand for?
5. State **two** features of growth stage in business cycle.

Sample question – worked example

T&U Partners produce building blocks made by recycling waste plastic. The blocks are very cheap to make. T&U partners believe the blocks are good for low cost housing. Rubbish was delivered to the site, twice a week. Demand has grown quickly from 1000 to 15 000 blocks per week.

But Usman, one of the owners, is concerned about the latest economic data he has seen in a newspaper. This is shown in the figure below.

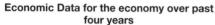

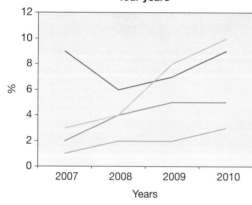

1. Do you think the economic data is favourable or not for T&U partners? Explain your answer. **[12]**

   Student's answer:
   Some of the data is very positive. The population is rising rapidly from 3% to 10%. This is good as people are likely to need more housing, so demand for blocks should continue to rise. Average income has also increased which is also good as more people have some income to buy a home, again increasing demand for blocks. As the economy has grown steadily from 1 to 3%, people are likely to be more happy to buy a house, as they will feel confident that their jobs are secure, and wages might rise so they can afford to buy expensive things like houses.
   There is some bad information. Interest rates have risen over the past 3 years to 9%. This could mean that people do not want to buy a house, as the interest rate will make the cost of a loan more expensive, so less people can afford to buy a house. Also as average income has gone up it could mean less demand for low cost housing. Anyone who can afford to buy a house might decide to buy a more expensive one.

   > Several good points explained about population, average income and interest rates.

Comment: This is a good answer. Several positive features have been correctly explained in context. Good application is shown through the correct use of data and the references to bricks and low cost housing. Both positive and negative effects of the data have been included.

But, the answer has not really addressed the evaluative part of the question as to whether the data is favourable or not. An overall assessment is required for all the marks to be given. For example, *"overall I think the data is fairly positive. Most of the indicators seem to be good for T&U Partners because they may lead to increased sales of bricks. A growing population will need housing, and if people are worried about interest rates, low cost housing is a safer option for them, which is the market they provide bricks for."*

Overall mark: 10/12

Key terms to learn

Economic boom: period in the business cycle when economic growth is rising rapidly.

Business cycle: refers to changes in the level of economic growth over time.

Economic growth: period in the business cycle when Gross Domestic Product is rising.

Pressure group: a group of people who come together with a common aim to try to influence the decisions and activities of businesses, local councils or the Government.

Recession: refers to a down swing in the level of economic activity within an economy.

Examination style questions for you to try

T&U Partners produce building blocks made by recycling waste plastic. The blocks are very cheap to make. They believe the blocks are ideal for low cost housing.

Rubbish was delivered to the site, twice a week. Demand has grown quickly from 1000 to 15 000 blocks per week. Usman, one of the owners is concerned that they might have to relocate. "We will need to triple the number of deliveries, and take on extra staff. The government are planning new pollution laws? It's all because of pressure groups again. We have to cope with rules for everything – workers, the quality of the bricks. When is it going to end? It all costs us more money. At this stage in the business cycle, I don't know what we should do! "

1. Identify **two** stages of the business cycle.

   Stage 1:

   Stage 2:   [2]

2. What is meant by a 'pressure group'? [2]

3. Identify and explain **two** ways that pressure groups try to influence the actions of businesses and government.

   Way 1:

   Way 2: [8]

4 T&U Partners are worried about the influence of pressure groups on their business. Do you think pressure groups always have an important role to play in influencing the actions of businesses like T&U partners? Explain your answer. [6]

Sample case studies

These questions are in the style of Cambridge examination questions but are written by the author to provide additional practice material.

Case study 1

Fizzed Fruits is a successful private limited company. It produces a wide range of fruit drinks. Its products are sold all over country F. The business is looking to expand overseas. Fizzed Fruits have invested a lot of money in new technology in order to meet the extra demand. All drinks are made using batch production. Many problems have led to a fall in productivity. Many workers are unhappy.

Fizzed Fruits have recently launched a new citrus drink called 'full on fruit'. The drink is targeted at the mass market, as a low price product. Its price is similar to other unbranded drinks on the market. The drink is sold in the popular Fizzed Fruits cartons and advertised locally on radio and through in-store promotions. The drinks are sold directly to small independent shops as the business think this is better than using wholesalers.

The Finance Director is disappointed with the initial sales of the new drink. He is concerned about its cash flow position, "What will this mean for working capital? Our suppliers are already complaining. Did the marketing department do any research?"

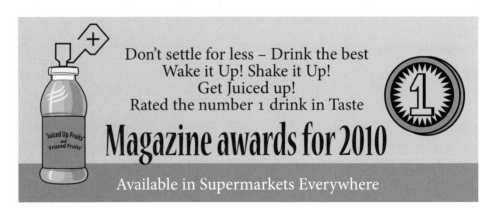

Don't settle for less – Drink the best
Wake it Up! Shake it Up!
Get Juiced up!
Rated the number 1 drink in Taste

Magazine awards for 2010

Available in Supermarkets Everywhere

Appendix 1: Advertising poster for Juiced up fruits

To: Finance Manager
From: Production department

Subject: Estimated production costs for 'juiced up fruits'.
(Costs per 1000 units – 1 litre cartons)

Raw material	$150
Labour costs	$200
Packaging	$50
Distribution costs	$100

The drinks are to be sold for $1 per carton

Materials costs are likely to be high as we have to import a lot of the fruit we use. The distinctive cartons are also expensive, but its part of the brand.

Appendix 2: Memo to Finance Director

Looking to trade overseas?

Do you want to apply for a subsidy? Or just want some advice.
It's easy.

YOUR GOVERNMENT CAN HELP

It's good for the country – we can all gain from economic growth, exchange rates and employment.

Let us help YOU to overcome any problems of entering new markets.

CONTACT OUR NEW DEPARTMENT TODAY.

Appendix 3: Government advertisement

Questions

1. (a) Explain **two** possible financial problems that might arise for Fizzed Fruits if the actual costs of the new product are higher than the estimated costs.

Problem 1: ....

....

....

....

....

....

....

....

Problem 2: ....

....

....

....

....

....

....

.... [8]

(b) Do you think the Finance Manager at Fizzed Fruits should be concerned about its cash flow position? Justify your answer.

....

....

....

....

....

....

....

....

....

....

....

....

....

....

....

....

....

....

....

....

....

.... [12]

2. (a) Identify and explain **one** advantage and **one** disadvantage of
batch production for Fizzed Fruits.

Advantage: ....

....

....

....

....

....

....

....

Disadvantage: ....

....

....

....

....

....

.... [8]

(b) Do you think the introduction of new technology is beneficial
for Fizzed Fruits? Justify your answer.

....

....

....

....

....

....

....

....

....

....

....

....

....

....

....

....

....

....

....

....

....

.... [12]

3. (a) Explain to the Marketing Manager how primary research could be carried out.

....

....

....

....

....

....

....

....

....

....

....

....

....

....

.... [8]

(b) The Marketing Manager thinks changes should be made to the marketing mix. Explain possible changes Fizzed Fruits could make. Justify your choices.

....

....

....

....

....

....

....

....

....

....

....

....

....

....

....

....

....

....

....

....

....

.... [12]

4. (a) Identify and explain **two** reasons why governments encourage exports.

Reason 1: ....

....

....

....

....

....

....

....

Reason 2: ....

....

....

....

....

....

....

.... [8]

(b) What do you think are the **three** most important factors for Fizzed Fruits to consider when deciding whether to trade overseas? Justify your answer.

Factor 1: ....

....

....

....

....

....

....

Factor 2: ....

....

....

....

....

....

....

....

Factor 3: ....

....

....

....

....

....

....

.... [12]

5. (a) Identify and explain **two** reasons why it is important for Fizzed
        Fruits to find more about competition in its market.   **[8]**

        Reason 1: ....

        ....

        ....

        ....

        ....

        ....

        ....

        Reason 2: ....

        ....

        ....

        ....

        ....

        ....

        .... **[8]**

    (b) Fizzed Fruits sell their products directly to retailers. Do you
        think this is the right channel for them to use? Justify your
        answer.

        ....

        ....

....
....
....
....
....
....
....
....
....
....
....
....
....
....
....
....
....
....
....
....
.... [12]

Case study 2

Solid Metal Mining (SMM) is a large company. They extract copper, nickel and other minerals in various locations around the world. Their main objective is profit. Last year they made net profits of $36m.

SMM uses hi-tech machinery and unskilled workers to extract the minerals. All workers do a 12 hour shift and are paid the minimum wage in each country. They also receive a bonus based on each mines' profits. All workers receive some basic training, but the health and safety record is bad and motivation is low.

Recently large amounts of copper have been found in country L. The area is remote, but ideal for the wildlife found there. Access to the site is poor and there is no electricity or water. There are few jobs for the local people. Some people are worried about the damage any mining will cause.

Opening this new mine will be expensive. Besides the cost of new equipment, the company will have to spend money improving the local roads and supplying the power and water to the site. Initial estimates put the cost at $20m. The project manager is not sure this is a good location.

Appendix 1: Extract from accounts

Balance sheet as at 31 December 2010 ($m)

Fixed assets		320
Current assets	60	
Current liabilities		
Overdraft	40	
Creditors	40	
	80	
Net assets		300
Financed by:		
Share capital	120	
Retained profit	105	
Long term loans	80	
Capital employed		300

Appendix 2: Protest poster or MAP

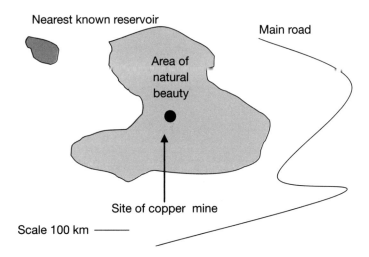

Appendix 3: Article in national newspaper

Mining row refuses to go away!

Environmental groups are protesting at the Government's decision to allow Solid Metal Mining to open a mine at the country's main beauty spot. Campaigners had hoped to obtain funding for an eco-tourism project instead.

A Government minister said "The jobs created by this major business are important for the future economic growth of our country. All these pressure groups care about is green space. We want our people to have a better standard of living."

Questions

1. (a) There are many accidents in the mining industry. Identify and explain **two** measures that SSM could change to improve their health and safety record.

    Measure 1: ....
    ....
    ....
    ....
    ....
    ....
    ....
    ....

    Measure 2: ....
    ....
    ....
    ....
    ....
    ....
    ....
    .... [8]

    (b) Do you think that bonuses are the most effective way of increasing motivation of workers at Solid Metal Mining? Justify your answer.

....

....

....

....

....

....

....

....

....

....

....

....

....

....

....

....

....

....

....

....

....

....

.... [12]

2. **(a)** Solid Metal Mining is a public limited company. Explain how the
   objectives of the company might be different if it was owned by
   the government.

....

....

....

....

....

....

....

....

....

....

....

....

....

....

.... [8]

(b) Do you think building the new mine will be beneficial to country L? Justify your answer.

....

....

....

....

....

....

....

....

....

....

....

....

....

....

....

....

....

....

....

....

....

.... [12]

3. (a) Identify and explain how **two** stakeholders would use the accounts of Solid Metal Mining.

Stakeholder 1: ....

....

....

....

....

....

....

....

Stakeholder 2: ....

....

....

....

....

....

....

.... [8]

(b) Using the information in Appendix 1, consider the advantages and disadvantages of the **three** possible sources of finance to use. Recommend to SMM the most suitable source of finance. Justify your answer.

Option 1: ....

....

....

....

....

....

Option 2: ....
....
....
....
....
....

Option 3: ....
....
....
....
....

Recommendation: ....
....
....
....
.... [12]

4. (a) SMM will need to recruit some workers for the mine. Explain the
        process of recruitment and selection they should follow.

....
....
....
....
....
....
....
....
....
....
....
....

....

....

....

.... [8]

(b) SMM plans to recruit people living in country L rather than transfer workers from their mines in other countries. Do you agree? Justify your answer.

....

....

....

....

....

....

....

....

....

....

....

....

....

....

....

....

....

....

....

....

....

....

.... [12]

5. **(a)** Mines have to be located where deposits are found. Identify and explain **two** other location factors which are important for SMM to consider when deciding where to locate. **[8]**

Factor 1: ....

....

....

....

....

....

....

Factor 2: ....

....

....

....

....

....

....

.... **[8]**

(b) Consider how **three** different stakeholder groups will be affected by the opening of the new mine. Which group do you think will be most affected? Justify your answer.

Stakeholder 1: ....

....

....

....

....

Stakeholder 2: ....

....

....

....

....

....

Stakeholder 3: ....

....

....

....

....

.... [12]

Answers to questions

Mark scheme for Case study 1

1.(a) *The marks available for this question are: 2 marks for knowledge; 4 marks for explanation/analysis; 2 marks for application*

Content:

- Break even point may be at a higher level of output – how increase sales if initial sales were disappointing.
- If costs are higher then profits may be lower – unhappy shareholders/less retained profit to help buy any more new technology.
- To keep profits the same they may have to increase price – could lead to reduced sales if prices are increased – as price similar to other unbranded items.
- Lower profits so difficult to raise share capital – problem of finding alternative, possibly more expensive, ways of raising capital.
- If costs are higher than expected then may become overdrawn – how finance cash flow problem – suppliers are already complaining.

Points for Application: price similar to unbranded items / disappointing initial sales / suppliers complaints/ (use of information in appendix two) imported material / packaging

1 mark for each problem identified; up to two further marks are available for explaining the nature of each problem; 2 application marks are also available

1.(b) *The marks available for this question are: 4 marks for knowledge; up to 6 marks for explanation/analysis and evaluation; 2 marks for application*

Content:

- Large cash outflows for technology – if financed by loans, more repayments going out.
- Cash inflows slow as initial sales are disappointing so lack of cash to pay costs.

- Suppliers will want to be paid for raw materials (fruit etc.) – could refuse to supply company so no juice for drinks. It might be difficult to arrange alternative suppliers as most fruit seems to be imported.
- Suppliers might refuse to offer credit terms which will increase cost.
- Successful business so only likely to be temporary problem so suppliers are more likely to give them time to pay.
- Successful business who sells a range of products – so other products could contribute to cash flow – there is no evidence to suggest these products are struggling so overall cash flow might be fine.
- Cash flow is an issue – even the most successful business can fail if cannot pay its debts as they fall due.
- Awareness of problem is good – as shows planning so is likely to have time to take action to solve any cash flow problem before it arises.

Points for Application: disappointing initial sales / suppliers complaining / imported materials / successful

Themes for evaluation: only one product in a wide range so no need to worry / should worry as even profitable businesses need cash for working capital / aware so have time to solve problem so not really an issue

Evaluation – justified decision made as to whether a problem based on analysis of points identified and discussed

2.(a) *The marks available for this question are: 2 marks for knowledge; 4 marks for explanation/analysis; 2 marks for application*

Content: Advantages:

- Flexible – can help FF respond effectively to a sudden change in demand – if sales increase they can adapt so gain higher revenue/profits.

- Production can be easily changed from one product to another – so FF able to respond quickly to changes in demand – sales will increase leading to higher revenue/profits.
- Workers will have some variety of jobs – making work more interesting so increased job satisfaction/more motivated/increased efficiency.

Disadvantages:

- Can be expensive – more equipment may need to be purchased as several different processes might need to be carried out to produce different drinks.
- Additional costs as more training needed – have been problems – maybe workers don't know what to do.
- Increased storage costs – as more warehouse space is required for drinks to be stored ready for shipment to customer. Might need refrigeration equipment for storage of fruit or finished drinks.
- Time delay while switch between batches – can slow down production – could be reason why productivity fallen. Lack of output could explain disappointing sales.
- A fault in a part of the batch can affect the whole batch.

Points for Application: disappointing initial sales / suppliers complaining / imported materials / successful

1 mark for each advantage/disadvantage identified; up to two further marks are available for explaining the nature of each advantage and disadvantage; 2 application marks are available

2.(b) *The marks available for this question are: 4 marks for knowledge; up to 6 marks for explanation/analysis and evaluation; 2 marks for application*

- Creates opportunities e.g. cost savings – They might reduce the number of employees needed because of their labour saving potential.
- Speed up production so more work to be completed in a given time period – overheads spread – so lower unit cost.
- New methods – FF introduced batch production – able to widen product range; e.g. machinery might be able to pit / skin fruits so can offer new flavours.
- New products – technology can make new products possible.
- New markets – increased output will allow FF to enter new overseas markets.

Problems:

- Training cost – workers will need to know how to use new technology before the business can make full use of the new system. This will increase costs and possibly cash outflows so worsening their cash flow position.

- Breakdowns – if machinery breaks down, the entire stage of batch production will have to stop. This will affect the level of output.
- Employees reaction to change – workers are unhappy. Some might fear their jobs or wages will be cut so could become de-motivated. This could lead to a fall in productivity – reducing the potential cost savings.

Points for Application: disappointing initial sales / workers unhappy / increased demand / fall in productivity / expand overseas / cash flow

Themes for evaluation: all change takes time to be effective – only initial problems. Long term advantages should outweigh disadvantages / it is a risk to change method of production at same time as introducing a new product so needs careful management if going to be beneficial

Evaluation – justified decision made as to whether new technology is beneficial based on analysis of points raised

3.(a) *The marks available for this question are: 2 marks for knowledge; 4 marks for explanation /analysis; 2 marks for application*

Content: Knowledge marks – e.g. primary research could include questionnaires, interviews, and consumer panels. 1 mark for each example – 2 max.

Explanation of how to carry out the research – e.g. need to design a questionnaire (1), set a budget to carry out the research (1), select the type of sample and sample size (1), decide where to carry out the research and when (1), go out to a shopping centre or local stores and carry out the questionnaire (1), collate and analyse the results (1), produce a report (1).

1 mark for each point of explanation of how to carry out the research (up to a maximum of 4 marks)

Points for application: – examples of questions asked e.g. 'What type of drinks do you like? Where do you buy drinks' what type of radio station do you listen to?

1 mark for each type of primary research method identified (2 marks max); up to 4 further marks are available for explaining how the research method(s) can be carried out; up to 2 application marks are available

3.(b) *The marks available for this question are: 4 marks for knowledge; up to 6 marks for explanation /analysis and evaluation; 2 marks for application*

Content: Product – increase the range of flavours sold – tropical or berry fruit drinks. Mass market customers might not like citrus fruits – disappointing initial sales. By changing the flavour to appeal to more customers – might increase in sales. Batch production would allow a variety of flavours to be made. FF could use limited edition flavours to test out demand for different drinks; change size of drink carton – to handy drink size to family packs or multi pack versions to increase amount of sales.

Price – low price ($1) ok as promotional pricing but not a long term strategy. FF is successful / known for their distinctive packaging. This suggests FF do not need to match unbranded prices. Low prices might infer lower quality so deter customers who will choose better quality of Juiced Up fruit – lead to lower sales. Could use competitive pricing as company established.

Promotion – advertising on local radio and in store promotions. But need to reach more people as aimed at mass market – Posters, leaflets and billboards, promotions (money off coupons) or free samples could be considered. If people can taste the drink and like it, this could encourage them to buy more.

Place – change from independent shops to supermarkets / other shops so more people in their target market can buy. Larger store might have space to have larger, more eye catching promotions. As the product is new, customer awareness is important. If customers cannot get to small independent stores they can't buy it leading to fewer sales for FF.

Points for Application: distinctive packaging / $1 / local radio / in store promotions / low price / mass market / small independent / sell directly to shops / juiced up fruit award

Evaluation: Clear and detailed explanation of the changes to be made to at least 1 element of the marketing mix. Why the changes are necessary and explanation of how the change would increase sales

4.(a) *The marks available for this question are: 2 marks for knowledge; 6 marks for explanation /analysis*

Content:

- Economic growth increased – as goods and services sold overseas, increases total value of goods and services produced by the country – should mean living standards rise, which is a government objective.

- Lower unemployment – as businesses need to produce more goods and services to meet customer demand in other countries, they will have to recruit more employees to increase production.

- Encouraging exports will lead to a stronger exchange rate – the more export sales businesses in a country achieve, the higher the demand would be from abroad to buy that country's currency and this would lead to an increase (appreciation) in the value of the local currency – A stronger exchange rate would make imports less expensive – and reduce risk of inflation in the country.

4.(b) *The marks available for this question are: 4 marks for knowledge; up to 6 marks for explanation /analysis and evaluation; 2 marks for application*

Content:

- Foreign competition – know number of competitors, and how powerful competitors are. Already have competition from Juiced up fruit, which could lower possible sales. If FF enters new markets, how will other competitors react? As have cash flow problems, FF might not be able to respond if a price war breaks out. Brand loyalty to other products will reduce possible sales.

- Quality standards overseas – need to know if there are different rules and regulations for production/ sales of fruit drinks. Higher standards in other countries could lead to higher costs for FF, as have cash flow problems can FF justify extra costs?

- Transport and distribution costs – need to pay to send products overseas. If refrigeration is required, this will add to cost.

- Different customer tastes – other countries might want different flavours, which the business will need to find out. If cannot satisfy individual country requirements they will lose sales. Extra market research could be required which will increase the cost.

- Projected profits – will potential revenue cover the additional costs incurred?

- Barriers to trade – quotas – restrict the amount that can be sold in certain countries; tariffs will add to the price charged, making their products less competitive in other countries so lower levels of sales possible.

- Currency fluctuations – already have to pay cost of importing fruit. Any changes in exchange rate will affect FF – a rise in currency will help as will lower import costs. Might lose out as exports become more expensive, resulting in potentially fewer sales.

- Risk of non payment – will not know customers in overseas markets so cannot automatically trust them.
- Size of overseas market – how profitable is export market? is it worthwhile exporting. Can production department cope with the additional output or different specifications of drinks for the export market? Will FF need new machinery – is this cost effective compared to extra sales.

Points for Application: disappointing initial sales / workers unhappy/ increased demand / fall in productivity / import fruit / citrus flavour / fruit

Evaluation: justified decisions made based on analysis of factors. At least 3 factors well explained as well as good judgement shown as to why these factors are important when deciding whether to export

5.(a) *The marks available for this question are: 2 marks for knowledge; 4 marks for explanation /analysis; 2 marks for application*

Content:

- Identify the level of competition – a highly competitive market is likely to be more difficult for.
- Level of Market share held by competitors – if Juiced Up or other competitors have a monopoly position in the market this will make it difficult for FF to compete. Brand loyalty to rival drinks will reduce the potential market for FF drinks.
- Size of market – so able to establish whether there is likely to be sufficient demand for a new product.
- Pricing – how much should they charge for their products – have set low price, is this right price for the level of competition in the market.
- Promotion – which methods should they use to attract attention? They might want to change where or how they advertise.
- Where are competitors products sold? Do they want to sell their products in the same supermarkets as Juiced up fruits drinks?

5.(b) *The marks available for this question are: 4 marks for knowledge; up to 6 marks for explanation /analysis and evaluation; 2 marks for application*

Content: Current system:

- Direct feedback received from retailers – which business can use to improve product.
- Full control of distribution – they are able to decide who and where drinks sold.
- Lower costs – as costs of wholesalers will need to be included in the price.
- Business is successful – is there any need to change?

Benefits of wholesalers:

- Advice given – wholesalers likely have more knowledge of drinks market – where to sell, which flavours are popular which could help FF increase level of sales.
- Saves storage space – warehouse space will not be needed on site to store drinks. This will free up space which could be used if extra production facilities are needed to meet overseas orders or reduce storage costs if able to rent smaller space.
- Saves transport costs – as distribution costs $100 per 1000 litres to independent stores no longer needed – reduce FF's so less pressure on cash flow and increased margins.
- Have one large customer rather than many small orders so save time.
- Receive money quicker as goods sold to wholesaler who sell on the stock – could help cash inflow as not waiting for payments from many small shops.
- Reducing costs of administration need less staff if only deal with a few large customers – this will reduce overhead costs.
- Allow FF to concentration on production – so more time to solve production problems as don't have to worry about distribution.

Points for Application: disappointing initial sales / distribution costs of $100/ increased demand / expand overseas / cash flow / successful / any market research

Themes for evaluation: disappointing sales suggest change is necessary – but is distribution the reason for the problem? / How much control does FF want over distribution / wholesalers will free up FF to specialise on production

Evaluation – justified decision made as to whether current method is right channel for Fizzed Fruits based on analysis of points raised

Mark scheme for Case study 2

1.(a) *Marks available for this question are: 2 marks for knowledge; 4 marks for explanation /analysis; 2 marks for application*

Content:

- Additional training – better understanding of what need to do – which would reduce mistakes – currently workers only receive basic training.
- Recruit more skilled workers to operate machinery – they might have a better understanding of how to use the equipment so reducing the accident level.
- Provide safety equipment such as goggles, gloves and helmets – if accidents happen, then workers have some protection which could reduce the number of serious accidents.
- Additional lighting – working down a dark is dangerous, with lights on helmets would be able to see dangers more easily.
- Posters and safety leaflets – workers would be informed about dangerous areas, can be made aware of what to do in case of an accident so help can be obtained more quickly.
- Reduce length of shift down from 12 hours – more accidents are likely if workers are tired.

Points for Application: bad record / basic training/ unskilled workers / 12 hour shift / hi tech machinery

1 mark for each problem identified; up to two further marks are available for explaining how the measure would help improve safety; 2 application marks are also available

1.(b) *The marks available for this question are: up to 4 marks for knowledge; up to 6 marks for explanation /analysis and evaluation; 2 marks for application*

Content: *advantages and disadvantages of various methods of motivation could be discussed*

Bonuses: extra paid in addition to wages based on meeting set target – incentive can motivate especially if the mine is profitable; but depends on amount, and nature of job as money alone not likely to be effective if basic needs not met.

- Basic needs such as food and shelter will be met by money, but other factors influence motivation which can be discussed – safety at the mine – record is bad; social

factors – it is an isolated site, so how many people will there be there to mix with?
- Motivation theories can be included in the answer e.g. McGregor, Maslow, and Taylor as different factors are likely to motivate each individual.
- Financial – profit sharing, performance related pay as well as bonuses which are currently used.
- Non-financial – health care paid for, free transport, pension paid, Praise for a job well done, job rotation, job enlargement, job enrichment.

Points for Application: minimum wage, motivation is low, bonus based on each mines profit, health and safety record

Themes for evaluation: depends on what motivates each individual worker, factors such as low motivation suggest that bonuses might not be the best method – money is little use if workers are fearful of their safety. Whether bonus is best method will depend on reasons behind poor motivation

Evaluation – justified decision made as to whether a problem based on analysis of points raised

2.(a) *The marks available for this question are: 4 marks for knowledge; 4 marks for explanation /analysis*

Content: Business objectives of a plc might be to make profits, growth, survival, diversification but the objectives if government owned might be to provide a service, to break-even, to provide employment.

1 mark for each different objective identified; up to four further marks are available for reasons how the objectives might be different are explained OR contrasts are drawn between the two types of ownership

2.(b) The marks available for this question are: up to 4 marks for knowledge; up to 6 marks for explanation /analysis and evaluation; 2 marks for application

Content: Advantages:

- Mine will provide power and improve roads which benefits local community /businesses – which could help development of remote location.
- Job created for local people – in an area where there are few jobs – can help improve standard of living.
- Provide jobs for wider community if road building and power supplies installed.

- Economic growth in Country L as output will be higher due to copper – proceeds from mine could help develop country.
- Improve reputation of country – seen as developing nation.

Disadvantages:

- Environmental damage – as this is an area of natural beauty and habitat for wildlife.
- Loss of eco-tourism – which might be more sustainable option for the site.
- What will happen to the area once all resources have been extracted? Project manager already questioning value of site.

Points for Application: growth; employment; no water or power, remote location, few jobs, $20m, eco-tourism, wildlife, pressure groups want green space

Evaluation – justified decision made as to whether mine is beneficial based on analysis of points raised (*should consider both advantages and disadvantages*)

3.(a) *The marks available for this question are:2 marks for knowledge; 4 marks for explanation /analysis; 2 marks for application*

Content:

- Owners – is business profitable ($36m) – want a good return on their investment to ensure investment is worthwhile.
- Lenders – is SMM able to repay loan / meet interest repayments. Level of gearing important as shows how risky lending would be – as only 27% SMM should be able to increase their gearing without too much additional risk.
- Investors – Potential new investors want to know if the business is profitable. How much y return on their investment can they expect – if low they won't invest.
- Employees / trade unions – level of profits ($36m) as this will help in negotiating their bonuses and any pay rises / profitable might suggest jobs are secure.
- Government – amount of tax likely to be paid, stability of business to ensure jobs are not at risk.

Points for Application: figures from appendix 1; bonuses, profit, $36m; ROCE 12%

1 mark for each stakeholder identified; up to two further marks are available for explaining how the stakeholder would use the accounts; 2 application marks are available

3.(b) *The marks available for this question are as follows: up to 4 marks for knowledge; up to 6 marks for explanation / analysis and evaluation; 2 marks for application*

Content: Options include:

- Bank loan – large amount available; interest paid; can be long term, no loss of control.
- Share issue – share profits; possible loss of control; no interest payable but may expect dividend payments which will reduce amount able to set aside as reserves. Business is however successful – made profit of $36m last year so should be no problem to attract investors.
- Retained profits – no interest payable, no loss of control, funds not available for other uses in emergency.

Points for Application: use financial information in appendix 1 – $80m, $105 m, $120 m, $20m is estimate only, $36m profit

Themes for evaluation: depends on whether feel control is an issue; all three options are possible so any sensible reasons will be considered

Evaluation – justified decision made based on analysis of points raised (*should consider both advantages and disadvantages*). Would need to say why one method is better than other two options for full marks

4.(a) *The marks available for this question are: 4 marks for knowledge; 4 marks for explanation /analysis*

Content: Stages that could be discussed: Job analysis/Job description, Job (person) specification/Job advertisement, send out application forms/CV & letters of application, Interviews, select the best applicants/ send out letter to make job offer.

1 mark for each stage plus a further mark for explaining how that stage is carried out

4.(b) *The marks available for this question are as follows: up to 4 marks for knowledge; up to 6 marks for explanation / analysis and evaluation; 2 marks for application*

Content:

Recruiting from Country L – For:

- Possibly lower wages as currently few jobs for local people – able to offer lower wages as workers need jobs.
- Can train them in the ways of SMM – they would not be confused by different approach used at other sites.

- Guaranteed to speak local language – so fewer communication problems which could increase risk of accidents.

Against:

- Training costs high if need a lot of workers – all workers would need basic training – adding to $20m cost of opening the mine.
- Recruitment costs – advertising and selection is an additional expense and no guarantee suitable workers can be found.

Transferring workers – For:

- Employees already known to the managers – more productive as procedures are likely to be understood.
- Have the required skills – No need to train workers therefore less expensive. If workers know what they are doing this will decrease the risk of accidents.
- May need to recruit from wider field anyway if not enough local people to work in mine.

Against:

- More expensive e.g. workers from other countries might receive higher wages which would increase labour costs for the mine.
- May not speak local language – communication problems with local workers.

Points for Application: some basic training, health and safety is bad, hi tech machinery, remote

Evaluation – justified decision made as to which is best approach based on analysis of points identified and discussed (a good answer should consider both advantages and disadvantages). Answer needs to say WHY one method is better than other one for full marks. Either option is possible.

5.(a) *The marks available for this question are: 2 marks for knowledge; 4 marks for explanation /analysis; 2 marks for applications*

Content: Market; Power; Government influence (regulations or grants); reaction of pressure groups, Availability of labour; Transport and communications; power

Points for Application: remote, unskilled workers, no power or water, access to site is poor, project manager is wondering

1 mark for each factor identified; up to two further marks are available for explaining why the factor is important for SMM to consider

5.(b) *The marks available for this question are as follows: up to 4 marks for knowledge; up to 6 marks for explanation / analysis and evaluation; 2 marks for application*

Content:

Shareholders/owners of SMM – want to know how much profit is available for dividends – a profitable mine might increase value of shares held so would also receive more money if they sold their shares.

- Bank and other lenders – Are SMM able to repay their loan, and meet interest repayments. If the mine is not successful, SMM might not be able to repay the loans so the lenders could face financial problems. Fixed assets $320m suggest there are enough assets to use as security for loan, so no great risk of loss.
- Government of Country L – would see development of area – improving prospects of economic growth, and living standards for local community. Development might raise profile of country which could lead to other businesses start up in country.
- Workers – better job security if business expands. Large deposits could be good news as if the mine is successful; they could receive better bonuses. But risks to safety, as the new mine is established.
- The community in the surrounding area – infrastructure (roads, power, and water)/ more jobs for the local people – could help improve their standard of living. However there are dangers – increased noise and air pollution, plus the loss of wildlife.

Pressure groups/environmental groups – would lose as loss of wildlife and green space – development would stop the eco-tourism scheme.

Points for Application: $20m is estimate only, $36m profit, loss of green space, eco tourism, jobs, power, water, roads, remote, financial information from appendix 1, economic growth

Themes for evaluation: Positive news for shareholders as likely to be profits; or negative for pressure groups who do not appear to have any positive gains from the opening. Community seems a sensible choice as they are directly affected. Many other stakeholders are indirectly affected but they don't live where the mine is located. Justified decision made as to most affected based on analysis of points raised. Would need to say why one group is more affected than other two for full marks.

Answers to section 1

UNIT 1

Progress check

1. Limited availability of resources to meet the unlimited wants of people; Any business owned, run or controlled by the Government; Cost of something in terms of the next best option.

2. Needs are items that we must have in order to live such as food or shelter. Wants are items that we would like to have, although they are not essential e.g. latest pair of fashionable shoes.

3. To provide the goods and services that people need or want.

4. Land – space for stall; Labour – the Market trader or assistant; Capital – till or table used to display goods; Entrepreneur – Market trader.

5. Added value is the difference between the costs of bought in resources and the price at which the "finished product" sells e.g. - difference between the costs of catching the fish and their market price.

6. Two from: Turning raw materials into finished goods; Branding; Packaging and Adding extra features to products.

Examination style question for you to try

1. Cost of something in terms of the next best option – it is the options not selected.

2. The difference between the selling price of a product and the cost of raw materials used to make it.

3. Branding – making a product stand out from its competitors. People will pay more for this good rather than buy cheaper alternatives increasing the amount of added value; Reduce costs with same price – if able to lower cost of bought in materials, this will increase the amount of value added.

Unit 2

Progress check

1. Primary – the sector of the economy which extracts or produces raw materials out of which finished products are made; Secondary – the sector which takes raw materials and turns them into finished goods; Tertiary – the sector of industry that provides services to businesses and individuals.

2. Examples include manufacturing, building, refining.

3. Examples include – accountancy, retail, distribution, hairdressing.

4. Students own answer.

Examination style question for you to try

1. Primary: farming, forestry, mining; Manufacturing: food processing, refining.

2. Country B might have limited natural resources – Primary only 2% labour force, compared to 43% in country A – if no natural resources in country, has to be fewer jobs available in this sector. Nearly ¾ of Country B workers found in service sector, 70% compared to 37% in country A – might have specialist skills such as financial or education that are better than other countries. Other reasons – cheaper food sources from other countries – so do not give jobs to primary; primary might be mechanised so few jobs created; large public sector – health and education sectors.

3. **Banking** – need account to make and receive payments easier; bank can offer services to ensure payments made if cash flow problem; tend to be trusted by all parties – if suppliers not paid they could stop or delay important deliveries. **Advertising agency** – to help promote their wide range of chocolates across the world – need to increase customers awareness / remind them of their products; **Market research agency** – as tastes changes, Kape must know so able to respond to changes in demand to maintain sales – hence purchase of Bradbury; **Insurance** – need to protect workers / equipment against accidents – which could mean expensive premiums – for premium, can offset this cost to limit impact on business – legal action could damage reputation; **Retailers** – shops where products are sold so customers able to buy their chocolates; wholesalers buy their chocolate to sell onto retailers; **Website designers** – set up and possibly maintain their site so able to keep stakeholders up to date with plans – important as sell in several countries. Also possible way to increase sales in future; **Accountants** – manage their accounts so comply with all financial reporting rules for large businesses; **Legal services** – if any complains about what they sell; **Transport businesses** – to move chocolates to and from customers / suppliers domestically and internationally; **Communication** – will need to

ensure can call or electronically contact wholesalers – particularly important as sell in many companies. Need Suppliers to maintain production – without orders / stock they would have nothing to sell to generate an income for themselves, or good customer relations to maintain reputation / market share.

4. Student's own answer – based on businesses selected. See question 3 for points to consider.

Unit 3

Progress check

1. When a business benefits from lower average costs per unit.
2. Workers feel too remote from management; more job security with a larger firm; Banks more willing to lend to a large firm as more chance of money being repaid; Government need to know effect of policy decisions on different sized businesses; Businesses want to know about size and strength of competition – could influence marketing decisions.
3. A merger – two businesses join together by agreement; a takeover – one firm buys out the other business. It is much quicker way to grow.
4. Sell more of current product in existing markets; Sell current product in new markets / segments; Launch a new product; Adapt an existing product.
5. Personal reasons, lack of finance, size of market.
6. Students own answer.

Examination style questions for you to try

1. When a business benefits from lower average casts per unit.
2. Communication problems, bureaucracy, motivation issues etc.
3. Problems include: larger firms harder to manage and control – could lead to diseconomies of scale e.g. communication problems – messages become distorted / lost as too many people to keep informed; bureaucracy – systems / structure cannot cope – lead to communication problems such as lost orders; motivation issues – workers feel too remote from decision makers – can lead to lower productivity or workers leaving; competition rules – Governments put legal restrictions in place to protect interests of consumers – add to business costs; Cash flow/ financial problems; effect on ownership – Owners might have to give up some or all control.

4. Sell more products in existing markets – increase number of glass products sold to existing customers or encouraging new customers through promotions or discounts; Sell current product in new markets / segments – target different markets e.g. overseas to attract a wider customer base; Launch a new product – a stronger glass or screens for computer products – able to appeal to more customers / enter new markets as well as spreading risk; adapt existing product – change the design of bottles to include larger or smaller items.

5. Students own answer – based on points discussed. Advantages include: possible economies of scale – lower average costs per unit; diversification / spread risk – less reliant on one market or product – if sales fall in one market, other products / markets to rely on which improves their chances of survival; financial reasons – larger firms are more likely to survive or be able to borrow money; personal objectives – power and status wanted by owners; Market domination – increased power or market share – able to influence prices more easily; Access new markets – windows. Plus problems outlined in question. Yes or no decision allowed.

Unit 4

Progress check

1. Internal disadvantages to the business of a decision, expressed in monetary terms; Externalities: the costs and benefits of business activity borne by the wider community.
2. Social costs are negative effects of a business decision on community whilst social benefits are positive features of a business decision for community.
3. Examples include – air and noise pollution, congestion, waste.
4. Students own answer. This refers to creation of economic wealth in a country which lead to growth in jobs /income and output – so ideas such as growth of important industries such as electronics, tourism; arrival of Multinational companies suitable.
5. Sustainable development is important because people have unlimited wants and there are limited resources. If all the resources are used up for production now, there will not be enough resources to meet the needs of future generations.

Examination style questions for you to try

1. Internal advantages to the business of a decision, expressed in monetary terms.

2. Benefits include: jobs – need extra staff; new employees likely to have better standard of living / available income which could be spent at local shops who would benefit from extra sales; extra work for delivery business – triple deliveries needed; economic growth – value of output produced increasing; increased business for other suppliers – need more waste material to turn into blocks; access to cheaper housing for local people – low cost housing – meet basic shelter needs, using up waste material so less rubbish left around to pollute / spoil the environment.

3. Benefits see question 2: Costs include: pollution – extra deliveries will mean air pollution, noise pollution – disturb local residents; road congestion – increased traffic accessing the site.

4. Students own answer based on points discussed. Social costs and benefits see question 2 and 3. Private sector business might also want to take into account financial costs: need to expand the site – costs of investment, can they afford it – as it all costs money. Cost of complying with government rules – add to business costs. Need to recruit extra workers – time and expense of hiring and training staff. Financial benefits – revenue received from 10000 extra blocks per week.

Themes for evaluation: Difficult to put money values to external costs and benefits. T&U can look at all issue to weigh up whether it is worthwhile. If the benefits exceed the costs, likely to go ahead; Other points could mention: if overall socially beneficial – government might help with social problems; personal aims of social responsibility.

Unit 5

Progress check

1. Objective a target which a business wants to achieve in order to fulfil its aims; public sector - any business owned, run or controlled by the Government; stakeholder - any group of individuals who have an interest in the activities of a business.

2. Provide a service, control natural monopolies and protect key industries.

3. a) profit, expansion, market share; b) survival, break even.

4. Students own answer.

5. More pay for workers might result in less profit available for shareholder dividends.

Examination style questions for you to try

1. Any business owned, run or controlled by private individuals for example sole trader, partnerships or limited companies.

2. Social responsibility – as green, profit – common aim for private sector businesses; survival – when set up; growth – as orders increased, and has order for 10000 extra bricks.

3. Objectives of a plc: profits, growth, survival, but the objectives if government owned might be services – provide low cost housing whereas T&U might sell the blocks for any purpose if customers willing to pay their prices; to break-even – sold cheap already, but T&U would still aim to make money to fund expansion whereas Government receive funding from taxation to make up any shortfall; to provide employment – extra jobs would be created so location would be important to Government – located near city centre – Government would want to ensure any location is likely to lead to maximum number of jobs. Whereas efficient use of employees to help lower costs is more a priority for private sector business.
Both groups could have social responsibility as an objective so don't refer to this in answer as the question only asks for differences.

4. Student's own answer based on choices made. Possible groups could include: employees – might benefit from promotion or different roles, pay rises and increased job security; lenders – as provide finance so able to earn more in fees / interest; community as jobs created or suffer due to increased noise pollution, congestion and disruption caused by the building of the expanding site; government as jobs / economic growth and tax revenue would help them meet stated objectives; Likely choices to be community, employees and financial groups.

Unit 6

Progress check

1. A general rise in the level of prices; Government spending on public spending and payments such as education and state benefits.

2. The Government influences the economy in order to control unemployment, inflation and economic growth.

3. It is a measure of how much as country produces. If it rises, it should mean that peoples' standard of living have improved.

4. The money supply is the amount of money in the economy.

5. People will have less income available to spend as more money will go to government. They will have less money to spend so can buy fewer goods and services so less sales for some businesses.

Examination style questions for you to try

1. Inflation refers to a general rise in the level of prices in the economy.

2. People have more income available to spend so will demand more products from Ronaldo – if they want new glass windows they are likely to go ahead with this expenditure as it would be cheaper to borrow the money needed. This will lead to increase in sales for Ronaldo so could mean higher profits. Ronaldo faces lower costs if they have borrowed money. Lower expenses could lead to higher profits. Lower interest rates reduce the cost of borrowing so more likely to borrow money to invest in business or if they need finance to support the merger plan.

3. Laws and regulations – legal restrictions will set guidelines on accepted levels of business behaviour. Businesses will have to abide by rules or face legal action; Financial support e.g. grants and subsidies to encourage businesses to set up in certain locations which can help create employment; Training and education schemes to provide workers with the necessary skills to find employment; Tariffs and quotas – these will restrict the level of imports into the country; fiscal (tax) – government can directly influence expenditure in the economy through how it spends its money; and monetary (interest rates) will influence the amount of money in the economy.

4. Students own answer based on points discussed. Points include: taxation will reduce amount that people have to spend so lower sales; businesses face higher costs and if prices do not rise to cover increase – lower profits; less retained profit to invest back into business – problem of trying to expand; higher costs could lead to job losses – higher unemployment so lower living standards for affected workers; taxation is used for government

projects – can benefit poorer members of society or pay for construction or development of roads or schools, subsidise production or goods and services.

NOTE the word 'Always'. Try to include points for both sides of the argument in your answer. This can help produce a more balanced response. There are likely to be both advantages and disadvantages.

Unit 7
Progress check

1. E-commerce – buying and selling of goods on line; ICT – Information and Communications Technology.

2. Less paper to file, templates for standard letters; accounts kept on spread sheets, communications sent by email or networks; attachments can be sent quickly without need to print out and send hard copy.

3. Need for additional training, new jobs might be boring; fear of change; lower skilled jobs might mean lower rates of pay.

4. Convenience – can view and buy from home; can check instantly whether goods are available – so less wasted time; More competition – can lead to lower prices; Choice – can select from wider range of products from around the world.

5. Training; communication – tell workers about planned changes; – involve workers in decision making.

Examination style questions for you to try

1. Improve productivity, provide faster information; more accurate information; reduce costs; improve quality.

2. Concerns about internet security – could mean less customers as people are concerned about typing their bank details into a computer. Additional costs: E-commerce could reduce the costs of having a shop – but other costs e.g. web design, IT support. To ensure reliable system, might need to upgrade computer system or install more secure payment methods – will add to the costs of introducing e-commerce.

3. For disadvantages see answer to question 4. Remember to apply the points to AB (see below).

4. Students own answer – Either viewpoint is possible. **Advantages include:** Improve productivity, provide faster information – able to send information anywhere at the press of a button; more accurate information – machinery could weigh out more accurately the quantities needed

so materials not wasted; reduce costs – lower labour costs/ no breaks - production can continue for longer – better able to meet increasing sales; improve quality as produce a consistent mix of ingredients so less chance of mistakes in the recipes – result in less wastage of materials to help keep production costs to a minimum. **Disadvantages include:** Cost of technology – can they afford it? AB – steady growth in sales (We do not know the actual level of sales) – But bakery items tend to be low priced items, so AB might have to sell large quantities to cover the cost of new technology; Savings not guaranteed – as other costs have to be considered; additional costs of training will add to the cost of new machinery – some older workers were worried – might reduce the effectiveness of training – could lead to lower productivity than expected – so cost savings not gained; maintenance – machinery will need regular inspections to check working properly – whilst checked, output likely to be affected – reduce amount of stock available for sale; to obtain full benefits might need to update technology regularly – further adding to the cost of new technology.

Application points – break down, increasing production again. Sales are steadily increasing. Older workers worried

Evaluation should focus on whether advantages for Any Baked are likely to be more than disadvantages explained.

Unit 8

Progress check

1. A place where buyers and sellers are brought together; What people are willing and able to buy.
2. Any three from price, income, taste, technological change, price of alternative goods, price of substitutes, seasonal factors, size of population and government policy.
3. Better quality of products – businesses compete to add new features or versions to encourage customers to buy their products rather than a rival.
4. Possible lower prices – more producers so price war as try to attract customers; wider range of products as businesses try to attract customers with new / more varied items.
5. Producing the right product means more money spent on research and development to match customer's

needs – increases costs. As more competition – unlikely to charge a high price to cover the extra costs – could mean lower profits.

6. Smaller producers might not be able to compete against the lower prices of so close down – reduce the choice for consumers / some products are no longer available.

Examination style questions for you to try

1. Place where there are many businesses in the same market wanting to sell to the same customers.
2. Taste – change towards higher quality chocolate – good for Bradbury as demand should rise; income – as people earn more money they can afford to spend more on luxury products such as chocolate; seasonal factors – people might buy less chocolate in hot weather or buy more around festivals as gifts for people; price – a rise in price could reduce the level of demand; price – a fall in price might suggest poorer quality so demand might fall.
3. Taste – tastes changing towards higher quality chocolate – good for Bradbury as demand should rise increasing sales. If people don't like their chocolate this will have a negative impact on sales. Income – as people earn more money they can afford to spend more on luxury products such as chocolate. As targeted at rich consumers – this is important because as people's incomes rise this should broaden their target market leading to increased sales

    Price – need to set the price carefully – A higher price might discourage sales as cannot afford it – lead to a fall in demand. BUT luxury chocolate – price too low – could damage 'luxury' image as people think it is poor quality. Any other sensible factor could be discussed. Likely options include government rules on food or seasonal factors.
4. Students own answer based on points discussed. Any reasonable points allowed. Factors include: price as policy is to sell cheap; price of alternatives as competitive market; seasonal factors – demand likely to rise at festival time; demand might fall at warmer times of year; government regulations could affect what ingredients they are able to use; income – as cheap, if incomes rise customers might be able to afford more expensive luxury / quality chocolates; taste as changing towards higher quality – if people don't like Kape chocolate, sales will fall. Price, taste, income are likely factors to be discussed.

Unit 9

Progress check

1. Economy where there is minimum government intervention as all resources are owned by private individuals.
2. Full state ownership of all resources.
3. Low prices due to the number of different businesses competing for customers; wide choice of products as businesses compete to attract customers to make profit.
4. Governments ensure vital goods and services are produced even if it is not profitable. Businesses might be forced to supply goods that are not cost effective to produce; stop customer exploitation - so not allowed to set very high prices for necessary goods. This can limit amount of profit made; Government influence to ensure minimum standards to protect consumers can lead to higher business costs.
5. Laws / regulations; fines; monitoring activities of business.

Examination style questions for you to try

1. An economy with both a public and private sector. There is both free enterprise and state control in this economy.
2. Choice – more producers so wider range to pick from; better quality – as businesses try to improve products to encourage customers to choose their goods over rivals, lower prices – as businesses use promotions or lower prices to encourage customers to buy their goods; new products as firms look to develop products to suit customer needs to encourage sales.
3. Consumers must travel two miles to the supermarket whereas the local stall more convenient – not everyone will have transport to get to the supermarket – cannot benefit from wider choice and lower prices; Supermarket might not offer the personal service of smaller business; Sylvia's stall might close down as cannot sell enough fruit to cover all costs; fewer sales could lead to more rotting food which Sylvia can't sell at normal price – less revenue (if any) from these items; small fruit stall – likely to benefit from economies of scale – so higher unit costs and higher prices charged.
4. Students own answer based points discussed. Points include: competition should result in: • lower prices so consumers can afford to buy more with same amount of money; • more consumer choice – as firms compete to gain

business they offer more / different goods – consumers are more likely to find exactly what they want; more promotional offers and deals – as businesses try to attract customers to choose their products over rivals – consumers can buy more for their money; better customer service; product innovation – try to develop new products or add more features to attract consumers. Consumers benefit from wider choice; better quality; increased business efficiency leading to lower costs enabling businesses to charge lower prices to consumers. However competition can also lead to: hidden costs such as reduced quality [to cut costs] – consumers might think better value for money but quality is actually lower; hard sell (by putting pressure on customers to buy) can force consumers to spend money on products they cannot afford or do not really need; too much choice can confuse customer, product differentiation can make comparisons between different brands difficult. On the whole likely to be beneficial as long as government rules ensure consumers are not exploited.

Unit 10

Progress check

1. The price of a country's currency in terms of another country's currency; import taxes put on the price of goods entering the country.
2. Tariffs increase the price of goods imported into a country whereas a quota limits the amount of goods that can be imported.
3. Exports become more expensive as other countries have to pay more to buy same amount of goods. Level of exports is likely to fall.
4. Two from: protect domestic producers to maintain jobs; raise money through tariffs; protect domestic businesses from unfair competition; protect important industries in the country; protect jobs in domestic industries.
5. Legal problems/ government controls, trade customs, level of competition in country, different tastes, costs of transport and distribution, lack of contacts, language.

Examination style questions for you to try

1. Allows access to a larger market – especially important if domestic (home) market for a product is small / in decline as it reduces the risk for the business if one market fails; growth from increased sales – increased production,

leading to economies of scale – lower costs / hopefully greater profits. Other options include spread risk, only a small market for tools in South Africa.

2. Absence of contacts in new market to give advice and guidance e.g. legal matters – could find that tools do not meet set standards in Asian market – can't be sold in some countries. National cultures and tastes differ – will customers in Asia want the tools? Costs of selling abroad, including distribution and trading costs can be expensive – might not be cost effective for a small business to sell in faraway countries – as will increase the costs lowering possible profit made unless can pass on the additional transport costs to customers in terms of higher prices – higher prices could mean lower demand. Other issues include: Language problems – no common language – this could create difficulties between the business and customers when trying to understand orders – need to hire additional employees or pay for training which will increase their costs which could be a problem for a smaller firm. Legal problems/ government controls are likely to be different in the respective countries; trade customs – where and how are the goods sold in the different countries; level of competition in country could mean different marketing strategy is required which will cost money and take time to develop.

3. Students own answer – depending on points discussed see questions 1 and 2. Answer can be either yes or no, as long as it is supported by reasoned argument. Other points to remember include – size of business, finance and appropriate skills within company to trade overseas, helpful that Managing director is keen to expand – but do they need to enter Asian market – are there any closer markets, have they undertaken any market research to know if there is sufficient demand.

4. See comments to question 3. Questions 3 and 4 cover similar points – just make sure you develop the points more fully to access all the analysis and evaluation marks.

Answers to section 2

UNIT 11

Progress check

1. Owners are only liable for the amount invested in a business. Their personal assets are safe if the business fails. A sole trader is a business owned by one person.

2. Someone who has the skill and risk taking ability to bring together the four factors of production to make goods or services.

3. Own boss, keep all profits, easiest form of business to set up as only one person; make all own decisions, unlimited liability, only one owner.

4. Unlimited liability; limited access to funds to finance business.

5. Owners can lose everything they own if the business fails. Business debts belong to the owner, so creditors take personal possessions if the business owes them money.

Examination style question for you to try

1. A partnership is an unincorporated business that is owned by two or more people (the partners).

2. Advantages: few legal regulations – easier to run the business / cheaper as Alejandro won't have to pay high costs to lawyers. Freedom of choice – Alejandro can take his holidays when he wants. Close contact with customers – can build up relationship with individual customers. Keeps all the profits – if he works hard and increases the businesses profits he doesn't have to share them with anyone else like a partner or other shareholders. Own accounts private – no need to publish the accounts unlike limited company. Own boss so able to make all the decisions so he has total control over the business – able to decide direction taken. Simplest form of business to set up as only one person.

3. Disadvantages: No one to discuss problems with – he might lack experience in running a business unlike his sister who knows how to run a small business – might be helpful to have a partner to discuss issues. Unlimited liability – if business fails, Alejandro could lose business AND his personal possessions. Limited capital – only has own money to invest in the business. If the business was a partnership or a limited company additional money available from partners or shareholders. Lack of customers – sister has more contacts.

4. Sole traders – see answers to question 2. Partnership: access to more funds – both can put money into the business so more money to invest; share workload – Alejandro can take time off; share responsibility – Can ask sister for advice on decisions; able to specialise

more as greater range of skills – accountant and new business advisor; Miranda able to bring in new customers; share ideas to help business develop; major problem of unlimited liability – partnership will not avoid this. <u>Application points include</u>: new business advisor / knows the problems of running a small business/ few customers arranged/ rent free premises.

<u>Themes for evaluation</u>: most new businesses start as sole trader or partnerships so either option is possible; A partnership seems most suitable option especially as business would benefit from her contacts and skills (obtaining rent free premise already) but he might like being his own boss.

Unit 12

Progress check

1. Business that exists separately from its owners – business has its own legal identity; A limited business whose shares can be freely bought and sold to the general public.
2. Limited liability; access to more funds to finance growth / run business.
3. Differences: Private limited company cannot raise funds through the stock exchange so has restricted access to funds to finance growth; A public limited company must publish detailed accounts every year but a private limited company does not have to disclose as much information to the public.
4. Simply refers to the fact that anyone can buy their shares in the business.
5. Restricted sale of shares – needs agreement of other shareholders to sell shares; cannot sell shares on stock market – so cannot raise as much capital as public limited companies; have to disclose some financial information – so cannot keep all accounts private unlike sole traders and partnerships.

Examination style question for you to try

1. A limited business whose shares cannot be sold to the general public.
2. Limited liability – so personal belongings are not at risk – if expansion into Asia does not work – only lose amount invested in business not personal assets like home; Able to attract more finance so business not dependent on Lars, Hans and Jacques for funds – easier to finance planned expansion; managers have opportunity to 'own'

the business they work for – this could help motivation as they will directly benefit from success of company.

3. Two from: many legal formalities to complete – takes time to complete and expensive; have to disclose accounts/information to any interested parties – rivals will be able to gain vital information about business; divorce between ownership and control more likely – owner will no longer have complete control over decision making; risk of takeover – as shares can be freely sold on the stock market anyone can buy them – if someone buys enough original owners lose ownership.
4. Disadvantages: see answers to question 3. Advantages: able to access more funds – better able to finance expansion into Asia; larger businesses able to benefit from economies of scale: managerial – afford specialists, purchasing – discounts for bulk purchasing, technical – cost effective to buy larger automated machinery, financial – seen as less risk so can get lower interest rates on loans. Themes for evaluation: if business wants to continue its expansion, good idea as able to raise additional finance; do they want to give up control or risk takeover? Cost of change; Judgement: Can decide for or against idea depending on points discussed – but must be supported by what has been written.

Unit 13

Progress check

1. A business granting a franchise; An enterprise undertake by two or more businesses pooling resources together.
2. A merger – two business join together to form one company, whereas Joint venture the two businesses remain separate, but work together as partners on a specific project.
3. Franchisee has less independence than a sole trader as they must follow guidelines set by franchisor; Franchisee has better chance of success because they have a proven product to sell, and support of large company behind them to help with advertising. A sole trader has to do all this themselves; A franchisee must make royalty payments to the franchisor whereas the sole trader can keep all profits made.
4. Different cultures and management styles could result in poor co-operation and arguments between them; profits have to be shared so not gain as much as if operate on own; have to compromise on ideas so best ideas might not be chosen.

Examination style questions for you to try

1. An agreement that allows one business to trade under the name of another business to sell the other company's products or services.

2. A business is able to expand without committing large amounts of its own resources; lower risk as risk is spread between both parties; get regular royalty payments from franchisee; retain a large say in how the business is run and what products sold.

3. Students own answer, based on issued discussed. Either option is possible. Possible factors: Business failure less likely as well – known brand name – fixit are the leading car repair business – customers are more likely to go to their business rather than risk a small new start up business. Franchisor carries out advertising – so Abraham will have to spend less money – which could reduce amount he has to borrow – can help his cash flow, which can be a problem for new businesses. Franchisor is established brand – more likely to obtain discounts or trade credit.

   Help and advice when setting up – Abraham is a mechanic, does he know how to run a business? Training for staff and owner provided – so help is readily available. Banks more willing to lend money as franchisor is likely to be trusted more than an individual.
   But: Decisions taken at FIXIT head office might not suit Abraham's location – little room to change them. Franchisee has less independence than a sole trader as they must follow guidelines set by franchisor. Cost - franchise will cost an extra $35000 – able to borrow? Has to pay royalties every year whereas a sole trader can keep all the profits made.

   Themes for evaluation – more chance of success if franchise as more support/ proven name; sole trader – has always wanted to be own boss – only sole trader will give him this freedom; much will depend on whether Abraham can raise sufficient funds for the franchise.

Unit 14

Progress check

1. A limited business whose shares cannot be sold to the general public; any business owned, run or controlled by the Government.

2. Profit, break even, survival, customer service.

3. Growth, profit, increased market share – any reasonable answer but not likely to be survival or break even unless in financial difficulty.

4. Type of ownership; the degree of control the owner requires; the amount of finance needed; how profits are to be used; the size of the business.

5. Private limited company.

Examination style questions for you to try

1. Financial problems – a business will need more working capital to finance the day to day operations; Risk of overtrading – this could lead to cash flow problems for the business; Operational – can they meet extra demand on time and within budget; might need to change production methods or recruit new staff to cope with the extra demand – takes time and money; communication problems – does everyone know what to do – can be difficult if systems are based on smaller organisation; Social responsibility; profit; diversification, enter new market.

2. Students own answer, based on points discussed. JV: less risk as share costs with other business - do not have to bear loss on own; Access to new technology, expertise and knowledge – National oil have expertise in fuel, TSG sugar; if objectives of venture not clear / known to all could lead to misunderstandings; objectives of companies could conflict – why are both parties doing this? Share profits – so both will make less if succeed whereas if only one business would gain all profit made; different cultures / management styles can affect level of cooperation – different approaches could mean conflicting objectives which could mean targets not met; Advantages of takeover such as merger would mean total control of project – so keep all profits; clearer set of objectives as only one set; conflict – who would be in charge of new company; Larger companies are more likely to experience diseconomies of scale such as coordination, organisation and communication issues. Other issues: some countries do not allow foreign ownership so Joint Venture might be only available route open to either business.

3. Themes for evaluation – either more advantages or disadvantages of joint venture; new area – National fuels don't have the skills with sugar, so safer option; merger better if management think it is such a good idea, as would have total control over project and would gain all profits.

NOTE: The same issues apply to both questions 3 and 4. It is only the level of detail required in the answer that is different.

Unit 15

Progress check

1. A business that has operations in more than one country; country in which multinational has overseas operations.
2. Cost cutting, increased profit; enter new markets; spread risk; access raw materials.
3. False.
4. Inflow of profits can help balance of payments; learn new production skills and techniques; business less reliant on home market so more secure.
5. Increased employment from the multinational establishing operations in the country raising the living standards for the local population; Access to a wider range of products made locally so country is less reliant on imports. Goods should hopefully be cheaper as well; Improved image for the country overseas – by association with international company could lead other businesses to invest in country.

Examination style questions for you to try

1. A business that has operations in more than one country; country in which multinational has overseas operations.
2. Increased employment – raising the living standards for the local population; Access to a wider range of products locally so could benefit from more choice; Lower cost of goods – as additional transport costs avoided if imported from other locations; Improved image for the country overseas – by association with international company could lead other businesses to invest in country; access to new technology and training – 300 jobs will be created; improvements in infrastructure could happen as business will look to ensure good access to the site, all locals will benefit.
3. and **4.** Students own answer based on points discussed. Advantages of multinational: New investment – will look to develop roads or energy which other citizens will also benefit from; more exports will happen as goods transferred from host country so improves balance of payments; fewer imports – could also lead to lower prices and more choice; jobs created – 300 jobs from Kape alone – more MNC will lead to more jobs increasing living standards; more competition – lower prices, more choice for consumers; taxes paid to the government used to fund other social projects.

    Disadvantages: Impact on existing firms – MNC can afford to lower prices – local businesses might have to

close as cannot compete; profits flow out of the country; often only unskilled jobs are created – so little benefit for workers; influence on government and economy – assistance does influence location – could demand large grants just to stay in the country; If MNC finds different country with cheaper labour – will they stay – always looking for new opportunities – unlikely to be loyal to a country if they only selected for business reasons.

Application: 300 jobs, government assistance, cheaply, always looking for new opportunities.

Themes for evaluation – more / less advantages so good or bad; only benefit as long as it suits the company, not all multinationals are bad so few good could help outweigh negatives.

NOTE: The same issues apply to both questions 3 and 4. It is only the level of detail required in the answer that is different.

Unit 16

Progress check

1. Structure where most of the decision making takes place at higher levels of management. Number of levels of responsibility in an organisation.
2. Shows working relationship between different sections – who is in charge; departments within organisation; Formal lines of communication – who to speak to if have a problem.
3. Size of organisation; the skills of the workers; the skill and style of manager; the type of work.
4. By product, by function or by region (also allow by market).
5. Improves motivation of workers as feel more involved in decision making; quicker decision making possible at a local level.

Examination style questions for you to try

1. Shows the number of people someone is responsible for.
2. Poorer communication as messages must pass through more levels to reach people; slower decision making as information requested must pass through more people, and decision given back – can take a long time; employees can become de-motivated as don't feel part of decision making process; managers can have difficulty knowing what is happening at lower levels of business – so could lead to wrong decisions as not aware of what is happening.

3. Advantages include: saves managers time as don't need to make all decisions so can focus on more important tasks; work more interesting for employees as involved in decision making; speeds up decision making as employees able to take instant decision without having to find manager first; motivation for employees – feel have an important part to play in business. Disadvantages: more time for manager to explain task at start – so little effective time saved; increased chance of mistakes if employees don't have all the information; need system to check everything which can increase time and cost.

4. Students own answer based on points discussed. Either viewpoint is possible. Points include: Able to react better and quicker to local issues affecting business in each region – could improve level of customer service – improve reputation – leading to increased sales; quicker decision making so opportunities identified in different regions are not lost due to waiting for head office decision; improves workers motivation at the 4 sites as feel involved in decisions made locally, not in a distant head office – could lead to higher productivity and higher quality work. BUT misunderstandings / problems of control and coordination if senior managers not aware of decisions taken elsewhere in business – could impact negatively on reputation or costly mistakes if orders duplicated; More expensive to set up as duplicate functions such as 4 sets of HR and marketing needed – do they have sufficient staff to cover all roles or need to recruit extra staff which will add to costs of business reorganisation; no guarantee that reorganisation will lead to improvements hoped for – might be a waste of time and resources.

Unit 17

Progress check

1. Communication – a method of sending a message from one person (sender) to another person /group (receiver); internal – all communications that take place between people within the same organisation.

2 To pass and receive messages; Give instructions ; Check and receive feedback and a method to discuss issues.

3. Formal communication is based on official systems set up by the business, whilst informal refers to all other methods of communication like – chatting in the corridor.

4. Two from; language, noise, problems with medium, sender or receiver, time, location, technical problems and breakdown.

5. Suppliers, customers, government, lenders include factoring house or creditors.

Examination style questions for you to try

1. All communication that takes place with people outside the organisation.

2. Text has many mistakes. Barriers include language – is not formal/ appropriate to the audience – gives wrong impression to suppliers; jargon such as depot, rendezvous which could confuse the reader; medium: will all supplier have a cell phone – otherwise will not receive message; does not ask for feedback so how check received?

3. Points depend on answer to question 2. Typical solutions might include – send out a letter, or phone or visit as only six suppliers – would be able to talk through changes ; text might be lost or misplaced so ask for feedback to ensure message has been received and understood; write in simple sentences to avoid technical language ' such as rendezvous, depot, which might confuse receiver.

Unit 18

Progress check

1. Person receiving the message is unable to reply to it; any communication involving speech.

2. Chance for feedback; Information can be quickly sent Understanding / feedback easy to obtain as direct contact; can use body language / gestures to support message; Some forms allow you to give same message to many people at same time.

3. Give two direct feedback is not always possible; wrong language can make understanding difficult; cannot always check if message received; some forms of written can be ignored or seen too late.

4. What is the message? Why is it being sent? Who needs to know? How quickly does it need to reach them.

5. Two way communications involves opportunity for feedback which one way does not.

Examination style questions for you to try

1. Examples include: letter, notice board, poster, fax.

2. Internal communication – all communications that take place between people within the same organisation.

3. Easier to implement policies – everyone in company will know that they plan to reorganise the company

by region; avoids confusion – if messages are clear and communicated to all everyone knows what to do even if they are in different locations; motivational impact – everyone feels involved in decisions or communication as the company has grown, it is easy for employees to feel that they are excluded from the decisions being made; increased co-ordination and efficiency as less chance of mistakes if people know what to do.

4. Meeting: chance for feedback, able to discuss ideas, can involve a large number of people; no guarantee that everyone is listening or had chance to ask questions. Letter – written copy for reference; less time consuming than other options, can send to many people at same time, no guarantee all understood letter especially if language not suitable; people might not receive letter.

   Telephone: feedback, chance to discuss issues with each individual; expensive in time and cost of calls especially if a lot of people, danger of giving different message to different people so adding to confusion.

   Could make case for all options. I would choose Meeting – as allows chance for everyone to hear information at the same time, there is no guarantee that everyone will receive the letters simultaneously, meetings will allow the workers the opportunity for feedback. The telephone also allows for feedback, but it is not feasible for growing company to call everyone. It is not a personal issue (like job loss) so for this issue, I think a meeting is the most suitable method to use.

   Note: when you make a decision, remember to say why you have not picked the other options as well.

Unit 19

Progress check

1. Costs a business must meet before it can start making and selling its goods or services; Money to cover day-to-day running costs of a business.
2. Expansion, start up, day to day costs, cash flow problems, buy new equipment.
3. Potters wheel, place to work from, kiln for firing the pots.
4. Paper, ink, heating, lighting, wages for workers.
5. Replace old equipment, buying extra equipment or moving to a new factory.

Examination style questions for you to try

1. Capital expenditure – as this is expected to last a long time.
2. Either: current assets minus current liabilities or money to cover day-to-day running costs of a business.
3. If a business cannot pay suppliers, could stop deliveries of materials – delay or stop production – might be an issue for a small business like Gee's as he is likely to have fewer spare resources – if too much of his working capital is tied up in stock or debtors he could face cash flow problems; If workers are not paid on time- might become de-motivated, which could affect the quality of work – this could lead to fewer sales so lower revenue. Lower efficiency could result from a de-motivated work force leading to increased costs or waste resources; all businesses need to have enough working capital to ensure the long term survival of their business as even profitable businesses can fail without enough cash to pay its creditors.

Unit 20

Progress check

1. Loan secured against an asset which if not repaid, can be taken; A facility arranged with a bank to allow a customer to make payments in excess of the cash in the account up to an agreed limit.
2. Owners funds, retained profit, sell fixed assets and various ways of managing working capital.
3. Loans are debt, whereas shares represent ownership of the business; loans need to be repaid with interest whereas shares do not have to be repaid, there is no interest but dividends might be paid.
4. Overdraft, factoring, trade credit, short term loan.
5. Share issue, debenture, long term loan, mortgage.

Examination style questions for you to try

1. Bank loans, overdraft, share capital, trade credit, leasing, hire purchase.
2. Advantages: able to buy stock to repair cars before Abraham has to pay so he can earn money to pay creditor; Creditor can offer discounts – help reduce costs of stock, so less expenses for a new business which might have cash flow issues; No interest paid so lower cost which can help cash flow. Disadvantages – if Abraham can't pay, will supplier still provide stock – he will need parts for vehicle repairs; No discounts could increase costs – could have a negative impact on a new business;

As a new business, would suppliers be willing to provide enough trade credit to Abraham.

3. How long is the money needed for – short or long term, the method should match; What is the money needed for – start up, working capital or expansion – different methods will be used for each; How much is needed – different sources will raise different amounts; what risk is involved – for example debt or shares. If sell shares there is a risk of takeover or loss of control; Type and size of business – not all options are available to all businesses – sole trader cannot sell shares; Cost of finance – interest has to be paid on some methods of finance.

4. Student's own answer based on points identified in question 3. The key issues to consider are what he is trying to buy – equipment is capital expenditure which is long lasting so time period (how Long) is

also likely to be relevant; type of business – Abraham is a sole trader, and a new start up so fewer options available.

5. Students own answer based on points discussed. Both are short term sources so either possible. Trade credit issues – see question 2 answers. Overdraft – advantages: only pay if overdrawn, easy to arrange, flexible, likely to be granted to new business. Disadvantages – interest is paid on amount overdrawn unlike trade credit, repayable at any time could lead to cash flow problems; might depend on how quickly he receives customer payment for work done, might be better to have overdraft for unplanned expenditure.

Evaluation: If able to secure trade credit – seems better option as no interest to pay. He has been mechanic so likely to have contacts that trust him.

Answers to section 3

Unit 21

Progress check

1. Smaller group of customers with similar characteristics and similar product needs; Mass market has a large number of customers for a standard product.
2. Price, promotion, pricing, market research and place.
3. Small level of sales, higher prices.
4. Develop products that better match specific customer requirements to increase sales and profits; Spot gaps in the market so providing opportunities to increase sales.
5. Ways include: size of households, interests, gender, income, location, age.

Examination style questions for you to try

1. Splitting up the market into particular groups of people.
2. 37% of $950000 = $351500
3. **Advantages:** Able to focus more closely on the needs of individual customers – People who like Bradbury's luxury chocolates will expect a higher quality product than Kape's mass market customers. Kape can tailor their products to suit the needs of different markets to increase sales. Geographical segmentation will allow Kape to meet cultural and taste differences of a country – if they can meet individual tastes, customers might continue to buy the chocolates as they suit their tastes – can help

develop brand loyalty leading to higher sales. Able to spot gaps in the market – which if only sold to mass market, they might miss out on sales opportunities to competitors.

4. Students own answer – based on points discussed. Either answer is possible. Reasons FOR: a competitive market – need to stay ahead of rivals – hence bought Bradbury's quality chocolate; Ensure products made meet customer demand – so increase / maintain sales and profit; Common approach due to increasing competition in most markets; businesses usually carry out market research first to find out customer needs – tastes can change so there is no guarantee people will always prefer better quality chocolate – so sales might fall – if they can anticipate these changes- more chance of success; **but** market research is expensive and no guarantee results correct so might be waste of money; luxury chocolate is only a small market – $950000 – is there much need for research; depends on what is sold – if only a niche or specialised market, might be fine to be product orientated.

Unit 22

Progress check

1. A small group of people meet regularly to give their views on products or issues; research which involves collecting new information that did not exist before.

2. Own sales information, government statistics, newspaper articles, internet, trade journals, existing research documents, market research agencies.

3. Interviews, questionnaires, observation, Consumer panels / focus groups experiments.

4. Open questions provide more detailed responses as allow person to give more information. Whereas closed questions only allow simple answers from a limited range of options.

5. What information do you want to find out – this will influence what is asked, and the type of questions used. Identify suitable questions to ask – the questions must gather the information required – if not, waste of time and money. Open or closed questions? Open questions provide more detailed responses. Closed questions only allow simple answers from a limited range of options. Questions asked must be clear and easy to understand – if people can't understand the question will lead to incomplete or inaccurate information which is little use. Avoid leading questions – questions must allow people to give their own opinions without too much guidance from the interviewer or question – or risk bias. Test questionnaire so problem questions can be identified and corrected before actual research undertaken.

Examination style questions for you to try

1. Primary research involves collecting new information that did not exist before.

2. Little use if it is inaccurate/irrelevant/inappropriate – wrong people asked or gather wrong information – as will not know potential customer's needs – wrong products developed which could reduce possible sales. Bias in research (how questions are asked / sample size too small so could misrepresent consumer attitudes. Tastes change over time – how useful is old information in today's market.

3. Provide a closer match between what is produced and what is required by their new customers – Kallis is new to Asian market – so as different country might need different tools, which Kallis will need to know if he is to make enough sales. Market research will allow Kallis to anticipate future needs and current trends – so able to respond customers' needs in different markets – as a small company must meet customer's needs to compete effectively against possibly larger rivals.

4. Students own answer based on points discussed. Case can be made for either if explained. Primary research: **Advantages:** First-hand information – so suit Kallis specific needs;

Specific to individual requirements – any other information might not focus on South African company entering Asian market so likely to be more useful; Information only available to them – could provide competitive advantage. **Disadvantages:** expensive to collect – as it is new information – only has small budget; Time consuming to collect – as information did not exist before – does Kallis have time before launch in three months' time.

5. Secondary research: **Advantages:** Quick – already available – information available before launch date (3 months) to guide company; cheaper than primary research – information is either free or available for not much money – fit into small budget; Little effort to obtain data as easily available – so small company won't need to hire specialist researchers which will add to their cost; secondary data can help identify questions. **Disadvantages:** Is information reliable as collected for another purpose – might not answer any or all the questions Kallis has – incomplete information might lead to the wrong decisions being made; unsure of aims of original research so data might have limited value for Kallis; available to competitors – so how helpful is information if looking to gain marketing advantage; out of date – if information is old, might not be relevant for current purposes; if research is from another country, cultural differences could affect reliability of results. The data must relate to the new Asian market if it is to be useful.

Evaluation: Choice depends on amount of time and money available and what Kallis wants to know. If K has time and money, primary is better option as likely to answer their specific questions. If only requires general population, interests of Asian people or income information secondary should be fine, as it is both readily available and cheap to obtain.

Unit 23

Progress check

1. Simple record of facts and figures presented in rows and columns.

2. Visual representation so easy to see relative importance of each segment; easy to understand.

3. Useful when want to show trends over time.

4. Easy to construct; easy to see results quickly; clear visual image.

5. Easy to construct; shows all the data collected; able to include a lot of information.

Examination style questions for you to try

1. Easy to construct – so anyone can produce one; shows all the data collected – able to see all information so can make informed decisions, includes lots of information. Disadvantages: Difficult to see trends quickly which can limit usefulness; too much information can make decision making difficult especially if user cannot understand how to use the information.

2. See chart. For all marks must include title and label axes.

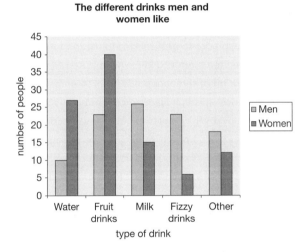

The different drinks men and women like

3. More women likely to drink fruit drinks than men – so women are a better target market for their drinks. Women drink more water than men, 27% compared to 10% of the men in the survey; more men drink fizzy drinks (28%) compared to 5-6% women; more men drink milk 26% compared to 15% women. The market research shows the size of the market segments and shows what different genders like – can target different drinks at different people. Information can help decide production levels and promotional activities/ advertising campaigns – which magazines or methods to use depending on whether men or women like the drink.

Unit 24

Progress check

1. The combination of product, price, place and promotion used to sell a good or service to consumers.

2. Price, product, promotion and place.

3. Product

4. No. Marketing mix blends together all the elements of the 4P's. It is like making a cake – you need butter, sugar, flour and eggs. If you overlook one ingredient it won't work properly. For a business, this could mean customers do not buy the product because the price is wrong. This will result in lower sales and profits for a business.

5. Distribution

Examination style questions for you to try

1. Describes all the activities that go together to make a customer decide to buy a product.

2. Any two of price, product, promotion place (and packaging).

3. Changes include: price promotions out of season, promotions such as book one holiday, get a second half price, one free activity included when you book; advertising – in holiday magazines or places aimed at active families; aim holidays at different groups of people to increase range of target market to boost sales.

Unit 25

Progress check

1. Involves giving a product a special name to create a unique identity; actions taken by business to try to boost the sales of the product to slow its rate of decline.

2. 'Fit for purpose' means that the good or service will do the job that it is intended for:

    *   Protect, inform, promote, comply with legal requirements, boost brand image, help extend product life cycle

    *   Launch / development, growth, maturity, saturation and decline

    *   Change a feature of the product; Sell the product in new markets; target a different market segment; add new features to 'improve' the product; change the packages to change its image; encourage customers to use product more often.

Examination style questions for you to try

1. Product not well known, sales slow. A lot of advertising needed to attract interest so costs high. Profit unlikely at this stage.

2. Four from: Protect the product – so it reaches the customer in perfect condition; Provide information – so customer knows how to use the product; Safety information, required by law – to inform or protect

customers; Means to attract customers – colour and shape can help a product stand out against competition; Help create unique identity – distinctive packaging gives the product an identity to attract customers; Quality of packaging can help boost brand image – customers expect luxury products to have expensive packaging; Help extend the life of the product – re-packaging can be used to remind / attract customers.

3. Students own answer based on points discussed. Points include: presentation can raise customer awareness as notice colour or design of the packaging; Means to attract customers – use of colour and shape can help products stand out against competition; Help create unique identity – distinctive packaging gives FF's products an identity to attract customers – which helps it stand out in a competitive market. Quality of packaging can help boost brand image – customers expect luxury products to have expensive packaging; Help extend the life of the product – re-packaging can be used to remind / attract customers. However, packaging is only one element of the mix, a successful product depends on the right blend of all 4P's, depends as well on product – not easy to package all items especially if sell services. One sided answers focusing solely on positives of packaging allowed.

4. Students own answer based on points discussed. **New product** development issues include: expensive and time consuming; no guarantee customers will like the product; new products can allow business to have a fresh start; if product in decline will extension strategies actually help if people don't like the product anymore; new technology allows the possibility of new, better products – if first to enter this market – could become market leader, increase sales. **Extension strategies** – likely to be cheaper than developing entirely new products; know product has basis for sales if popular before – customers just need reminding about it, fashions change – a new colour could be enough to boost sales in short term. Other issues – could have both as extension could fill gap whilst business develops new products – bringing in vital funds.

Unit 26

Progress check

1. Responsiveness of demand to a change in price; Price is set lower initially to enter a new market.

2. Sales will rise by <u>less</u> than percentage change in price, so lower profits likely.

3. Useful to guarantee a certain amount of profit or not in competitive market.

4. Able to recover development costs quicker due to high price; reinforce quality image for product.

5. Possible loss of revenue as prices set lower; price charged might not cover costs; longer time to recover development costs of new product; if business tries to increase price, customers might buy from rivals so loss of revenue.

Examination style questions for you to try

1. Product is priced at or just below a competitor's price to try to gain more of the market.

2. If demand is elastic, sales will fall by more than extra raised by price rise – so profits likely to fall more. If demand is inelastic, Sales will fall by <u>less</u> than percentage change in price so profits likely to rise (opposite effects also credited if refer to fall in price).

3. Description of three methods from: Skimming – set high price – distinctive carton might allow for some brand loyalty, high costs so help recover costs quicker if successful; Competitive pricing – very competitive, mass market – so if price in line with competitors might help sales, and at least won't loose market share to rivals; cost plus pricing – ensure all costs covered and make a profit, high costs – so price likely to be high so is this sensible in view of competitive market?; Penetration pricing – competitive so low price might attract attention from customers to try drink, if likely they might continue to buy even when price increased; promotional pricing – but only for short period of time – as established company possible to consider; Psychological pricing – set a price based on perception want to create – high price if want image of quality – the company is popular. <u>Application points to consider include:</u> competitive market, popular, distinctive cartons, expensive to make and mass market. Choices depend on which options selected. Likely options are cost plus, competitive or penetration. Any sensible options could be discussed or chosen.

Unit 27

Progress check

1. It refers to where the product is sold and the methods used to get the product there. Retailer is anyone or outlet for selling goods to consumers.

2. Producer to consumer.

3. Overseas trade

4. Producer to consumer; producer – wholesaler – consumer; producer – wholesaler – retailer – consumer; ; producer – retailer – consumer.

5. Cost, size of business, nature of product, location of market.

Examination style questions for you to try

1. A middleman who buys goods from a producer to sell on to the retailer or customer.

2. Wholesaler breaks bulk for retailer – so ABC only buy what need; reduced storage costs – as do not have to hold more stock than needed; wholesalers can offer credit terms – this could helps cash flow; offer delivery so lower transport costs for ABC; don't have to deal with lots of suppliers which saves time.

3. Student's own answer based on points discussed. Either answer is possible. Points for wholesaler see answer 2; Missing out the wholesaler is usually faster (less links in distribution chain) and cheaper (fewer groups will want share of profit); wholesaler might not deal with all the suppliers that they want to use; Food can benefit from a more direct channel – depends on what is sold; difficult to obtain lots of high quality items; Could discuss other options such as producer – retailer – consumer – lower costs, more control.

    Application points: small, quality, wide range of products, free delivery.

    Themes for evaluation – retain current method as only small/ wide range so other channels will be time consuming and expensive to set up (extra staff to meet suppliers); different system – save costs so prices might be more competitive – increase sales?

Unit 28

Progress check

1. Any promotion that involves the use of the media; Business gives money or support to an event, project or people.

2. Options include free gifts, price promotions, samples, point of sales, competitions.

3. Options include television, radio, posters, billboards, leaflets, newspapers.

4. It can provide information about your product, persuade customers to buy your product, create good image of

product or company, increase awareness of new or existing products or services.

5. Cost – how much can you afford to spend; where are customers – local, national or international; what is the message – if trying to inform would use different techniques to persuade.

Examination style questions for you to try

1. Refers to all activities that are designed to make customers aware their products so that they are encouraged buying them.

2. Features to highlight: families – show people together; happy faces to show enjoyment; activity holiday – action images. Other information: name of business; price; contact details; experience of the business; guarantee; high quality product; location.

3. Options include: Local or national television, Local or National newspapers, posters, leaflets, specialist magazines, price promotions – short term reductions, competitions, discounts, open days (similar to demonstrations); sponsorship, website. Application: free use of swimming pool, competitive prices, good reputation, low cost housing, families, health and safety.

4. Students own answer based on points discussed. Either viewpoint is possible. Advantages of current methods: cheap – able to afford to place more posters in more locations, visual so more impact so likely to attract attention – **but** difficult to ensure people will notice it; limited information, difficult to target – so cannot guarantee families interested in activity holidays will see it As want to increase sales, could consider other options: local TV / radio if can afford it – as plenty of competition in market - more varied promotion might be necessary. Depends on what competitors do, and what they can afford.

Unit 29

Progress check

1. A financial plan for the marketing of a product for a set period of time; Looking at the strengths, weaknesses, opportunities and threats facing a business or product.

2. Set business objectives, gather marketing information, set marketing objectives; plan and implement activities, monitor and review.

3. Allows for better use of resources so not wasting time or money on unnecessary activities, Helps decision

making so identify right marketing mix to use, Allows business to anticipate changes in market and customer needs. Able to take advantage of new opportunities and minimise threats; Helps monitor progress towards overall business objectives; Allows them to anticipate threats so able to take appropriate action to avoid danger.

4. Options include: market penetration, product or market development.

Examination style questions for you to try

1. A statement of the actions a business will take in order to achieve its marketing objectives.

2. Student's own answer, based on points discussed. Either viewpoint possible, but NO more likely. Marketing covers a range of activities so that a business learns more about customers and competitors so that products that are produced are the right ones/at the right price/in the right place. Good products do not simply sell themselves because they have to be promoted and customers made aware of their existence and value. A good product is important as it's the basis of good marketing -Bradbury successful in past (37% market share) so could argue that good products can sell themselves.

3. Four elements must be covered: Price – skimming as high price will suggest quality; or cost plus pricing as ingredients used might be high quality so more expensive to buy; Promotion – leaflets, tasting, advertising in specialist magazines; Place – specialist shops in area where rich people live or shop; or wider range of shops if want to attract larger market, sell direct via mail order; Product – high quality chocolate, expensive packaging to reinforce image; Must explain choice in context of Bradbury's.

Unit 30

Progress check

1. Producing a number of similar items in groups or sets; when production uses high proportion of capital (machinery) to make goods.

2. High cost, specialist workers, single items, unique products.

3. Production is simply the process of converting raw materials or components into finished goods.

4. Flow

5. Flow

Examination style questions for you to try

1. Producing large numbers of same product continually.

2. Can be inflexible – difficult to change products if orders change; expensive system to set up as a lot of expensive machinery needed if flow to work effectively; machines break down ALL production likely to stop as continuous flow broken; problem of worker motivation – repetitive / less interesting work; Cost – can business afford flow as machinery can be expensive to buy; training costs – workers need to know how to operate equipment.

3. Students own answer based on points discussed. Either option possible, if supported. For points see question 4.

4. Students own answer based on points discussed. Either option possible, if supported. Advantages of batch – some flexibility as different varieties can be made; cheaper than job as some economies of scale but not as cheap as flow; flow allows for large scale production – KC sell around the world; flow can give lowest unit cost – help keep costs down so low prices can be charged; Disadvantages of flow: see question 2;

    Themes for Evaluation: depends on actual volumes – enough demand for flow to be cost effective. If not, could lead to stock piling – not good for perishable chocolate; plus increase storage costs. Job not appropriate – most expensive method – unlikely to have cheap chocolate; enough output to meet demand; no economies of scale to lower average costs for Kape; the product does not have to be unique.

Unit 31

Progress check

1. Level of output where total costs equals total revenue; total cost of production divided by total output.

2. Examples include: rent, interest on loans, salaries.

3. Overheads

4. Information based on forecasted costs and revenues might not be accurate; assumes all goods sold, but is this true for fashion or seasonal goods.

5. Increase break-even point.

Examination style questions for you to try

1. Variable cost: timber/materials used in furniture, wages, nails, glue. Fixed cost: rent of the shops, salaries, general heating and lighting costs.

2. Break even at 1500 chairs, both axes should be labelled as should fixed costs, variable costs, and total cost. 1 mark per correct feature.

3. **Advantages:** simple tool – anyone at WW can use it to help make better decisions; help decide level of output and sales needed to cover its costs. If produce and sell more than the break-even output, will make profit. Shows the minimum amount of products sold to just cover costs – set target number of chairs to avoid loss; monitor performance – can show if they need to boost sales e.g. lower price from $25 or try to cut $15 costs.

   Disadvantages: Based on assumption that everything made is sold – not always true – orders cancelled or new designs mean that demand changes; Costs or prices could change so results misleading e.g. if import / export chairs or parts vulnerable to exchange rates; Forecast – are the figures accurate enough for decision making – business is growing quickly.

4. Students own answer based on points discussed. Either viewpoint is possible. For points see question 3.
   <u>Themes for evaluation</u>: yes – information is helpful to aid decision making; useful tools – help financial success as if unable to plan how much to produce could order wrong amount of stock, produce too much waste – costs time and money. However limited value as inaccurate – so not reliable so wrong decisions could be taken which results in lower sales or expensive mistakes in what is produced.

Unit 32

Progress check

1. Any three from cost, tradition, customers, suppliers, competition, legislation, the environment, infrastructure, available workforce.

2. Issues such as transport, power and energy, communication.

3. Options include: competition, access to parking, proximity of customers, cost.

4. Certain products like food stuffs need specific conditions to grow.

5. Options include transport, availability of workers, power, space, government.

Examination style questions for you to try

1. Grants, rent rebates, or tax incentives, legislation, regulations.

2. Offer grants, rent rebates or tax incentives to businesses locating to areas of high unemployment – persuade company to locate in particular place – to benefit from lower costs. ALSO restrict where businesses can be sited – legislation / regulations if think business activities could have negative effect on society / environment.

3. Availability of suitable vacant shop; What other shops are nearby – competitors/other shops which attract customers/busy retail area, Availability of customer parking nearby so easy for customers to visit shop. Security of area and shop – don't want extra costs of security. Rent paid and other local charges – high rent will increase costs. Access for delivery vehicles – need to near road so suppliers can bring all the materials, flour can be heavy if carried a long way.

Unit 33

Progress check

1. Lean production involves using techniques to cut down waste in a business improves efficiency. Just in time – Production is carefully planned to ensure materials arrive at the right time in the production process.

2. Higher efficiency – as costs per unit are lower so making better use of available inputs.

3. Sickness, machine breakdown, Industrial action, skill level of workers, level of worker motivation, capital or labour intensive business.

4. Groups of workers are given responsibility for making either parts or the whole product.

5. Specialist – higher quality products; Business at full capacity so cannot produce enough goods themselves; Cheaper to produce – e.g., lower cost provider, no need to hire additional staff or machinery; Save time as goods might already be available; Increased flexibility – orders might be seasonal or one off order. Only need temporary increase in output.

Examination style questions for you to try

1. Productivity – is simply output measured against input. It is usually measured in terms of output per unit of labour or per item of machinery. If productivity improves, it means it is getting better – good – means more output per input.

2. Two options from: work study – examine how work carried out to identify ways to improve how each task is

done – result in redesign of layout or job done; training – better skilled workers – fewer mistakes are made – might improve productivity so that the costs of training are more than offset by increased profits. Introduce team working – workers are split into groups who are responsible for making either a specific part or the whole product; economies of scale e.g. purchasing able to buy stock in bulk to receive discounts to lower average cost.

3.   Students own answer based on points made. Either viewpoint possible. **Benefits** of new technology include: improve quality / increase output / improves productivity / way to reduce labour costs / machines do not need breaks / faster production – which could be important as need to increase production again / can handle more complex work – so might be able to introduce more variety of products which would help increase sales / current machines keep breaking down, so need to change equipment anyway. **Problems:** Replacing employees is expensive in terms of redundancy, retraining and the possible impact on motivation of the remaining employees so could limit potential savings if workers not willing to adapt to change – workers were concerned; New technology is constantly changing so it is expensive – finance manager concerned about cost – can business afford it? Will need to continually update equipment to gain the maximum benefits of new technology.

<u>Themes for evaluation</u> – need to replace old equipment so do they have a choice? Can business afford to introduce new technology as gearing is already high; more advantages so yes, or more disadvantages explained so no.

Unit 34

Progress check

1.   The difference between cash inflows and outflows over the period; a financial plan for a future period of time.
2.   Show when a business can expect cash flow problems, so have time to take steps to avoid them.
3.   Includes wages, rent, material costs, heating, lighting, transport, advertising, tax and interest payments.
4.   Overdraft, short term loan, trade credit, factoring, ask debtors to pay quicker, take longer to pay creditors.
5.   Two from: Help plan and coordinate activities; enable business to set targets to help achieve business objectives; Motivate workers by setting targets to work towards;

Help highlight differences between planned and actual costs. Business can then take action to solve problems; Review previous activities; Control cost; monitor different departments.

Examination style questions for you to try

1.   Closing balance – $70; net cash flow is $40
2.   Sylvia has a lot of competition from supermarket so sales are not stable – down $30 in February alone – reduced cash inflow needed to pay her outflows. If continues to fall - possible as extra competition – she could run out of cash. Rent could increase, if it went up to $100 she might not have enough cash inflows from sales to pay it – sales are falling. Other issues: amount of wasted fruit / or sold at reduced price so reduced inflows.
3.   Options include – arrange overdraft so that they have access to cash as and when needed to pay creditors; or short term loan from bank so have funds for set period of time so can pay short term debts, try to reduce costs such as pay out less on stock or wages; try to spread cost of rent over the year – no single large expense paid in a single month; ask creditors for more time to pay so have more time for inflows from sales; ask debtors to pay quicker so cash inflows are received sooner; factoring so receive proceeds from any credit sales before actual payment made; sell surplus fixed assets to release cash tied up in equipment or land; sell some stock cheaply to gain cash quickly.
4.   Students own answer based on points discussed. Points include: cash-flow statement used to show any gaps, or shortfalls, between cash receipts and payments. If shortfalls known – have time to arrange extra funds to cover. Most businesses will need additional funds at some time. Concern is good – shows she is aware of the issue – bank is more likely to consider a loan request if there is evidence able to pay them back. She knows sales aren't guaranteed, so it is important to plan more carefully. Cash flow is still positive every month so she can cover all costs, if her estimates are correct – March $160 left. Has little money – but small business might not need much more cash to operate. Sales up in March; was February temporary drop – is she is worrying over nothing? Sells different produce to supermarket – regional produce – so is it a competitor? Cash flow is a problem for any business so yes she is right to be worried, but she seems better placed to cope than many businesses without a cash flow forecast.

Unit 35

Progress check

1. Current Liabilities: Debts which have to be paid back in less than one year;
   Cost of sales: shows how much the direct costs of making items are.
2. Trading account, profit and loss account.
3. Fixed assets, current assets, shareholder funds, current liabilities, long term liabilities.
4. Working capital
5. Net assets

Examination style questions for you to try

1. Current assets might be stock/debtors/cash. Fixed assets might be remises/machinery/vehicles. Answer can also be a practical example such as bars of chocolate [current asset] since the company is a chocolate manufacturer.
2. Creditors – businesses that Kape have bought supplies from but as yet have not paid for – $15m. Represent a short term liability for the business.
3. Profits are a necessary reward for risk taking – Kape's shareholders will expect a return on their investment – part of $126m given out in dividends?; provide source of funds for future investment – want to buy company – cheap source as no interest is paid; is $126m enough to pay for takeover? Reason for existence – all businesses in private sector seek profit as an objective. Necessary for long term survival – as any business that fails to make a profit will have to close down eventually if it cannot make a profit.
4. Content from: Cash flow forecast tries to show when how much and when cash will enter and leave a business. It can help Kape as it will show them when they need more cash, and how much. Operate on such a large scale, always going to be many outflows. Even a PLC with profits of $126m can fail without sufficient cash flow. Aid financial planning – if know when might have a problem, can ask for help before they need it – Creditors might want $15m back before have cash. If they can show they have has a plan, banks are more likely to lend. Profit and loss account shows whether the business has made a profit or a loss over year; compare results to previous years ($15m to $126) to see how successful Kape have been; owners can see if they will get a return on their investment – so will continue to invest. Possibility of retained profit for investment –

fund takeover of Bradbury / expansion into new countries; measure of the success of the business – can compare the level of net profit made to other companies to see how well they are performing. Break even analysis shows the minimum number of chocolates that business have to sell to just cover costs – target amount to ensure a loss is not made; monitor the business – show if need to boost sales. Focus on low prices – so important to ensure enough items are produced to satisfy demand – otherwise they might need to build another factory or add more machines to ensure meet anticipated demand; can look at different scenarios to see what price or output is possible before changes have to be made. It is therefore an important planning tool for the business.

To gain the evaluation marks, you must make it clear why each document is important.

Unit 36

Progress check

1. Liquidity: ability of a business to meet its short term debts; Return on capital employed (ROCE): Measures how efficiently a business uses its capital to make a profit.
2. Current ratio; acid test
3. Net profit / sales times 100; gross profit / sales times 100; net profit / capital employed times 100.
4. Helps judge how well business has performed, compare with previous years' accounts or with the accounts of other businesses.
5. Any from workers (pay or bonuses); lenders – able to repay / risk; shareholders – risk, amount of dividend; government – tax or jobs; community – jobs.

Examination style questions for you to try

1. Net profit: 40/500 = 8%
2. Shows the amount of profit made for every $1 of sales after allowing for expenses. A higher % shows that the business was able to control its overheads better – but FF has fallen slightly by 0.33% – so didn't control their overheads as well as last year. It can be compared to other similar businesses or against other years.
3. Financial success is often measured in terms of return on assets [ROCE] – [but you don't have information to work this ratio out] Net profit margin can be used – as profits

are sometimes seen as an indicator of success. This shows 2009 30/360 = 8.33% 2010 = 8%. Thus, 2010 not obviously better as less able to control overheads compared to 2009. So sales are up ($140m) and profit is up ($10m) but margins down. So there is no clear answer as to whether 2010 is better as figures show different things. Profit rose by 33% while sales rose by 38%. On balance probably was a successful year but could argue that falling margin is not a good sign.

4. Creditors want to know how secure their money is, and whether the company would have trouble repaying them in an emergency. Employees want to see how well their employer is doing in order to judge their job security. An

employee's job is likely to be safer in a successful company. A profitable company is also more likely to be able to afford to give out pay rises, or bonuses. Lenders want to see if business able to repay any loans taken out. Investors – see possible returns on investment – how much are they likely to receive from $40m profit.

How would this type of question be marked?

For simple statements like profit and sales up so business was successful [up to 2 marks.] Identification of ratios and formula i.e. use of correct figures [up to 2 marks]. Use information to make a supported judgement including some consideration as to what successful means [Up to 2 marks].

Answers to section 4

Unit 37

Progress check

1. System of pay where workers paid by amount of output they produce; Something that makes people wants to work.
2. Fair pay, safe conditions, reasonable hours.
3. Physical, safety, social, self-esteem and self-fulfilment.
4. Theory X – all workers are lazy and only work for money. Theory Y – workers are motivated by many things, they have ambitions and want to succeed.
5. False – all methods of reward can cost the business money.

Examination style questions for you to try

1. System of pay where workers paid a set amount for each hour worked.
2. Reasons might include: dislike nature of the work – tasks might not challenge them or use all their skills, don't like low rates or method of pay – unable to earn enough to satisfy their needs; unhappy with conditions – health and safety standards good for customers but what about other facilities for staff, do not like other workers / management – so social needs are not met; do not like style of management – might prefer to be told what to do / don't want boss to know personal details; lack of promotion prospects – everyone is equal so how do they progress?
3. Students own answer. Either yes or no possible if supported. Issues include: Praise is Maslow level four – self

esteem as good work is recognised; this is a higher order need so will only work if physical, social and security needs already met. If not praise unlikely to be effective as other basic needs must be satisfied first. Also depends on what is important to individual workers – if theory X, only money is likely to work but theory Y people are motivated by many things. It is unlikely that praise on its own will be effective.

4. Students own answer. Any option possible if supported. **Bonuses** – sum of money paid to workers, in addition to their basic pay if they reach certain performance targets – workers encouraged to work harder to meet targets to earn the extra money – workers will feel part of the business as they share financially in the success of the business. Bonuses are not guaranteed, so if external factors (e.g. recession) affect business, workers could receive nothing despite hard work. They are seen as important, and have a role to play in good customer service. **Job enrichment** – Employee is given more difficult tasks to do or encouraged to take part in the decision-making – motivated as work is more challenging and feel valued so raising self-esteem. Rewards gained by individual actions – not external factors which they have little control over. Could increase costs as training might be needed. Could affect team idea, as unlikely everyone can be given extra jobs. **Fringe Benefits** – extra incentives given to employees e.g. discounts, insurance or company car. Given in addition to wages such as discounts on holidays / extra

activities at sites, or insurance cover in case injured at work. Can help boost morale, and pride in business so more productive. If offer insurance could reassure workers in case of accidents that they are protected so could help keep good staff. Security is a basic need in Maslow's hierarchy – important as employees role in business is part of their success. Workers might expect these anyway, so will they increase motivation? Fringe benefits add to costs of the business, discounts on holidays, insurance as not free.

Unit 38

Progress check

1. Managers make decisions after consultation with workers; style of management where manager gives workers the freedom to make all day to day decisions, with few guidelines and little direction.
2. Delegation, consultation, experienced and skilled workers, workers involved in decision making, two way communication.
3. Planning, problem solving, making decisions and co-ordinating the efforts of the staff for whom the manager is responsible.
4. Effective when staff are ready and willing to take on responsibility, they are motivated, and can be trusted to do their jobs.
5. Students own answer.

Examination style questions for you to try

1. Managers make all the decisions without any discussion with workers.
2. It costs a lot of time and money to replace staff. Costs of recruitment/ training new employees. If a lot of staff are leaving these costs will rise as more replacements will be needed. If lose experienced staff, new staff might not be able to work as quickly – productivity and output could suffer. Mistakes more likely with new staff – could affect reputation and sales. Poor reputation – harder to recruit people. Cost of advertising for new employees; cost of training new employees – the business does not seem able to offer benefits – can they afford the ongoing expense of recruitment? production problems if staff leaves suddenly – already struggling to meet orders; morale low for existing employees as workload for them

might have to increase to cope with the shortage of 40 workers.

3. Students own answer based on points discussed. Either viewpoint is possible. Point to consider include: **Reasons to lower turnover** – reduced recruitment costs which will add to business costs; reduced training costs, saving of time on recruitment and training; opportunity costs – what money spent on recruit / training could have been used for e.g. to help fund expansion; loss of 40 skilled workers – might be difficult to replace. **Reasons to support turnover:** new ideas / skills brought by new craftsmen could produce new designs for business; enthusiasm – want to work for company; better skilled workers so better quality work possible; able to pay lower wages as new so not earn extra yet for loyalty. Themes for evaluation: problem if unable to replace skilled workers, looking to expand so need more, it could be important to retain experience. No – if workers want to leave, it is difficult to stop them. If they remain they might be de-motivated and produce poor quality work or affect other workers. Depends on how easy it is to recruit replacement workers.

4. Many options including increase wages; change to piece-rate; increase fringe benefits; give longer holidays; provide safer working condition – so less risk of injury; introduce worker participation; introduce job enlargement. Plus ways to increase motivation – change of management style, team working. Any sensible suggestion which is supported would be allowed.

   Application points include: other local businesses offer piece-rate, long holidays, pensions and safe working conditions, they can't afford to match, 160, 40 leave, skilled workers, autocratic, growing business.

Unit 39

Progress check

1. Training occurs away from the work place; training aimed at introducing new employees to the business and its procedures.
2. Person specification.
3. FALSE – all training costs money. It costs money to set up in house training centres or send people away for college or training courses. Whilst people are away from the work place, potential output could be lost.

4. Benefits – work with experienced worker, familiar with environment; might be cheaper; some work done whilst training happens.

5. Off-the-job: broad range of skills taught; experienced and qualified trainer so more effective? Work of other employees is not disrupted whilst training occurs.

Examination style questions for you to try

1. Main features: Name of the employer and employee, job title, date of commencement of employment, hours of work, details about pay and other benefits, such as pension and sick schemes and holiday entitlement, amount of notice of termination and details of grievance and disciplinary procedures.

2. Content: Furniture should be built correctly (quality product) – with the furniture being hand finished skilled workers are needed as not everyone will have the skills needed to produce a quality product. Skilled workers are needed to help maintain the growing reputation of WW – if sub standard chairs are made, this will reflect badly on the business and they could lose sales. Unskilled workers might not be able to produce work at a high enough level to meet the standard set. Idea of furniture built and sent out quickly (efficiency) – this wil speed up operations, and ensure orders are met on time, if not reputation could be affected.

    <u>Application points include:</u> furniture; successful, efficiency, hand finished, quality, safe. Note for all marks to be awarded, you will need to explain why having skilled workers is important.

3. Students own answer based on points discussed. Either option is possible. Internal points include: motivation for existing employees – as have chance to progress; likely to have good knowledge of business so no costly induction training required so fewer expenses; generates stability within company – which with a high turnover of workers might help support image; already know workers so able to fit into structure and practices quicker than someone who has no knowledge of this business.

    External points include: wider pool of candidates to draw from; bring in new skills and ideas - could benefit

company; growing rapidly - do existing workers have the necessary skills / expertise to cope with job requirements? friction with existing workers who will feel overlooked for post – could lead others to leave, and turnover is already high so stability is important – to help protect growing reputation; clash of management styles could hinder progress towards goals; would external candidates want to join business in view of high turnover?

<u>Themes for evaluation:</u> internal so motivational for existing workers – can progress in business, costs likely to be lower as no induction training; know business so start immediately: External – if don't have skills – if rapidly growing, managing finance for a larger business is not the same as for a small business, new ideas brought in.

4. Job description: outlines the tasks and responsibilities of a specific job – so applicants know what the job involves - so Rico's time isn't wasted going through lots of unsuitable application forms,. This allows Rico to draw up a job specification with suitable skills, etc. required.

    Job specification: outlines the required skills, qualifications, personal qualities, etc. for a specific job – to ensure a suitably qualified person is appointed and that they have the skills etc. to do the job required. Rico must find suitably qualified carpenters who can hand finish furniture.

    Advertisement: informs people of job vacancy – informs people what job involves, qualifications, etc. needed if want to apply. Details about the job (such as wages) are given so only suitable candidates apply. The advertisement must be placed in a location so suitable applicants see it. As they are struggling to find enough workers locally, need to advertise in all four regions or specialist publications to attract the attention of skilled carpenters.

    Interviews: where the applicants are seen face to face and asked a series of questions – to make sure person hasn't lied on their CV/ able to do job advertised / could fit in with the other employees. Rico has to check that they are skilled workers otherwise the reputation of business at risk.

Answers to section 5

Unit 40

Progress check

1. Involves transfer of business from private to public sector; controlling amount of money in economy through interest rates to help manage rate of inflation.

2. Ensure provision of essential services such as education or health; ensure prices charged are affordable; protect jobs if a company is a large employer; control of some industries is part of wider government objectives.

3. Two from: ensure essential goods and services are available at reasonable cost; ban / control the supply of harmful products; protect interests of customers; reduce level of unemployment, control level of inflation, encourage economic growth, encourage domestic and international trade, control negative effects of business activity on environment.

4. Monopolies will try to limit the choice and increase prices for consumers so government try to prevent the exploitation of consumers.

5. More competition so more choice and lower prices for consumers, increase trade for domestic businesses, improve balance of payments, job creation if output increases for domestic firms.

Examination style questions for you to try

1. Options include various employment laws, consumer protection laws, location regulations (planning controls); competition laws, quotas, tariffs, rules and regulations.

2. Encourage jobs, provide new services, competition can lead to lower prices for customers, help businesses locate in certain locations.

3. Students own answer based on points discussed. Whilst both viewpoints are possible, the word always means it is more likely that a no conclusion should be drawn. Points to consider include: Competition laws set minimum standards or rules that all businesses should follow. These are designed to protect customer against dangerous products, misleading advertising. Customers have legal rights should laws be broken so this should benefit consumers; Competition also helps consumers to benefit from lower prices as firms compete to gain sales, better

quality and more choice; Governments try to restrict or control monopolies as they try to limit the choice and increase prices for consumers so many benefits. However too much competition can lead smaller businesses to fail which could reduce choice or lead to loss of unique items; businesses cut corners to lower costs so able to charge lower prices so quality might suffer although products still safe to buy; on whole positive but there are some disadvantages.

4. Students own answer, depending on points discussed. Content: possible reasons for government controls on business include: protection of employees – working conditions – plastic could give off fumes depending on process used; H and S – delivery lorries will be entering the site at all times – how will workers or visitors be protected, if there are fumes let off from the process – ventilation or other safety equipment might be necessary; minimum wage rules which will increase the costs for the business. Location decisions – influence where businesses choose to locate – T&U might need to relocate so they could face planning controls especially as the number of deliveries will create more pollution; access to the site is important as the number of deliveries rise, To protect consumers – the bricks should be safe to use – especially as they will used for housing, they will need to be strong enough so there is no risk of the houses collapsing and injuring people

To score highly on this question, there needs to be a good discussion of government controls and what they are intended to achieve. There must to be a clear judgement made as to how they could affect T&U's business, which is supported for full marks to be achieved.

Unit 41

Progress check

1. Ethics: is concerned about behaving in a way which is right and fair; Collective bargaining: the union represents all members in negotiations with management rather than each individual workers representing themselves.

2. Members

3. False, like pressure groups they only have the power of influence only governments can set laws.

4. Go slow, work to rule, overtime ban, strike.

5. Fair wages can help attract and retain workers, ethically sourced goods can improve image and possible sales; operate at higher standards means less danger of breaking laws so avoid additional costs or damage to reputation.

Examination style questions for you to try

1. Dangers might include use of dangerous machinery/ inappropriate clothing/lack of protective clothing/noise/ hygiene/atmospheric pollution/working excessive hours/ temperature (1 mark per danger identified).

2. Actions include: training so understand how to use equipment better, provision of safety equipment e.g. goggles, harnesses and overalls; improved lighting and ventilation; rest breaks so not tired; job rotation to reduce monotony of tasks; adding guards to equipment so sharp edges are not exposed.

3. Students own answer based on points discussed. Either answer is possible if explained. Points to consider: Much depends on the nature of the issues facing the business. If it is failing to comply with the minimum requirements of the law then changes must be made otherwise it faces legal action. If minimum standards have already been met then the issue is not so clear cut. If accidents are occurring in spite of training then it implies that the processes used are dangerous and might need changing. Are the accidents simply minor ones (are they actually due to the workplace?) or more serious. Failure to do so might lead to compensation claims which will further add to business costs. Does the training need to be improved? There are also moral issues concerning things like ethical employee obligations. Perhaps accidents occur due to long hours of work (40 hours). Solving this would increase costs. As sales are already falling, they might be able to afford the extra money, so more jobs could be at risk if they try to make labour savings to pay for extra health and safety. But overall, yes is more likely as money probably does need to be spent in order to save money in the longer term.

4. Students own answer based on points discussed. Either answer is possible if explained. Unions exist to protect the interests of its members. These new laws could make conditions of employment worse for employees. They might receive less benefits such as less holiday

entitlement or discounts which would reduce the overall payment package received by workers; wages may be lowered – they only receive 25c above minimum wage, if minimum wage is lowered, this might reduce the pay received by workers of the company, so members have less income available to spend which the Union would be opposed to. They are looking to raise wage rates not see them lowered. New laws would make it easier to sack workers, which Union would oppose. Health and Safety may be worse accident rate might increase from 31 so workers are more at risk so they feel less secure in their jobs; workers have less protection. What if the next step is to restrict the role of trade unions? However more jobs could be created by the introduction of more multinational companies, so creating more job opportunities for people. There is no evidence to suggest that Snappers will reduce the wage rate paid to its employees – they pay above the minimum rate anyway. It might be an issue for workers of other companies not Snappers. Overall, the Union is right to be concerned, as the dangers are greater than the possible benefits for its members of the proposed law changes.

Unit 42

Progress check

1. Deliberate decision to avoid purchasing particular products; the lowest point in the economic cycle where demand at lowest, unemployment at highest level.

2. Trade cycle

3. Trade unions, competitors, government, pressure groups, customers, global factors.

4. Gross Domestic Product – Records value of goods and services produced in a country over a year.

5. GDP rising ; sales and profits should rise; levels of output rise; costs rise to meet growing demand.

Examination style questions for you to try

1. Recession, slump, growth and boom.

2. A group of people who come together with a common aim to try to influence the decisions and activities of businesses, local councils or the Government.

3. They try and achieve their goals by – generating bad publicity – so create a bad image for businesses – customers might not buy from them so sales are reduced . Organise

boycotts of products – customers choose not buy from them so sales are reduced. Visible protesting – marches and poster campaigns to raise awareness of the cause. Lobbying the government for changes – petitions sent and campaigning to get laws changed.

4. Students own answer based on points discussed. Whilst both viewpoints are possible, the word always means a No conclusion is more likely. Points to mention include: A pressure group is a group of people who come together with a common aim to try to influence the activities and decisions of businesses or government. Pressure groups can campaign for any issue. Typical issues include environmental, health and location of businesses – so pollution caused by T&U's factory likely to attract their attention. Groups will either lobby governments or run campaigns which can affect the reputation of a business. They aim to create enough awareness to make the business change what they do – in this case possibly lobbying the government to introduce laws. T&U will be unhappy as changes suggested could lead to higher costs. However pressure groups do not have the power to make laws BUT businesses often have to listen to pressure groups or risk losing sales and customers. Businesses MUST do what the Governments say or face legal action. Depends as well on business – some will already try to act in a responsible way – whether pressure groups exist or not.

Index